STUDIES IN CHRISTIANITY

STUDIES
IN CHRISTIANITY

BY

BORDEN PARKER BOWNE

BOSTON AND NEW YORK
HOUGHTON MIFFLIN COMPANY
The Riverside Press Cambridge
1909

47391

Published March 1909

PREFACE

THE first three of these Essays have been separately published before. As they here appear they have been revised and considerably extended.

The Essays have not been written for specialists, nor for professional unbelievers, but solely to relieve some of the difficulties under which popular religious thought labors because of misunderstanding. Indeed, the entire volume might be described as an aid to progressive orthodoxy, or as an attempt to combine the new theology with the old religion. That the future as well as the past belongs to the old religion I am perfectly sure. This religion has often been ignorantly and inadequately conceived, and even caricatured at times by its disciples, but it has the advantage over all its competitors and proposed substitutes of *being alive;* and life counts for much in organic history, spiritual as well as physical. At the same time the old religion may need a new theology for its better expression and formulation, and in this sense a new theology may be a valuable aid to the old religion.

Quite unsuspected by the noiser champions, the problems of religious debate are fast chang-

ing their form. The old-fashioned naturalism,
with its naïve fancy, the more nature the less
God, is falling into discredit. The immanence
of God in natural processes permits us to affirm
a supernatural natural and a natural supernatural, to which the old-time naturalistic objections
have no application. For the same reason the
old-fashioned supernaturalism, which was purely
an accident of the deistic philosophy, has under-
gone a parallel transformation. The supernaturalism of to-day is concerned only to find
God in nature, life, history, miracle,—no matter
where so long as it finds him; but it finds him
predominantly in law and life. This is produc-
ing a sanity of religious thought beyond anything known in the past, and it is prophetic of
still better things to come.

With the progressive moralizing of religion
a corresponding change is taking place in the
inner life itself. Selfishness can work in any field,
and it has made in religion some of its most
odious manifestations. The desire to escape
punishment and to " get off," or be " let off," has
been unpleasantly prominent in religious history.
This also is passing away. Not merely to get
something from God, but to work with him and
be like him, is becoming more generally the religious ideal. Thus the element of gratitude and

active aspiration is taking precedence of the selfish factor. And our thought of religion itself is more and more passing from the conception of a yoke and a burden to which we must submit for fear of something worse, to the conception of religion as the summit and crown of our being, as indeed the supreme condition of large, joyous, and abundant life. Thus the old religion, while remaining true to type, is gradually freeing itself from the crudities of early thought, manifesting its essential nature, and building itself into its ideal form. To help toward this consummation is the purpose of this book.

BORDEN PARKER BOWNE.

February 22, 1909.

CONTENTS

I

THE CHRISTIAN REVELATION

STUDIES IN CHRISTIANITY

I

THE CHRISTIAN REVELATION

OUR Christian faith is, that God, at sundry times and in divers manners, spake unto the fathers by the prophets, and that, in the fullness of time, he revealed himself unto men by his Son. This faith will last as long as the Christian Church; I believe it will last as long as the human race. Nevertheless, it is possible to conceive the revelation, its mode and meaning, in such a way as to obscure the truth and seriously to embarrass faith. There is enough of this misconception in popular religious thought to warrant a brief discussion of the subject. It is not, then, a question as to the reality of revelation, but solely as to the manner of conceiving it.

Of God's self-revealing movement the Bible is the historical and literary product and record. This does not mean that God has not revealed himself elsewhere and in other manners; but of that revealing movement which culminated in Christianity the Bible is the product and record.

It is the literature which grew out of and around
the revelation, and it mediates for us a knowledge of the revelation. But on turning to the
Bible, we soon become conscious of needing some
guiding principle for its interpretation. Except
from the right standpoint, the Bible is a most
embarrassing book. Much of it seems to have no
connection with those moral and religious interests which, we suppose, give revelation its motive
and value. Instead of a compact expression of
doctrines to be believed and of duties to be done,
we have a heterogeneous collection of history,
geography, biography, genealogy, statistics, liturgy, poetry, prophecy, sermons, stories, parables,
letters, and such like. And when questions of conduct are touched upon, they seem to have little
significance for us. Temple rites, idol worship,
the tiresome purifications of the Mosaic law, the
disputes between Pharisees and Sadducees, the
eating of things offered to idols, — these, and
similar obsolete questions, are the matters dwelt
upon ; and for us these questions are as dead
as the men who raised them. What concern have
we with prophetic burdens of Egypt, or Moab, or
Tyre ?   And what practical wisdom do we gain
from them for the guidance of our own lives?
By following out this line of thought, one might
easily reach the conclusion that the Bible is, for

us, obsolete and worthless. The antiquarian and student of ancient life might possibly find his advantage in it, but the plain, every-day man and woman have to worry along about the same with the Bible as without it. Indeed, unless we use it wisely, we may be even worse off with it than without it. Illustration is found in the dementalized textarians and their whims with which the history of the Bible abounds. The use of the Bible as a book for vaticination on all manner of subjects is familiar to every one. It would be hard also to find a single step of progress, ethical, intellectual, religious, political, which has not been resisted and condemned by texts from the Bible. As Dryden put it: —

> The fly-blown text conceives an alien brood,
> And turns to maggots what was meant for food.

Thus we see how the Bible may be an embarrassing and incredible book, conceived as a divine revelation, unless we get the right point of view. For this insight we need no profound scholarship, or long and close communion with the higher critics; the conclusion lies on the surface for every one. We obviously need, then, to seek for some central idea, which shall unify and illuminate the whole, if we are to find any supreme value in it. And such an idea must be sought in

a better conception of the purpose and contents
of revelation. Only thus can we give these dead
questions and this vanished life any abiding significance for present and future times.

What, then, is the Christian Revelation? To
this question many answers might be given;
but the one which best sums up the truth, and
best brings out the great and abiding value
of Christian teaching, is this: The Christian
revelation is essentially a revelation of God. It
teaches us what God is, and what he means. It
is, primarily and fundamentally, a revelation of
the righteousness and grace of God. It tells us
how God feels toward us; what he has made
us for; what he has done and is doing for
us; how we are to think of life and its meaning,
of death and destiny, of our mutual human
relations also, and the spirit in which we are to
live. The answer to these questions constitutes
the gist of the Christian revelation; and this
answer the Church forever repeats in its profession of faith in God the Father, in his Son our
Savior and Lord, in the inspiring and sanctifying
Spirit, in the forgiveness of sins, in the kingdom
of God upon earth, and in the life everlasting.
These ideas are at the heart of the Christian
religion and of Christian civilization; and these

ideas have come with abiding power and definiteness and fullness into the world's thought and life only along the line of God's revelation of himself through the prophets and through his Son.

The Christian revelation, then, is not the Bible, though it is in the Bible. It consists essentially in certain ways of thinking about God, his character, his purpose in our creation, and his relation to us. It has these great ideas for its contents, and it is to be approached, studied, and understood only in connection with these ideas. They constitute its chief value for us. However the pentateuchal question might fall out, or whatever our view concerning the second Isaiah, we are Christian so long as we hold the Christian view of God and man and their mutual relations; and the only abiding significance of the Bible lies in helping us to this view. With this view, we can dispense with everything else; and without this view, it matters little what else we have. And if the Bible helps us to this view; if this long history is an illustration and object lesson whereby we may discern what God is and what he means, — then its value and perennial significance begin to appear. And if we further find that nowhere else can the divine character and purpose be so clearly discerned, then it is manifest that in the historic movement out of which Christianity has come, we have a revelation of God which outranks in value all others which he may have made, or which men may have feigned or imagined.

It is from this point of view that the need and value of the Christian revelation are to be determined. When we consider it as a dogmatic treatise in abstract speculative theology, or as a text-book in ethics, or as anything but a revelation of God, it is easy to doubt whether it has any special and abiding religious value. As thus conceived, the matter seems neither particularly new nor especially profitable. By carrying the abstraction far enough, we can make all religions look alike. It is also easy to pick out detached ethical precepts and deep mystical sayings from ancient life and literature, and especially from the sacred books of other religions, and thus finally to present those religions as rivaling Christianity itself. But the matter is very different when we consider revelation as the self-revelation of God, and when we consider its fundamental and central ideas and inspirations. Then we first begin to get some conception of its deep meaning and inestimable value; and some conception also of the world-wide difference between the Bible and all other scriptures, between Christ and all other masters. The questions men most need to have answered are questions about God, his character, his purpose in our creation, and his relation to us. We can find out from conscience and experience how to live together in the daily round; but what does life itself mean, and what is its outcome to be? With these questions the earnest thought of the world, the religions and philosophies, have busied themselves from the beginning; and to these questions every well-instructed Christian child has a distinct and sublime answer which the sages and philosophers of the non-Christian world have sought in vain to find. And the deepest lack of that world is the lack of just those ways of thinking about God and his relation to us which we have learned from his revelation of himself. This lack is the great source of the failure of the heathen world, the source of its moral and speculative aberrations, of its hopelessness also, and of its blinding and withering superstitions. What that world most of all needs is the good news of God. This only can break the spells and disperse the illusions, because of which the people sit in darkness and the shadow of death, being bound in affliction and iron. They do not need the Bible considered as a book. They need the Christian way of thinking about God and his purposes concerning men; and they need the Bible only as it helps them to this view. And it helps beyond all estimate in this regard. We have so wrangled over the geology of Genesis as utterly to miss the immense significance of the first verse, " In the beginning God created the heavens and the earth." With that all pantheism, polytheism, and idolatry vanish. "No Osiris, Isis, and Set; no Anu, Hea, and Bel; no Sun, Moon, and Venus; no Moloch, Rimmon, and Ashtoreth," whose worship defiled the nations for ages, but God, the Everlasting Father and Lord. The more we study religious history, the greater the value of the Bible appears.

There has been, and still is, a great deal of superficial thought in judging of revelation. Since the comparative study of religion began, many have hoped, and more have feared, that Christianity would suffer when brought face to face with the other great religious systems. Enthusiastic students have eagerly studied the sacred books of the East, and have found abundant traces that God has never left himself without a witness. And they have gathered up golden words and profound sayings from the ancient sages, without giving us any hint of the mountain of chaff or dross in which they were hidden.

In this way the impression has become quite general that those sacred books are full of ancient wisdom and religious insight, and are patterns of sound and wholesome moral teaching. In the popular mind, indeed, purely imaginative works, like " The Light of Asia," have passed for literal reproductions of those venerable faiths. In this way many hopes and fears, both equally groundless, have been raised; and prejudice has taken the place of scholarly study and criticism. Fortunately, the translation of the various sacred books of the race is changing this state of things, and is bringing the study of those ancient and outlying faiths back into that wholesome, matter-of-fact atmosphere in which alone it can reach any valuable and permanent results. Max Müller, in the general preface to the translation of the Sacred Books of the East, calls attention to the extravagant fancies which have been cherished concerning the contents of these old books, and says: " Readers who have been led to believe that the Vedas of the ancient Brahmins, the Avesta of the Zoroastrians, the Tripitaka of the Buddhists, the Kings of Confucius, or the Koran of Mohammed, are books full of primeval wisdom and religious enthusiasm, or at least of sound and simple moral teaching, will be disappointed on consulting these volumes."

In another passage he says: "By the side of so much that is fresh, natural, simple, beautiful, true, they contain so much that is not only unmeaning, artificial, and silly, but even hideous and repellent."

The comparison of the Christian Scriptures with the other sacred books of the world has too often been made in a partisan interest. Sometimes those books have been rejected outright as manifest works of darkness, with the aim of exalting the Christian revelation. Sometimes, with equal unwisdom, they have been extravagantly praised as altogether comparable with our own Scriptures. But in both cases there has been oversight of the fact that the central idea in any religion is its idea of God. Hence, both parties have wasted time and strength over false issues. Christian partisans have ransacked ancient history and literature for religious superstitions and practical abominations, as specimens of what man can do without revelation. And anti-Christian partisans have done the same thing in order to gather fine sentiments with which to confound their opponents. Both parties were equally in error. Scattered ethical maxims and stray religious truths do not make a religion; we must rather judge it by its general theory of things, by its thought of God, of creation, of man, of life, of destiny, and by the inspiration which it furnishes. These things are the essence of a religion and the root of its power. Different systems might have many ethical precepts in common and many similar expressions of piety; but so long as they differ in their fundamental aims and ideas, only the utmost superficiality would think of identifying them. In a sense religious feeling can attach itself to anything, as a fetish or totem; but a religion for developed humanity, and which develops humanity, must be a religion for the whole man. It must satisfy the intellect, the conscience, the affections, and must furnish the will with a supreme inspiration. Any religious system is imperfect in the measure in which it falls below this requirement.

Applying this standard, we see the mighty gulf between the Christian and other systems in their adaptation to human needs. The banks of the stream of time are lined with religions which have perished because they could not keep pace with intellectual development; and many of the Asiatic religions are dying before our eyes from this cause. The truth that is in them is wrapped up with so much that is puerile, stupid, and revolting, that they are doomed to perish. They are in a worse plight in relation to conscience. They have so debased the thought of God, and have sanctioned so much of vileness, that as soon as conscience awakes, it revolts against them. And they are especially lacking in respect to any stimulus for noble living. Their predominant note is pessimism and despair. They find no worthy ethical purpose in creation, but only an endless and aimless doing and undoing, weaving and unweaving, without any justifying outcome. The supreme hope which the great Indian religions hold out for man is to escape from personal existence, either by absorption or annihilation. There is no hint of a Father in heaven in the Christian sense, no hint of a divine meaning in the world, no hint of a divine deliverance wrought out by a divine Deliverer, no hint of an ever-present Spirit leading souls to righteousness and perfecting them in goodness, no hint of life eternal in which the faithful soul shall glorify God and enjoy him forever. To drop into darkness, and escape the woe and burden of this illusion we call our life, is their great hope for the race. The Christian view of God and the world and the meaning of life is the precise and exact contradiction of all this; and yet, because of scattered moral maxims and stray gleams of religious insight, many have been pleased to hold that Christianity has nothing new or valuable to offer. The superficiality of such a view appears as soon as we ask for the central ideas and inspirations of the religious systems. And it is to be desired that the admirers of the Asiatic religions who now and then appear among us would be at the pains to master those ideas before beginning their work as apostles. If we would understand Hinduism, or Buddhism, or Confucianism, we must study them in their basal ideas and in the civilizations they have made. By their fruits ye shall know them.

I am in full sympathy with the desire to find the non-Christian religions as elevated as possible. I have no objection even to parliaments of religions, provided they do not hide the facts behind vague and general phrases, and provided they escape the defiling touch of the advertising harpy. There is no good reason why a Christian should not rejoice at finding traces of God's presence and inspiration everywhere among men, especially as his own Bible teaches him that there is a Light which lighteneth every man that cometh into the world. And for both a Christian and a theist it must be clear that the great non-Christian systems have had a place in the divine purpose for men. But this does not imply their perfection or their finality. As Judaism was the beginning and not the end, and would have been a failure if it had not merged into the broader thought of Christianity, so these other systems, at best, were only for a time. They never could make man perfect, or build him to his best estate. There is no call to blacken, and also none to whitewash. After all that charity or sympathy can truly say in their behalf, it must be admitted that their earlier forms were their best and purest, and that they have fallen below recovery. They have no power to save others or themselves. We may say, for instance, that the early Hindus set out on their way toward God, and that their religious literature is the record of their Godward journey; but when we consider the abominations of the Hindu pantheon and of the popular Hindu religion, we must admit that somehow or other they grievously missed their way. The thwarting, paralyzing, and defiling influences of Hindu society have concentrated and incarnated themselves in the Hindu religion. India is socially, industrially, and politically paralyzed by her religion. Caste is sanctified, the masses are hopeless, the people are divided by all manner of impassable gulfs due to their religion. If the Hindu mind could be swept clean of all its religious conceptions and their place taken by the ideas of the Lord's Prayer and the Sermon on the Mount, it would be for India a blessing great beyond all comparison. And it is hard to see how any political or social or industrial progress can be made in India until the present religious conceptions have been swept away or profoundly modified. After all, fruit is the final test; when any religious system has had a people under its influence for ages, it may rightly be judged by its fruits. Tried by this standard, Asia, past and present, is the sufficient condemnation of the Asiatic religions.

The general good nature with which the outlying religious systems are now commonly regarded must not lead us into overlooking these facts. As we have before said, if we carry the abstraction far enough, we may make all religions seem alike. Thus, we may discover that they all believe in God, and hence we may conclude that at bottom there is no difference. But this is only a verbal illusion, and does not remove the fact that the conception of God, and his purposes, and his relation to us, may exhibit world-wide differences in different religious systems. Or, again, we may say that all religions have an adaptation to their adherents, so that there is no one religion that is best for all; but this too is an abstract verbalism. The deification of evil and superstition can never be sanctified, or made other than destructive, by such reflections. Religions may be defiled and defiling. Finally, under the influence of some vague notions of the divine immanence, we may say that God has revealed himself in all of these systems. But unless we are willing to put all revelations on the same plane, and to deny man all influence in the unfolding of religious thought and activity, we gain nothing from this contention. Religious thinkers who have attained to any ethical insight would not be willing to look upon the gross immoralities and depraving abominations of many of the ethnic religions as revelations of the divine character and will. And when these are eliminated, we still have to admit that the revelation in the several systems is of varying degrees of adequacy and completeness. And then we have to inquire which of the various revelations brings us nearest to God, gives us the highest thought of God and man, of their mutual relations, and of the divine purpose in the creation of man, and furnishes the highest and most effective inspiration for human living.

Put in this way, the problem solves itself. However divine we may think the extra-Christian religions, the Christian religion is diviner still. Whatever service they may have done in the ruder and cruder stages of life, they are quite unable to make man or society perfect, or build them into perfection. Our sincerest admirers of Buddhism or Confucianism prefer to admire afar off. They would not care to live in a community developed from and dominated by the systems in question. For it is perfectly plain that when the mental and moral nature is developed, we must make demands upon any religion which claims our allegiance which these systems can never meet. As already pointed out, a religion for developed humanity, and one capable of developing humanity, must satisfy man's entire nature — the intellect, the conscience, the affections — and must furnish the will with a supreme end and inspiration. It is, then, right that we should be well-disposed toward all non-Christian religions, and we should be glad to recognize any good that may be in them; but this must not lead us to overlook their imperfection and practical inefficiency, and the resulting necessity of replacing them by something better. As soon as they come into contact with our Western thought, science, and individualism, it becomes apparent that their day is done, and that the final alternative will be Christianity or irreligion.

When we compare Christianity with the outlying religions, we feel its measureless superiority. We feel it equally when we compare it with the revelation of nature. Anti-Christian speculators in Christian countries have always been accustomed to emphasize this revelation, and to claim that it gives us all the light we need. Now, that there is a revelation in nature, in the mind, in history, the wise Christian gladly admits and steadfastly maintains; but that it is so adequate and complete as to leave nothing more to be desired is not so clear. In a Christian community, where Christian thought prevails, a philosopher may succeed in giving reasons for a faith otherwise learned, and may conclude that he has deduced it for himself. But this is illusory, even for speculative truth, which lies within the possible range of the reflective faculty. Thus, the unity of God, the doctrine without which rational science would perish, has come to men mainly through the influence of Christian teaching. Philosophy has followed after, and found reasons for the doctrine; but the doctrine itself has reached the mind of the modern world chiefly through Christian teaching, which has made it a fixed tradition and possession of modern thought.

Still more doubtful is the revelation of nature with respect to the divine character and purpose. The difficulties that meet us here are such that of late years the revelation of nature has been less confidently appealed to, and the more earnest skeptics have scoffed at it, or have greeted it with moody and scornful laughter. A revelation of power or skill alone furnishes no basis for religion. We need, in addition, a revelation of moral character and of moral purpose. And here it is that the revelation of nature is ambiguous and incomplete. This fact was never felt so keenly as at present. The easy-going optimism of the past and the naïve anthropomorphic interpretations of the world are daily growing more difficult. The advance of knowledge has revealed so many aspects of evil and so much that we cannot rationally interpret. We consider the raven and rapine of nature, the apparently meaningless aspects of things, also, and the long ages in which fire and slag and slime held barren sway. Of the lower forms of life, how few seem to have any meaning? We look at them in amazement and astonishment, and ask ourselves, How can these things be? Nor is human history much more intelligible. For the great mass of men there has been no history, but only animal need and craving, mostly unsatisfied. The many races, their alienations, their unending wars, their mutual slaughter, furnish a grim and difficult problem. And the few races which have climbed to some measure of civilization have soon grown weary of the burden as something too heavy to be borne. It is hard indeed to see how any one can look seriously at the history of India, of Egypt, of Central and Western Asia, of the nations and races that have lived on the shores of the Mediterranean Sea, without great disquietude of spirit. With our Christian faith we can indeed get on by postponing the problem and falling back on trust in God, but a purely inductive study without such faith could hardly fail to "lend evil dreams."

When we consider the general forms of nature, organic and inorganic, and the general facts of history, we are left in great uncertainty as to their meaning. And we are no better off when we look at the life of the individual. The general form of our life, with its marked prominence of the physical and the animal, is itself a stumbling-block. There seems to be something almost grotesque in this utter subjection of spiritual beings to animal needs. Then we note the uncertainty of our life and lot, the seeming accidents of health and fortune, the many turnings and overturnings in which we can discern no plan, the things which have impressed men with the sense of a blind fate or a blinder chance, which sports with men, and by which our best plans are often thwarted and brought to naught.

Thus in no realm does the great cosmic order seem to be working definitely at any intelligible task, least of all at any moral task. These facts are not incompatible with the divine wisdom and goodness. Our trouble with them may be only the shadow of our own ignorance; yet as they appear they point to neither wisdom nor goodness. Because of our thoughtless optimism we have generally ignored these facts, or we have regarded them from the standpoint of Christian teaching; and thus we have failed to get the impression of dismay which a purely logical study of the facts would furnish. This explains the pessimism which has seized upon so many earnest minds which have abandoned the Christian faith.

It is definitely settled at last that whoever has words of eternal life, science and philosophy have them not. The conceptions of God which are necessary to love and trust must be sought elsewhere. It was a favorite thought with Lessing, and has often been repeated, that the need of revelation will pass with time, as reason will gradually penetrate to the rational ground of all religious truth, and will at last stand in its own right. But this may be doubted for a double reason : First, the basal factors of the Christian religion are not merely rational truths to be discovered by reflection ; they are also, and more especially, facts to be learned by evidence. God's goodness and righteousness and his gracious

purpose towards men are questions of fact to be
answered by no introspection, but only by consulting his word and works. In the next place,
it is very doubtful if the human mind will ever
attain during its earthly existence to any satisfactory interpretation of God's methods in the
universe. Their mystery and impenetrability grow
more and more marked; and the impression
deepens that his ways are not as our ways, nor his
thoughts as our thoughts. The problem grows
faster than our knowledge; and more than ever,
for faith and trust in this awful God, do we need
the historic revelation of God in Jesus Christ.
Here we have, not indeed a God whom we understand, but one whom we can trust while we do
not understand. I do not think that Christianity
removes many, if any, of the intellectual difficulties we feel in contemplating life and the world;
it rather outflanks them by a revelation of God
which makes it possible to trust and love him,
notwithstanding the mystery of his ways, and
which assures us that all good things are safe,
and are moving on and up,

> Through graves and ruins and the wrecks of things,
> Borne ever Godward with increasing might.

The great significance of the Christian revelation, then, does not lie in its contribution to
ethics or to speculative theology, though it has

done something in both of these realms; but
rather in this, that back of the mystery and
uncertainty of our own lives, back of the apparent aimlessness of much history, and back of
the woe and horror of much more, it reveals
God, the almighty Friend and Lover of men,
the Chief of burden-bearers, and the Leader of
all in self-sacrifice. Over the seething chaos there
broods a Spirit divine; and from everlasting to
everlasting there stretches a broad bow of promise
and of light.

Such is the Christian revelation — a revelation
of God, of his righteousness, his love, his gracious purpose, and his gracious work. As such
it is

> The fountain light of all our day,
> A master light of all our seeing.

It is a great spiritual force at the head of all
the beneficent and inspiring forces which make
for the upbuilding of men and the bringing in
of the kingdom of God. If we would know some
things we must turn to nature, or to history, or
to psychology ; but if we would know what God
is, and what he means for men, we must come to
the Christian revelation, especially as completed
in Jesus Christ. Here only do we find the Father
adequately revealed.

The system of Christian thought about God

and man and their mutual relations, when seen
in its simplicity, is worthy of all acceptation. If
it be a dream it is the greatest dream humanity
has ever dreamed. Our hope for ourselves and
for our race is inseparably bound up with it. If
God be such a being as Christianity declares, we
have a sure foundation for the highest faith and
the noblest endeavor. But we often fail duly to
appreciate this revelation, or we make ourselves
needless difficulties in understanding it, because
of sundry misconceptions; which we now proceed to consider.

As the world is very different from what we
should expect a work of perfect wisdom, power,
and goodness would be, so God's revelation of
himself is very different in its mode and instruments from what we should have expected. And
we have commonly come to the study of the subject with various preconceived notions concerning revelation, and these have proved scarcely
less disastrous in biblical study than similar
notions have proved in physical science. It is
very easy, in an abstract way, to determine what
revelation must be, and these abstract determi-
nations often make it difficult to perceive what
revelation really is. And we are not willing to
allow it to be what examination shows it to be;

but we insist on wresting it into some conformity with our preconceived notions of what revelation must be.

The simplest and clearest notion of revelation identifies it with the Bible, and makes it the Word of God. Various reasons, historical and exegetical, unite in recommending this conception. This Word, again, was given by inspiration, and this, in turn, is most easily conceived as dictation. When the things thus dictated were written down and gathered up into a single volume, they formed the one infallible Word of God. This notion is level to the lowest understanding, and a great many biblical phrases readily lend themselves to it. With such a conception it was only natural to expect to find everything in the book as perfect and complete as its divine author. Infallibility was a necessary consequence. To admit error of any kind was to abandon the Bible altogether. For a long time it was held that even the language was perfect ; and the suggestion that the Greek of the New Testament was not classical was resented as little less than heresy. It certainly was not to be thought of, that the Holy Spirit did not write as good Greek as mortal men, and heathens at that.

This conception of a dictated book has always ruled popular theological thought, and for manifest reasons. The notion of a revelation through history, through the moral life of a community, through the insight of godly men, is comparatively difficult and uncertain. It is not so easy to see where and how the Divine comes in, or how to distinguish it from the human. It admits, too, of no such definite statutory formulation, and it cannot be so readily used in dogmatic construction, and especially in dogmatic fulmination. A formal verbal statement, on the other hand, is something sure and steadfast. It is convenient and portable also, and when prefaced by "thus saith the Lord," it cannot fail to put to flight the armies of the aliens. Nevertheless, this conception is a mistake, and a great part of our difficulties in this field are due to its implicit or explicit presence. For clearing up this matter, a word is needed concerning inspiration.

That the Scriptures are the product of inspiration is the firm faith of the Church. The authors were not left to their own devices, or to the blind gropings of their own understanding; but they spoke and wrote under the actuating influence of the Holy Spirit. So much clearly appears from a study of the writings themselves, and more especially from a comparison of them with the other sacred writings of the race. This divine influence and guidance are more manifest to-day than ever before; for we see more clearly how difficult was the problem to be solved. While other writers lost themselves in wild cosmogonies, and fictitious science, and fantastic dreams, the writers of the Bible maintain the most extraordinary soberness and reticence on these points. The errors into which they may have fallen are comparatively few in any case, and they in no way defeat the revelation of God at which the writers aim. The unique character of the Scriptures in this respect can be appreciated only by comparison with the other bibles of the race.

So, then, we may say that the Scriptures were inspired; that is, were written by men who were moved and enlightened by the Holy Spirit. But this does not mean that they were dictated by an Infallible Intelligence. The presence of inspiration is discernible in the product; but the meaning and measure of inspiration cannot be decided by abstract reflection, but only by study of the outcome. What inspiration is must be learned from what it does. We have no apriori conception of inspiration from which we can infer its essential nature. Neither are we permitted to say that inspiration always means the same thing; for inspiration may have different degrees. For instance, the degree of inspiration necessary to write the Book of Esther would be very different from that needed for the prophecies of Isaiah or the Pauline epistles. Hence we must not determine the character of the books from the inspiration, but must rather determine the nature of the inspiration from the books.

But how can there be inspiration without dictation? To this question there is no theoretical answer. The influence of one human mind upon another is a mystery; much more so is the influence of the Divine Spirit upon the human spirit. We can only fall back here upon the analogies of our own experience. In a perfectly real sense a teacher may inspire his pupils, or a philosopher his disciples, so that they remain themselves and yet are lifted to an insight to which of themselves they would never attain. We cannot tell how it is done, but the fact is familiar. In like manner, a preacher is often spoken of as inspired when he attains to some special insight or deep spiritual fervor. And the inspiration may well be real; but it does not turn the man into the passive instrument of a power above him; it rather lifts the man himself to a higher power. It is inspiration, not dictation. It is in accordance with these analogies that we must think of the inspiration of the Scriptures. God did not dictate the Scriptures, he inspired them; and that in such a way that the authors were at once themselves and also attained to a higher insight than was possible to their unaided powers.

But now it will be said that this is very loose indeed. Such a conception of inspiration does well enough for vague popular speech, but it is all too uncertain for the source of revelation. This demands something more definite and objective, something which can be fixed in a scientific definition; and this must finally be found in the notion of infallible dictation.

Without doubt this notion of dictation is the only conception of inspiration which is perfectly clear; all others shade away into indefiniteness and refuse to be fixed in a hard-and-fast definition. But equally without doubt this notion is absolutely untenable when applied to the received canon of the Old and New Testaments. Let us admit the literal truth of the passages where it is said that the word of the Lord came to prophets or apostles and which they were commanded to write down, it is still clear that this is very far from establishing the dictation of all the books of the Old and New Testaments. That some prophetic vision came to Isaiah as the word of the Lord may well be believed; but there is no connection between this fact and the claim that the books of Chronicles or the books of Esther and Ruth were written at the dictation of the Holy Spirit. The doctrine of dictation, as held by traditional theology, applies to the whole canon; and this doctrine is groundless. The Scriptures themselves make and warrant no such claim. Nothing would reveal the absurdity more strikingly than the attempt to conceive the Holy Spirit as the real author of the various utterances of the many speakers and writers. Speaking in their own person, they are intelligible; conceived as masks through which the Holy Spirit speaks, nothing could well be more puzzling and unprofitable. In the introduction to the Gospel of Luke and to the Book of Acts, the writer sets forth his reasons for writing and his acquaintance with the facts, like any other historical writer, and he shows no suspicion of being an amanuensis of the Holy Spirit. To such confusion the notion of dictation inevitably leads us; and when we lay aside this notion, there is nothing left but the vaguer yet more manageable notion of inspiration.

The traditional doctrine of inspiration, we have said, was not formed upon any study of the Scriptures themselves, but rather upon apriori assumptions as to what inspiration must be. To this may be added sundry influences from non-Christian sources. The Greeks and Romans had their revelations through various oracles; and these were commonly pathological performances in which the oracle raved and babbled under the influence of the " divine afflatus," and supposedly with little or no knowledge of what was said. The words spoken were words of the god. This conception was carried over into Christianity by some of the early Christian writers on inspiration. This view, together with the apriori assumption referred to, for a long time shut up the Church to the notion of a dictated book, of which the writers were only "the inspired penmen" while God himself was the real author, no matter whose name might appear as the writer. The Helvetic Formula pushed this dependence so far as to make words, letters, and punctuation marks alike inspired of God.

A very slight acquaintance with the text disposes of such a doctrine. If the Holy Spirit were the sole author of all the accounts we should expect them to agree, which of course is not the case. But it may occur to us that there is an important element in inspiration which has not yet been mentioned, and which is really the essential thing. This is infallibility. Dictation is important only as securing infallibility; and we may give it up, provided the infallibility is retained. The psychological state of the Scripture writers, then, is not a matter of supreme importance. They may have spoken or written in a state of ecstasy, or they may have received direct dictation from the Holy Spirit, or they may have been left to choose their own thoughts and words according to their mental type and experience, subject of course to the "supervision" or "superintendence" of the Spirit ; but however this may have been, the product of their inspiration must have been infallible if we are to have any confidence in it. If this be denied we might as well give up inspiration altogether. Accordingly we find, in the complicated and varying theories of inspiration which have been held in the Church, this notion of infallibility commonly underlying them, at least for all essential factors of revelation. In this claim all church authorities have generally agreed. The late Pope and the present Pope have both formally denounced the notion that there can be any error in Scripture, and Protestant leaders have generally done the same.

Abstractly considered, this seems conclusive. A fallible guide would seem to be none, or worse than none. We must, then, consider the supposed necessity of maintaining the infallibility of the Scriptures.

If we should discuss this question of inerrancy abstractly, it would be easy to make out a strong case for the necessity of the doctrine. We might say that the divine origin of the Scriptures im-

plies it, or that without it we should be all at
sea, and might as well have no revelation. But
we should be very careful in pressing such reasoning ; for, if sound, it can only result in the overthrow of all faith. It is beyond any question that
we have no inerrant Scriptures at present, whether
in the original languages or in the later versions.
Let any one who insists on inerrancy on the
basis of such abstract reasoning come out of his
closet long enough to consider the condition of
the manuscripts, early and late, and the variations of the versions, ancient and modern; and
unless he be given over he will see that strict
inerrancy in any Scriptures we have, or ever can
have, is a fiction. If, again, he insist on historic
inerrancy at least, let him suspend his insistence
until he has made the books of Chronicles and
the books of Kings tell accurately the same story.

Considerations of this kind have led many to
abandon the claim of inerrancy in the existing
Scriptures, and to confine it to "some original
manuscript." But if inerrancy is a matter of
practical importance, this view leaves us without the necessary guidance. Some original manuscript, which has vanished beyond any hope of
recovery, was infallible ; but the existing manuscripts and versions are not. What gain, then, do
we get from the vanished infallibility ? We may

possibly fancy that we have saved the divine veracity, but for practical purposes we are as badly off as ever.

And even if we had an infallible manuscript, which had descended from the earliest time, of how much use would it be to us without certain other infallibilities which not even the dullest would venture to claim? If infallibility be necessary, we should need not merely to reproduce ancient words, but ancient modes of thought and feeling as well. Unless our translators did this, we should still be exposed to error. And after the ancient words had been reproduced in exact modern equivalents, they would next need to be understood. Even those who have agreed in the inerrancy of the Scriptures have had disagreement enough in their interpretation. Theology, past and present, sufficiently illustrates this fact. The nature of language itself makes it impossible that there should be any hard-and-fast objective interpretation. The necessarily metaphorical nature of all language applying to spiritual relations bars the way.

Thus the original infallibility with which we started disperses and loses itself in the general uncertainties of translation and of language itself, and in the wranglings of theologians. We could hardly be worse off with any permissible admission of errancy than we actually have been with the stiffest doctrine of inerrancy. Even when pieced out with the doctrine of an infallible church, inerrancy has not saved us from divers winds of doctrine in the infallible church itself. Maintainers of inerrancy, then, ought to be put under bonds to tell us, in the face of the undeniable facts of biblical study and theological history, what their view has done for us, or can do for us; especially now that the "original manuscript" is lost.

Well, then, we have no revelation; and every one is free to do as he pleases with the Scriptures! This is a "logical consequence" of admitting errancy which cannot be evaded, and which, when properly flourished before the appropriate audience, is always effective. In reply we should say that this is a piece of closet logic, a verbal intimidation, resulting from considering the subject in an abstract and academic fashion. It is the exact parallel of a similar objection in the theory of knowledge. We may ask if our senses ever deceive us; and the answer must be, Yes. And then we may continue, with true closet logic: Well, if our senses may deceive us, how do we know that they do not always deceive us? And the answer must be that we cannot tell. And then, of course, the conclusion is drawn that we have no standard for distinguishing truth from error, and that skepticism overwhelming is upon us.

Now academically this is all right. This problem admits of no abstract theoretical solution. If we stay in the closet we can argue forever, and draw the most fearful logical consequences. But the problem solves itself in practice. We know both that the senses deceive us and that they help us to most valuable knowledge. We find out that they can thus help us, not by theorizing about them, but by using them.

The application to the case before us is manifest. The abstract problem, how an imperfect record can yet be an authority, admits of no theoretical solution. Like the problem of knowledge, it must be solved in practice. The value of the Bible must be determined, not by abstract theories of what it must be, but rather by study of what it proves itself to be in the religious life of the world. And tested in this way, nothing is clearer than its supreme significance. Whatever spots we find on it, it still remains the sun.

And thus it appears how barren and practically irrelevant is the abstract question as to the inerrancy of the Bible. As already said, if the doctrine is important we are in a bad way, because we have no inerrant Bible at present. If we grant the doctrine, we can make nothing of it; and we are as badly off with it as without it. But these manifest and palpable facts are hidden from us through the deceit of closet discussion, whereby we attempt to decide what must be, instead of inquiring what is. The doctrine is really of no practical interest. It owes its supposed importance to an abstract and academic treatment, which overlooks the concrete facts of the case and confuses itself with drawing fictitious "logical consequences." We meet all such difficulties by coming out of the closet and looking at the concrete facts. And then many a thing which may be difficult in theory is found perfectly simple in practice. Plato expounded the abstract impossibility of motion; and Diogenes refuted him by walking up and down before him. Concrete matters must be concretely tested; and abstract objections may often be removed by walking.

These misconceptions of the Bible, and the abstract and verbal discussions thence resulting, have greatly tended to obscure the meaning and to hinder the acceptance of the divine revelation. We have supposed ourselves bound to maintain the infallibility of the Bible, to find a revelation in every detail, and to defend the divineness of all that is attributed to God. In

truth, the revelation consists in what we have
learned concerning God, his character, and his
purposes; and the revelation is mainly made by
a great historical movement. Of this movement
the Bible is at once the product and the historical and literary record. The truth of the revelation depends on the general truth of the history,
and not at all on the infallibility of the record.
But we identify the record and the revelation,
and make ourselves additional difficulties by a
hard-and-fast theory of our own invention concerning the inspiration of the record. In this way
the Bible itself has often been made an obstacle
to the acceptance of the revelation. This is especially the case when ignorant ark-savers, without
suspicion that the Bible is a literature and a
library, and having never so much as heard of
the history of the canon, begin to flourish such
phrases as the " Word of God," as if all questions
were settled thereby. What such persons believe
about the Bible amounts to as little as what
Brother Jasper believed about astronomy. From
the same confusion of the record and the revelation even scholars have often lost all sense of
perspective and of relative values, and often
have missed the good news of God altogether in
disputes about dates, authorship, and swarms of
insignificant details; so that we cannot see the

great Christian facts from being taken up with the question whether Moses wrote the account of his own death, or whether the dead man really did come to life when his corpse touched the bones of the Prophet Elisha, or whether the lost axe really did swim when the prophet threw a stick into the water. And when we discuss the evidences of revelation we proceed in an abstract and ineffective way. We begin with a scholastic discussion of miracles and prophecy, and seek to establish the truth of revelation by these abstract considerations.

Now, this is inverted in every way, and we need to bring forth fruits meet for repentance. We must see that the revelation consists essentially in the new ideas concerning God and his will for men, and that all else — the history and the writing — are but means of setting forth and preserving these ideas. The Church was Christian long before it had the Bible, as the Christian ideas long preceded the completion of the biblical canon. The Church is Christian because of the effective presence of these ideas, not because of its doctrine of Scripture. And we must also see that any fruitful and convincing discussion of revelation for us must proceed from its fundamental ideas, and from its actual presence and power in the world. Miracle and prophecy can

never furnish a satisfactory starting-point nowadays for such a discussion. These things are too
far away to affect us. Even when we think we
believe them, we at once perceive that we do so
only because of their connection with a great
historical order now existing. If Christianity
were not a world-power, a great spiritual force
here and now, its origin would be a matter of
profound indifference, and nothing that happened thousands of years ago would ever make
it credible to us. We should not even take the
trouble to deny it; we should ignore it. But
when we find it to be such a power; when we
trace its progress, like a mighty gulf-stream,
through the ocean of human history; when we
compare its literature with that of other religious
systems, — then we have a great historical and
psychological problem for solution, and we find
no adequate solution except in the insight that
God has been revealing himself and establishing
a divine kingdom in the earth. The present fact
accords with the ancient history, and the ancient
history throws light upon the present fact. It is
their harmony and reciprocal implication, and the
moral and spiritual grandeur of the emerging system, upon which our conviction finally rests. In
this large way the doctrine of Scripture and the
evidences of Christianity must be discussed, if

any valuable result is to be reached. We must pass from abstract and scholastic discussions of a book to the concrete discussion of the Christian history and outcome.

Into such a discussion the question of biblical inerrancy need not enter at all. We need only consider the general truthfulness of the record. Moreover, the movement is to be studied as a whole; not only in its crude beginnings, but also in its outcome. The significance of the early stages of the revealing movement is not to be discerned by any abstract study of them or of their supernatural attendants, but rather by what has historically come out of them. Taken by themselves, they are crude enough. Taken abstractly, they are easily made to seem absurd. Taken without reference to what has grown out of them, they appear worthless. But taken historically, and in connection with the system of which they are a part, they are seen in their deep significance.

There is a good deal of logical delusion at this point on the part of both radicals and conservatives. On the one hand, we often fancy that the inerrancy of the Bible is the great affirmation of Christianity; and, on the other, we fancy that if we show errors of any kind, we have overthrown Christianity. In both cases we blunder. Chris-

tianity does not affirm an infallible Bible, but a
self-revealing God. It holds that God was in the
historical movement out of which the Bible came,
and in it in such a way that out of it we have
won a supremely valuable knowledge of God.
Whatever else was or was not there, God was
there, guiding the movement for his own self-
revelation. This is the true and only Christian
faith in this matter. And this faith is not affected
by the discovery of error and legend in the Scriptures. If we admit their existence, we also have
to admit that the great, fruitful, living, and life-
giving ideas concerning God and his purposes
have come to us along this historical line. The
spots on the sun have not hindered its shining.
However we insist on the presence of mythical
and unhistorical matter in the Bible, it has not
prevented God's highest revelation of himself.
This is the treasure which the vessel of Scripture,
however earthen, demonstrably contains. What
the Christian thinker should maintain is the
divine presence and guidance in the revealing
movement as a whole. He need not concern himself about details, whether for better or for worse.
All we can insist upon is, that the error, the
legend, the myth, if there be such, shall not obscure the purpose of the whole — the revelation
of God. And the objector also, if he wishes to

say anything to the purpose, should fix his attention on the central ideas, and not on details. The idea of an historical movement for the self-revelation of God is the great supernatural factor in the case, and this is not disposed of by any criticism of particulars. The essential Christian thought is of a world with God in it, of humanity with God in it, of history with God in it, of a great world movement from God through humanity to God again, where God is all and in all. In the presence of a great thought like this, it seems little less than intellectual indecency to make an issue over the speaking ass, or the talking serpent, or the rib that was made into a woman, whether to affirm or to deny.

By thus separating the religious system of ideas from questions of date, authorship, and questions of textual record, we may remain Christians in spite of the higher critics. Some of the critics have done wild work, and criticism has sometimes run to leaves without bearing any valuable fruit. The polychrome edition of the Bible, for instance, its minute partition of the text and even of texts, shows a faith beyond anything in Israel. Any one with a sense of logical responsibility and with a knowledge of the limitations of the evidence in the case knows that this pretended accuracy is a vagary of the imagination. But the general results of critical study have done only good and not harm. It is no longer permitted to teach that the Bible was infallibly dictated, or that the several works were written down once for all by the men whose names they bear, and were never revised afterwards ; but the Bible is no less profitable as revelation of God than before. Only now, instead of a simple dictation or single composition, we have an historical process, and the complex religious thought and consciousness of the ancient Church.

But now it will be asked again, How can a book containing error be trusted at all? This is that academic difficulty which arises from a closet discussion of the subject. We have already referred to it in treating of the infallibility of the Bible. We recur to it again in the hope that we may now be better able to discern its purely verbal and scholastic character. The same question may be asked concerning the use of our faculties, or our trust in any evidence or testimony. All of these things are affected with fallibility, and if we should attempt to find an abstract standard which should warrant our trust in our faculties or in one another, we should only land ourselves in universal skepticism. But when, instead of theorizing about our faculties, we use them, we get on very comfortably. The problem which is insoluble in theory, solves itself in practice.

In fact, the general problem of the criterion of knowledge, in whatever field, is practical rather than speculative. Academic discussion is futile and barren. In both religion and philosophy there has been a deal of abstract theorizing about the ultimate standard of truth or authority, as if there were some simple standard which, by external application, would reveal the truth. But there is no such standard. The mind itself, alert and critical, and with all its furniture of experienced life, is the only standard, and this can never be brought into any single and compendious expression. The mind has no standard of certainty, but it is certain about various things. Practical certainty is all we can hope for in concrete matters; and this is born, not of closet speculation, but of actual contact with reality. Concerning this certainty we can always raise formal doubts and cavils; but they disappear in practice. And any one who will use the Scriptures in this practical way, and with the aim of learning how to think about God and his relations to us and his purposes concerning us, will have no difficulty in discerning their great religious value, however much of mythical and unhistorical matter they may be thought to contain.

This insight into the practical nature of certainty is becoming general in the speculative world, and marks a very important step forward. The professional skeptic finds his occupation going, if not gone; for his objections have commonly been of the abstract, academic type, and these are now seen in their perennial barrenness and fatuity. It will be a great gain when the same insight becomes general in the religious world. The search for this abstract, infallible standard, and the claim to possess it, have caused, and still cause, no little confusion. That there is no such thing is manifest, and that it would harm rather than help, if we had it, is equally clear. A standard which left no room for choice, for love and loyalty, would defeat the moral ends of life. The heart and will have nothing to do with the acceptance of the multiplication-table, and no spiritual truth would have any value which could be thus accepted.

Parallel to this question of a standard, and partly coincident with it, is the question of authority in religion. Abstractly considered, it seems evident that without some final authority we must be all at sea. Practically considered, it is equally plain that the mass of men must live by authority in religion, as in everything else. The great majority of unbelievers as well as of believers are such by hearsay and authority, and not by any real insight or understanding. The form of life and its development make this necessary. Children, of course, cannot think for themselves; and from the lack of time and faculty the case is much the same with most men. Authority, imitation, and social contagion are the great sources of actual belief. These general facts make confusion possible; and the possibility has been abundantly realized. Of course no one imagines that authority *makes* anything true; but it is not an irrational supposition that authority can *declare* a thing to be true, so that because of our faith in the authority we can accept the thing declared, even when we do not clearly see the reasons for ourselves. In such cases authority is only a means for giving ignorance the benefit of knowledge, which it could not reach or hold of itself.

But when we come to apply these considerations to religion, confusion sets in again. Some will have it that the Church is the seat of authority; others find it in the Scriptures, and still others find it in reason and conscience. Abstractly considered, quite an argument could be made for each of these positions. Has not the Church, it might be asked, historically been the pillar and ground of the truth? Could Christian truth itself long survive the decay of the institution? But equally it might be pointed out that without the constant appeal and return to the Scriptures the Church itself is sure to go astray; and much historical evidence could be adduced in support of this claim.

Finally, it might be urged that reason and conscience are the final court of appeal; and much might be said to prove it. Martineau wrote a large volume, the weakest of all his works, in defense of this view. But all of these positions are abstract and partial. They are cases of the fallacy of "either, or," whereas the truth is "both, and." Practically, there is a measure of truth in each of these views; but practically, again, the whole truth is found only in all three taken together. The stiffest doctrine of Scripture inerrancy has not prevented warring interpretations; and those who would place the seat of authority in reason and conscience are forced to admit that outside illumination may do much for both. In mathematics the final seat of authority for each learner is most certainly in his reason; and yet without the teacher, this reason, which testeth all things, would not get far in most cases. Much more is this true in religion. Sabatier has written a very able work on "Religions of Authority," which religions are contrasted, to their discredit, with the "religion of the Spirit"; but in his zeal against authority, Sabatier fails to notice that historically authority has been and is a very necessary fact in religious development.

But, on the other hand, it is equally plain historically that book and church have had to yield again and again to the growing spiritual insight of the religious community. The stoutest verbalist and ecclesiastic to-day would not tolerate things on which once they vehemently insisted, but which have been outgrown, although the texts once relied on still exist. "If a man abide not in me, he is cast forth as a branch, and is withered; and men gather them, and cast them into the fire, and they are burned." This was long the standard text on the manner of dealing with heretics, but it has long since gone out of commission. "Compel them to come in" is another text that did great service in the past, but has been humanized in modern times. Back in the fifteenth century there was a great controversy whether the blood of Christ that was shed on the cross lost its hypostatic union with the Divine Logos and its world-saving quality while it lay on the ground at the foot of the cross, and a great debate was held at Rome for the decision of the question. Such a controversy is unthinkable to-day, even in the most orthodox circles. All interpretations of words must be functions of the interpreters, as well as of dictionaries and

grammars. When Caliban studies natural theology he finds Setebos, who is simply Caliban
enlarged. When Caliban interprets Scripture
he does the same thing. Plainly, no mechanical
religious standards can escape appealing to the
complex life of the religious community as the
real interpreter and judge of the standards themselves, and of their permissible meaning and
application. Apart from this, the old gibe is
literally true of the Bible: —

> This is the book where each his doctrine seeks,
> And this the book where each his doctrine finds.

Of course, if one takes a mechanical view of
salvation, and supposes that our safety depends
on some accuracy of ritual, or some exact orthodoxy of belief, such a person needs an absolute
standard or authority, in order to make sure that
no mistake has been made and the requirement
punctually fulfilled. Such notions obtain in many
non-Christian religions, and they are by no means
unknown in Christian history ; but they are nonexistent for one who has reached a moral and
spiritual conception of Christianity.

In all this polemical discussion of the Bible,
one commonly finds on both sides oversight of
the fact that the great significance of the Bible
is to help men to God. This is its religious use

and this is the main thing with the majority of Christians. It is their book of religion. The questions of criticism have no existence for them; but they read, — "The Lord is my shepherd; I shall not want." "God is our refuge and strength, a very present help in trouble." "This is a faithful saying . . . that Christ Jesus came into the world to save sinners." "For we know if the earthly house of this tabernacle be dissolved, we have a building of God, a house not made with hands, eternal in the heavens." "Let not your heart be troubled . . . In my Father's house are many mansions . . . I go to prepare a place for you." On passages like these the Christian world has lived, and in the strength of them a multitude of saints have died. They knew nothing of criticism, higher or lower; but they found God in the Bible, and God found them in the Bible, and they knew whom they had believed. No one is fit to give an opinion on the value of the Scriptures who overlooks this religious use of them, and the fact that by this use the great majority of God's saints have been nourished and are still nourished. It is to explain this fact that devout scholars have long spoken of the *testimonium spiritus sancti* as the great warrant of Scripture. A book that did not find us, to use the expression of Coleridge, would not long command our

attention or assent; but a book that does find
us in the deepest places and springs of life will
always command the allegiance of those who
seek to live in the spirit. No errors of science
or history will diminish its religious value for
the devout and religious heart. Of course, we
all understand the moral imperfection of the
Old Testament. A great many things jar on us
as falling short of the spirit of Christ, for
instance, the imprecatory psalms. And yet our
fundamental human needs and religious aspirations often find perfect and permanent expression
in the words of prophet and psalmist, so that we
turn to those words as humanity's classical religious utterance, and as being just as fresh and
living to-day as when they were uttered twenty-
five hundred years ago. " The Lord is my shepherd " ; " God is our refuge and strength ; " Bless
the Lord, O my soul " ; " Unto thee, O Lord, will
I lift up my soul " ; " The Lord is my Light " ; —
these are specimens of the Old Testament as a religious book, and as expressing humanity's search
after God in all its perennial moods and phases
of triumph and depression, of joy and sorrow
and misery. These words come to us across the
ages, and they pierce us through and through
with their insight into human needs in all ages;
and this gives them their imperishable vitality.

The possibility of combining effective religious teaching with error as to matter of fact may be seen in the following verse from Addison's hymn: —

> What though in solemn silence all
> Move round the dark terrestrial ball ?
> What though no real voice nor sound
> Amid the radiant orbs be found ?
> In reason's ear they all rejoice,
> And utter forth a glorious voice ;
> Forever singing as they shine
> " The hand that made us is divine."

The false astronomy of the first two lines does not diminish the religious value of the hymn. Had this verse occurred in a psalm, the traditionalists would have dealt with it after this fashion : Some would have maintained the geocentric theory as a divine revelation, and would have anathematized all other views. Others, longing to reconcile religion and science, would have held that the writer really knew the true theory, as it is not to be thought of that an "inspired penman" should be in error, but that, though knowing better, he described the fact as it appears. Thus the divine veracity and the infallibility of the Scripture writer would be saved. And still others might hold, on the warrant of common sense, that whether in the psalm or in the hymn, the religious value is independent of astronomic theory. Of course, the traditional rationalist would see nothing but the bad astronomy; all else would fall upon the blind spot of his intellect.

In the traditional discussion of revelation the antithesis of natural and supernatural has played a great part, and has been the source of much confusion. This antithesis has played a great part in the traditional discussion of revelation, and has been the source of much confusion. The traditionalist has commonly charged those who differ from him with denying the supernatural, and with attempting a purely naturalistic interpretation of the Bible. With him a variety of schemes pass for " bald naturalism." It is well to clear up our thought on this subject.

Without doubt there has been a deal of naturalism at one time and another which was " bald," and even worse. Such is the naturalism which assumes that there is a blind and impersonal system, called Nature, which does a great variety of unintended things on its own account, so that they represent no divine thought or purpose, but are simply by-products of the natural mechanism. In this sense the natural excludes purpose and intelligence altogether, and warrants the dislike and fear with which popular religious thought regards it. This conception of the natural grows up spontaneously in the field of sense thought which has not been duly chastened by criticism; but it is really an idol of the sense tribe. Philosophical criticism is rapidly leading to the insight that this nature is only a fiction of unenlightened thought. A painted devil may give one a turn, if supposed to be real ; but it becomes harmless when seen in its true nature. Critical thought will not hear of an independent or self-running nature in any case. It follows, then, that whatever nature does, represents that which it has been determined to do by a power beyond it. And if that power be intelligent, as the theist believes, then nature is simply doing that which God wills. Thus nature becomes simply the expression of the divine thought; and all the details of nature's working are as rooted in the divine purpose as they would be if executed by immediate fiat. And a still deeper metaphysics makes it doubtful if nature have any proper energy whatever in itself, or be anything more than the system of phenomena whose cause must be sought beyond itself. On this view there are two distinct questions concerning what we call nature. The first concerns the phenomena themselves, their nature, laws, and interrelations in general. The second concerns the causality in which this system is founded or from which it proceeds. The first question can be answered only by inductive science; the second belongs to metaphysics.

Theism is the only answer to the second question. In God all that we mean by nature lives and moves and has its being. The independent, self-administering nature vanishes; and all that remains of nature is the phenomenal order, and this has its efficient ground in God. But this order is an important object of study. After we have decided that the world is God's work, we have still to learn what the world is, and how God works in it; what the laws are according to which he proceeds, and how events are connected in space and time. Without some knowledge of this kind, the world would be impenetrable to our intelligence; indeed, we could not live at all. On this view, nature is only a general name for the system of phenomena; and events are natural in the form and circumstances of their occurrence, but supernatural in their causality. The events which arise in accordance with the established laws of the system are natural; but the causality is supernatural throughout. The most familiar fact is as supernatural in its causation as any miracle would be. The difference would lie only in the phenomenal relations.

With this result we no longer set up the natural and the supernatural in mutual exclusion.

A natural event is one in which we trace familiar laws, not one in which there is no divine
causality or purpose. And a supernatural event
would be one which, from its form or the circumstances of its occurrence, would more or less
clearly indicate a divine presence and purpose;
but in its causality it would be no more truly
divine than any routine happening. In its essential causality nothing whatever is explained by
"known natural laws," or by "unknown natural
laws," but only by the will and purpose of God.
The most familiar event proceeds as directly
from the divine will as the most extraordinary and
miraculous. The causality of the natural is supernatural, that is, divine. The method of the supernatural is natural, that is, God proceeds according to orderly methods. But whatever happens, be
it the maintenance of the familiar routine or miraculous departure from it, happens not of itself
or because of some mechanical law or system,
but because in the divine purpose and wisdom
that is the thing demanded. And in all things
alike God is equally present and equally near.

Thus, in the general field of theism, we are
compelled to distinguish the question of causality
from the question of method; and we see that
neither question answers the other. It is only
through mental confusion that we can fancy that

the decision as to causality decides the method
of procedure, or that the discovery of method
reveals the essential causality. Something of the
same distinction may be made in our study of
revelation. Our conviction that God is immanent
in the revealing movement does not decide the
form of the movement; and we are left free to
inquire as to this form, and to see to what extent
we can trace in it the familiar laws of history and
of the human mind. We are all the more free to
do this from the fact that the Scripture writers
largely described the facts from their conception
of the divine causality rather than from the phenomenal standpoint. It was their habit to refer
events directly to God without mention of sec-
ondary or intermediate causes or natural laws.
In this they were quite right as to the causality,
but we get a wrong impression as to the appearance of the event. There was certainly no such
phenomenal departure from the familiar order of
law in every case as the language of the reporters would lead us, with our different habit of
thought, to expect. If an Armada had sailed from
Tyre for a descent on the coast of Palestine and
had been dispersed and sunk in a storm, a Jewish
patriot would have ascribed the result directly to
God, and in this he might have been right; but
if we had been there we should have seen only a

storm. This would not indeed disprove the divine agency, but it would modify our conception of its form and method. The causality would be supernatural, but the method would be natural.

Without doubt this is the case with much of the supernatural reported in the Scriptures. It is to be understood from the standpoint of causality and purpose rather than from the standpoint of phenomena. And this is said, not from any aversion to miracle, but as being the conclusion to which a study of the reports themselves and of the habits of thought of the reporters naturally leads. And when we come to the distinctly miraculous, to that which breaks with the natural order and reveals the presence of a supernatural power, we may still look for some of the familiar natural continuities. Miracles which broke with all law would be nothing intelligible. We can understand miracles as signs whereby sense-bound minds are made aware of a divine power and purpose which they would otherwise miss, in their subjection to the mechanical movement of nature; but we cannot suppose them wrought at random and without any reference to the antecedents and environment. Thus, if we suppose God should design to make a revelation of higher mathematical truth, even by way of miracle, it is clear that the miracle would not be wrought among the Patagonians or Hottentots, but rather there where the development of civilization and of mathematical knowledge had made a place for the reception of the revelation. Even seed divinely sown needs a prepared soil, if there is to be any worthy fruitage; and thorny and stony ground does not furnish such a soil.

Hence, if we admit, not only the supernatural but also the miraculous element in revelation, it is plain that the revealing movement admits of being studied from the natural standpoint; that is, we may seek to trace the familiar laws of life and thought and history and human development in the progress and unfolding of the movement. And such study, when thought is clear, has no tendency to cast doubt on the supernatural source of the movement. On the other hand, it lends an absorbing human and rational interest to the problem, which is impossible when the human is paralyzed by the divine, and the natural is replaced by unintelligible arbitrariness. Naturalism, then, which displaces God and erects impersonal law into a mechanical and self-administering system which knows neither itself nor its products, we cast out with assured conviction, and that on the authority of both religion and philosophy; but naturalism, which attempts to trace the continuity of law and rational connection through all the works of God, whether in nature or revelation, is to be approved and welcomed.

Such naturalism never gives a causal explanation, but it is good as far as it goes. Its nature and value may be seen from the following illustration: It is very common to say that a man is explained by his time and environment. For instance, Newton would have been impossible among the Bushmen. His work demanded the existence of civilization and the work of previous mathematicians. This is undoubted; and, in this sense, Newton is explained by his time and environment. But it would be highly superficial to rest in this. The time and environment were the same for every mathematician in England; but they were ineffective until combined with the special genius of Newton; and this is something which time and environment never account for. Hence, in studying a man's life, we certainly need to consider his antecedents and surroundings. But the man himself is a factor apart, connected with these things, but not to be confounded with them or deduced from them. In the same way the naturalistic study of revelation can show important preparations, historical continuities, pyschological uniformities, rational harmonies; but we reach nothing final until we come to the immanent, self-revealing God.

The doctrine of the divine immanence, which is being reëstablished in philosophic thought once more, relieves many of the traditional difficulties of this discussion. Our Western thought has been largely ruled by the deistic conception of an absentee God and a mechanical universe. The chief part of our intellectual puzzles in this field are due to this obsolete notion. Religion is really concerned only to affirm a divine causality and meaning in the world; and science is really concerned only with the method by which that causality proceeds. These are two separate questions, and neither can conflict with the other. When this is better understood, the religious world will lose its fear of naturalism and its dread of law, because of the insight that God is working through the law and the order which he has made. And naturalism, on the other hand, will lose its dread of the supernatural, as it will recognize that the natural is only the form under which the Ever-living, Ever-acting God works his will.

The difficulties just dealt with have a logical and metaphysical root. We now come to others of a literary and linguistic character.

Another great hindrance to the understanding of revelation has been a misconception of the way in which language is used. The language

of the Bible has been taken in a hard-and-fast,
logical sense, as if it were evidence in a court
of law, or a theorem in geometry, and the most
grotesque distortions have resulted in consequence.

We are gradually learning that there is a language of poetry, of conscience, of emotion, of
aspiration, of religion, as well as a language of
the logical understanding. And the former language is absurd and incredible when tested by
the canons of the latter. Such language can be
understood only on its own plane and by the life
which generates it. The difference might be illustrated by our speech concerning the national
flag. One viewing the flag as a symbol of the
nation — its life, its history, its aspirations —
might say a great many things about it which
would be perfectly true from the standpoint of
sentiment and patriotic devotion, and perfectly
absurd from the standpoint of sense. For sense,
the flag is simply a variously-colored textile fabric;
but "Old Glory" is more than a textile fabric,
though it needs life and imagination to see it.

Now this distinction, so important in the living
use of language and so prominent in religious
speech, has been lamentably ignored in the study
of the Scriptures. A mathematician once read
"Paradise Lost," and reported that he did not see

that it proved anything. The Scriptures have
been studied in much the same spirit. The tendency has been to interpret every statement as a
statutory dogma, often without any reference to
the context, or the mode of thought of the time,
or the writer's purpose. Of course, we are all
familiar with the numberless petty sects based
on such Philistine interpretation, but the blunder
has never been lacking in the great orthodox
bodies. The result is as absurd as would be produced by a similar interpretation of our language
about the national flag.

As an illustration, consider the doctrine of
salvation by grace through faith. Every one, of
any moral development whatever, is ready to
renounce all claims to merit before God on the
ground of his own good works, and to affirm
that, if he have any place in the divine favor,
it must be based on the undeserved and condescending grace of God. Equally plain is it that,
if we are to be lifted out of our low life into the
life and fellowship of the Spirit, it must be, not
by any mechanical performance of external rites,
but by faith and trust in the grace which is
above us, and in the ideal which that grace
reveals. However we stumble or fall, we must
believe in that, and ever struggle toward it.
There is no deeper or more vital truth in the

moral and religious life. But it must be understood from the side of life. It must be vitally, ethically, spiritually apprehended. And when this is not done, and this doctrine is turned into a scheme of salvation on the model of criminal law, it loses its life-giving character altogether, and becomes incredible and pernicious. Mechanical interpretations of the atonement have often lent themselves to immoral conclusions, and nothing but a wholesome moral instinct has prevented it in every case.

A history of interpretation and of interpretations would be highly instructive. From this mechanical way of dealing with the subject it has often happened that those most familiar with the text have made the worst blunders as to the meaning. Out of this confusion we are gradually emerging, by the discovery that the Bible is not merely, nor mainly, a book of dogmas, but a body of religious literature also, which must be interpreted by universal literary methods.

A further specification of the same error about language is in overlooking the metaphorical nature of all language respecting invisible things. We have no way of expressing moral and spiritual truth except through some figure borrowed from our physical life and experience. But in such cases thought must be on its guard against taking the metaphor for the thing, or an exegesis of the metaphor for an exegesis of the thing. From oversight here a large part of traditional theology has been little more than an exegesis of misunderstood metaphors. The warning which Jesus gave, and which indeed lies on the surface, that the letter killeth, and the spirit only profiteth and giveth life, has been ignored, and history has been deluged with confusion and strife and bloodshed in consequence. It would lead to a great clarification of Christian thought if there were a general attempt to reduce the metaphors of Christian speech to their net significance. We should continue to use them thereafter, for there is nothing else to use; but we should be freed from bondage to them, and it might also turn out that there is a choice in metaphors. A great many metaphors of ancient religious speech are unimpressive or distasteful to us because the customs on which they rested have passed away, and we need new metaphors for the best expression of our thought.

There are a few persons who say that they take the Bible just as it reads; but that only means that they take their interpretation for the Bible. It reads : " He rode upon a cherub, and did fly ; yea, he did fly upon the wings of the wind." It reads : " He shall cover thee with his feathers, and under his wings shalt thou trust." Now there is probably no one who fancies such passages are to be taken as they read. Any one can see that such language must be taken for its meaning, and not for what it says; but not every one sees that a great many other readings are in the same case. Not every one sees that, as soon as we leave the plane of the senses, every statement has its element of "wings" and "feathers." There is no such thing as a hard-and-fast interpretation of such language. What we find in it will depend very much on ourselves, and on the presuppositions which we bring with us. And, in general, the progress of theology has consisted in adjusting *readings* to those fundamental principles of good sense and good morals to which revelation must conform, if it is to be of any value for us. These adjustments have commonly been resisted by the cry that the Word of God was being made of no effect; but Christian thought will always insist on interpreting the letter of the Bible in accordance with God's spiritual revelation of himself, both in the Bible and in the spiritual life of his children. An indefinite amount of historical theology, for which many texts could be adduced, has drifted away forever; not because we have become better grammarians and exegetes, but because it rested on an obsolete way of thinking about God and the Bible. In this way the Spirit leads us into truth. The realization of the spiritual life gives law to the exegesis of the Book.

And if any one should think that this must tend to fatal looseness, he may steady himself in two ways: First, he should remember that the value of the Scriptures can be determined only by using them in the earnest desire to know the mind and will of God. The frightful logical consequences which may be deduced from this view, as already pointed out, result entirely from viewing the matter academically and abstractly; and similar conclusions can be drawn from any theory of knowledge whatever. But certainty is a practical problem, and is to be reached only in practice and in contact with reality. When the Scriptures are used in this way, they have always vindicated themselves, and they always will. The only persons who will experience any sense of loss in this view are the dealers in proof-texts and detailed information concerning the divine plans and government. The detailed dogmatic constructions of the past are no longer possible, and we have to confine ourselves to the more general insight into what God is and what he means, and to the effort on our part to realize the divine kingdom upon earth. For this, we have all the information and inspiration needed; and this is enough.

And the second steadying consideration is

found in a look into history. There has hardly
been a step of progress — social, scientific, economic, religious — which has not been resisted as
fatal to the claims of the Bible. Ignorance in
high places has often made the Bible a menace to
humanity, and ignorance in low places has still
oftener made it a nuisance. This sort of thing fills
up the pages of Buckle and Draper and Lecky
and White. The humiliating history would be
a profitable subject of reflection for any one who
is inclined to resist any departure from his view
as fatal to the Bible. Texts have been arrayed
against astronomy, geology, political economy,
philosophy, geography, religious toleration, anti-
slavery, mercy to decrepit old women called
witches, anatomy, medicine, vaccination, anæs-
thetics, fanning-mills, lightning-rods, life-insur-
ance, women speaking in church and going to the
General Conference. All of these, particularly the
last, have been declared, solemnly and with much
emotion, to make the Word of God of none effect.

But all of us have got beyond most of these
things, and most of us have got beyond all of
them; and we count ourselves Christians still. For
us the Word of God is not the text of the Bible,
but that revelation of what God is and what he
means, which he has made to us through the
prophets and through his Son. The faith in this

revelation has survived across many changes of view concerning the Bible itself, and may survive many more.

Difficulty in understanding revelation often arises because of the failure to note its historical and progressive character. Being a revelation of deed as well as of word, it necessarily took on an historical form ; and being a revelation to immature men, it was adapted to their immaturity and shared in their imperfection. Jesus declares that God allowed some things which were not good, because of the hardness of the people's heart. Paul speaks of the old ritual as beggarly beginnings, and Peter calls it an intolerable yoke. But it was fitted to the times of ignorance at which God had to wink. The morality was imperfect, as indeed it must be so long as men are imperfect. In the abnormal relations of imperfect and willful men the thing to be done must always be unideal and can only be a choice between evils. But we forget all this and look for the insight at the beginning which came only at the end. For us, Christ completes the revelation and is the only standard.

A specification of the same objection is the difficulty felt with the character of the Old Testament saints, who, it is thought, were altogether unworthy of divine notice, and especially of divine approbation. Now there is no doubt that many of these ancient worthies do make a sorry show when judged by the Christian standard, and that if God were a Pharisee and careful of his reputation with other Pharisees he would have nothing to do with them. But as God was revealing himself as a God of grace, it seems to be quite in the order of things that he should condescend to sinners. Indeed, there was no other class to deal with, as there is no other class still. The ancient saints were earthly enough, and so are the modern saints. That God receiveth sinners is the essence of the gospel. The fact that he bore with the imperfect saints of ancient times is our great encouragement to hope that he will bear with the imperfect saints of to-day.

A great deal of mistaken criticism has been visited upon Old Testament morality from misunderstanding of this matter. Certainly many of the savageries reported are very far from ideal; and the reporters may often have idealized their origin. But in any case, so long as men are imperfect, their actual code, even if directly imposed by God himself, must share in their imperfection. God might conceivably have made men over all at once by fiat; but in that case it would have been a magical rather than a

moral revelation. If he is to develop men into
righteousness, he must regard the laws and limitations of humanity. God is in all history,
ancient and modern; and if the modern were
written from the divine standpoint, we should
find as doubtful instruments and as unideal
methods as we find in the ancient. As long as
the hardness of the people's heart remains, there
will be corresponding imperfection in the code.
If God is in history at all, we must say that he
wills both that a great many things bad in themselves shall be done, and that they shall be done
away with. And as for the saints, even the
modern saint commonly looks better at a distance
than on close inspection. The perfect has nowhere come. The forgiveness of sins is still an
important part of the gospel.

We are probably better able to understand this
matter to-day than ever before. The general conception of evolution has made us familiar with the
thought of slow progress in human development
as well as elsewhere. No one would now expect
a people to step at once from savagery to civilization. No one would now expect a people to
change all its customs and ideas and practical
modes of living and acting in a day. Even admitting a miraculous factor, we should not expect
any such magical departure from all the psycho-

logical and historical uniformities and continuities. If, then, God should begin with savages for the revelation of himself, he would descend to their savage plane; and his work would have to be judged by its tendencies and outcome and final form rather than by its early phases. The initial morality would be savage; the initial ideas would be crude; the initial saints would be barbarous. The morality would be slowly reformed. The myths, the legends, the dreams, would slowly be made the vehicles of a higher truth and would gradually fall away, or would receive a higher interpretation. Meanwhile, the saints would be far from ideal. The tradition, the environment, the custom, would, to some extent, be reproduced in them, with a highly composite result. The author of the hymn, "In the cross of Christ I glory," was also prominent in the opium war and conducted the negotiations that fastened the opium traffic on China. In our civil war there were undoubtedly good Christians on both sides who had the root of the matter in them; but they were doing their best to kill one another upon occasion. The spirit only slowly comes to appropriate manifestation; and yet all the while the leaven is leavening the lump — in which process, moreover, both the life of the leaven and the lumpishness of the lump are fully manifested.

If, then, any one is distressed over the crude morality and religious savagery of the Old Testament, the reply to him would be twofold. First, the old saints are no models for us. The fact that they did certain things is no warrant for our doing them. It is well known to what abominations and cruelties the following of Old Testament standards has led. For us the spirit of Christ is the only standard. But, secondly, it does not follow from this that God was not in the Old Testament history and even in the savagery, not of course as approving it as ideal, but as using it because of the hardness of men's hearts. Either that, or we must withdraw God from our thought of history altogether. A glance at cosmic ethics as revealed in all history will show it to be quite as grim as anything in Hebrew history. If these savageries were presented to us as divine ideals or as abiding standards for our imitation, our revolt could not be too instant and uncompromising; and in any case it requires some nerve and mental steadiness to contemplate human history, even to-day, without disquietude. Only the outcome can justify it.

But if God be a God of grace, and if this revelation be so valuable, why was it limited to so few and not rather conferred at once upon the many? This limitation has its mystery, but it is of a piece with the divine method in general. Mediation is the great form of divine communication. New truth is not painted on the sky or given to all at once, but it begins in the thought of one or of a few, and thence spreads. This is the form in which God's revelation of himself is spread abroad. The source of our trouble with this method is a back-lying misconception. It is supposed that God is made good by his revelation, and that he is not gracious toward those to whom the good news has not come. This notion has indeed been held, but it is rapidly passing into the class of extinct blasphemies. God is not made good by the revelation; he is shown to be good; and the goodness and grace exist and determine the divine action, whether revealed or not. The God who is dealing with the human race, in all its branches and individuals, is the God and Father of our Lord Jesus Christ, the Father of whom every fatherhood in heaven and in earth is named. We have got as far beyond the wholesale damnation of the heathen as we have beyond the damnation of infants, whether unbaptized or not.

The revelation of God, I said, was completed in Christ. This is true only of the objective manifestation. The revelation of that revelation is still going on. Christ's words were a leaven, a

seed; and their meaning and transforming influence were only slowly to be manifested in the
growing life and insight of his disciples under
the tuition of the Holy Spirit. In the deepest
sense, truth is revealed only when it is understood; and in this sense the revelation is still
going on. This revelation can never be put into
a book, so that any one who can read may discern it; it is possible only to, and in, the prepared
heart. Hence the spiritual meaning of Christianity only slowly enters the minds of men. The
truth is hidden by blindness, or is warped into
some image of our narrowness, until the inner
illumination is reached. Then new truth breaks
forth out of the Word. The Lord looketh at the
heart. God is a spirit, and they that worship him
must worship him in spirit and in truth. These
words have been with us for ages; and yet how
slowly do we free ourselves from the notion that
God is a stickler for etiquette, that certain rites
and formulas are necessary to secure his favor,
and that only certain persons can effectually
administer or pronounce them — a notion which
intellectually and morally is on the level of sorcery and incantation.

But there has been a very great and wholesome growth in Christian thought in recent years.
Under the guidance of the promised Spirit, we

are coming nearer to the truth of God. The elaborate constructions and interpretations of earlier creeds are falling away ; but in their place we have something infinitely better, — a clearer apprehension of that Fatherhood of which every fatherhood in heaven and earth is named, of God's moral purpose in the world, of his up-building kingdom, and his nearness to every faithful soul. The mechanical and artificial conception of salvation also is falling away, and we are coming to see that the end of the law is love; that is, the purpose of the law is to beget love in the heart and life. Or again, more concretely and comprehensively, Christ is the end of the law; that is, the fundamental aim is to reproduce Christ in the disciple. And this insight is gradually transforming Christian thought from an incredible mechanism of words and rites to a living and life-giving conception of what God is and what he means.

The mental life tends to equilibrium. The customary is clear and right; and clear and right often because customary. With the passive mind any departure from the customary is wrong and disastrous. The most beneficent modifications of opinion and custom have been viewed with alarm. In like manner the religious life adjusts itself to current customs and conceptions ; and any departure from them is thought to be fatal. But experience shows that life can abide across many changes of conception, and even that the new conception may be more favorable to life than the old. And this is true of the newer views of the Bible and revelation. Because of the fact just mentioned these were thought by many to be destructive, but now that we are used to them we find them genuine aids to faith. There is nothing in them that detracts from the value of revelation, but rather much that makes revelation more living and effective. We have indeed no longer a dictated and infallible book, but we have the record of the self-revelation of God in history and in the thought and feeling of holy men. With this change the intellectual scandals and incredibilities which infest the former view have vanished; and in its place has come a blessed and growing insight into what God is and what he means, which is our great and chief source of hope and inspiration.

It is a great change that has taken place in passing from the old view of the Bible to the new, and one readily understands that it would involve much friction and misunderstanding. The traditional conception was clear, but it has been finally discredited by the facts, and in its place we have something more vital indeed, but also more complex and less easily formulated. We now see that the revelation has taken place through a long historical process, through God's dealings with a chosen people, through the inspiration of holy men, through the songs of psalmists and the sermons and aspiration of prophets, and above all and more especially through the manifestation of the Divine Son. It was nothing mechanically given or rigidly fixed; it grew and it grew out of historical conditions through the working of the Holy Spirit upon the minds and hearts of holy men. We see that it was conditioned by the imperfections of the men to whom it came. They did not understand it. They had no such conception of the divine meaning as we possess. God is the great exegete, and he makes clear now what he meant then, but the men in the midst of the process had no clear vision. The meaning was not communicated with the exactness of a statute; it has become clear only in the unfolding of history.

And the facts that lead to this view may easily be pressed into the service of denial. They do lead to the rejection of the traditional view, and so long as that was thought to be the only possible view, they made for the rejection of revelation altogether. Some of these facts have been urged by unbelievers for centuries and have suffered in reputation on that account. Hence when Christian scholars began to insist on them as reasons for modifying the traditional view, they were thought to have gone over to the "infidels," and were slandered and libeled accordingly. All this was unfortunate, but not unintelligible; for the scholars themselves were not always happy in their way of putting things and often made the impression of denying revelation altogether. We have had the same experience in the biblical field that we have had with evolution. The latter doctrine, now that it is understood and duly limited to the facts, is seen to be at least harmless and even a veritable aid to theistic faith; but the doctrine as taught by a great many of its holders a generation ago was pure materialism and atheism. Ignorant teaching was met with ignorant rejection. More careful thought has changed all this, so that only a belated mind would be frightened at evolution, or would find in it an all-explaining formula.

Similar progress in the biblical field is fast enabling us to accept all the facts which unbelievers have marshaled against revelation, and is turning them into veritable aids to faith. Unwittingly unbelievers have built on the false antithesis of the natural and the supernatural, and have fancied that when natural laws were traced in the revealing movement, all supernatural meaning was denied. This fancy vanishes when we rise to the thought that the natural itself is no self-running mechanism, but only the orderly form of the divine working. We may still believe that God spake at sundry times and in divers manners unto the fathers by the prophets and by his Son, and that still by his Spirit he speaks unto the children and leads them into larger and fuller truth and life.

A recent report of a liberal religious gathering for the discussion of the Bible sums up the result by saying that we have discovered that the Bible is no revelation by God to man, but a revelation by man to man. Evidently the writer thought this a complete and perfect disjunction. If so, he was in the toils of the false natural and the false supernatural. God is no longer so easily ruled out by a verbal antithesis. It is still permitted to believe in a revelation *by* God *through* man *to* man for the better knowledge of God and the greater blessing of men. In the human world God is less a *with-worker* than a *through-worker*, but he works nevertheless to will and to work of his good pleasure.

II

THE
INCARNATION AND THE ATONEMENT

THE INCARNATION AND THE ATONEMENT

In his second letter to the Corinthian church St. Paul interrupts his general discussion to appeal for a collection in behalf of the persecuted Christians of Judea. He first mentions the liberality of the Macedonian churches; but with his delicacy of feeling and his belief in freedom he declines to lay down any rule for their gifts. The Corinthian brethren must decide for themselves. Still, in making their decision, he would have them remember the grace of the Lord Jesus and his divine sacrifice for them. "For ye know the grace of our Lord Jesus Christ, that, though he was rich, yet for your sakes he became poor, that ye through his poverty might become rich."

This word of St. Paul's is very interesting for both its matter and its manner. Its matter is essentially the doctrine of the incarnation of the Divine Son for the redemption of men. Its manner shows it to be the faith of the Corinthian church at that time. The doctrine is not presented as something new and strange, but is assumed as something known and accepted. "For ye know

the grace of our Lord Jesus Christ," etc. Our
Lord had existed before his incarnation. He had
been rich, rich in the ineffable divine fellowship
of the Father with the Son, rich in the glory
which he had with the Father before the world
was. As Paul declares in another passage, our
Lord had originally been in the form of God, yet
had not thought equality with God a thing to be
insisted on, but emptied himself, taking the form
of a bond-servant and becoming obedient unto
death, even the death of the cross. And all this
had been done for our sakes. For us he became
poor. For us he laid aside the glory which he had
with the Father, and became subject to human
limitations and conditions. And all was done in
order that by this infinite love and sacrifice we
might be lifted up to God. For Paul at least,
and for the early Christians also, our Lord's existence did not begin in Judea or in the stable at
Bethlehem.

This in brief is the doctrine of the incarnation
and atonement as continuously told by the Christian Church, with scantiest variations, from its
beginning until now. It is the essential doctrine of
Christianity and the abiding source of its power.
The doctrine has often been crudely held and
sometimes caricatured, but Christian thought has
always returned to it as its chief treasure. The

present study aims to rescue this doctrine from
some of the misunderstandings that have gathered around it. And first we consider the incarnation, its meaning and religious significance.

It is very easy to ⸻ take this doctrine. We
are often tempted ⸻ ret it by the imagination, and to c⸻ Lord as spatially
inclosed wit⸻ human form. Of
course i⸻ e arise as to
how h⸻ fined, and
su⸻ that the

⸻ as assum-
⸻ that nature
⸻ elf which was
⸻ equally insoluble
⸻ mutual relation of his
⸻ ature, his divine and his
⸻ gain we have an insoluble
di⸻ as the problem is presented in
this c⸻ .. This impossible duality appeared
at an e⸻ date in Christian thought, and has
commonly been eliminated by being ignored.
But these difficulties arise from picture thinking.
The unpicturable problems of thought always
seem absurd when intrusted to the imagination
for solution, and we especially need to be on our
guard in this matter against the misleading sug-

gestions of this faculty. We speak of ourselves
as being in the body, thus using a spatial form
of speech; but we are not in the body as something that contains us. Being in the body means
simply and only having a type of experience
which is physically conditioned. Being in this
world means only having a certain type of experience with certain forms and laws. Passing
out of this world would mean only passing from
one type and condition of experience to another.
And being a man, in general, means only existence under certain conditions and laws. And
if any being should become subject to the conditions, laws, and limitations of human life, that
being would by that fact, and so far forth, become, in the only intelligible sense of the phrase,
a human being. The assumption of human nature has the same meaning. That nature is not
a separate something to be put on like a garment, or joined on by some metaphysical hyphen.
It is simply the general law of humanity, and
if any being should become subject to that general law he would to that extent assume human
nature.

Hence by the incarnation of our Lord we do
not mean that an infinite being was compressed
into the limits of a human form, or that in some
picturable way he put on our humanity like an

external covering. We mean rather that he became subject to the conditions, laws, and limitations of human life, and thus became in the truest sense of the word a man. In this sense he assumed our nature and lived our life. Of course no language on such a subject is to be pressed beyond its general significance. It would not tend to edification to ask how far such limitation goes. The question could not be answered in any case. Human nature has higher ranges as well as lower ones, and there is no need to think of a descent into imbecility in order to become man. It suffices to affirm a subjection to the law of humanity such that we may best express the fact by saying, "The Word became flesh, and dwelt among us." This in the sense described is intelligible, at least in its meaning, and this is enough. When we say more than this, we soon lose ourselves in words and bad metaphysics.

If now we ask how this limitation is possible, the answer must be that we do not know; but just as little do we know how it is impossible. The progress of both scientific and philosophic reflection is making the problems of fundamental existence more and more mysterious, and, by revealing the limitations and relativity of our thought, is making thoughtful men more and

more careful of pronouncing on what is possible
or impossible apart from the indications of experience. This only we can say : There must be
some community between the divine and the
human to make this incarnation possible. If these
were strictly opposites, there could be no such
assumption of human nature.

It may also be added that the doctrine is
equally impossible except as we assume the subordination of the Son. The formula of Chalcedon
on this point goes beyond both Scripture and
reason. With this limitation, the net result of
theological thought is that while God in his
absolute existence must always remain a fath-
omless mystery to us, we come nearest to the
truth when we think of the Father, the Son,
and the Spirit. This is the doctrine of the Trinity, a doctrine mysterious enough no doubt, yet,
after all, the line of least resistance, both from
the biblical and from the philosophical standpoint. There is no view that is not attended with
great difficulty when we try to think it through.
The conception of a community of persons in the
unity of the divine existence is no worse off in
this respect than the conception of a single and
lonely personality without the eternal fellowship
which moral life demands. The conception of the
lonely God with no personal community in the

divine unity tends to run off either into agnosticism or into some form of pantheism. Likewise, the net result of Christological thought is that Jesus was not merely the Son of Mary, but was also the Son of God, who took upon him the laws and limitations of the human lot and thus became man in order that he might lift us to God. This is the doctrine of the Incarnation, which depends for its possibility on the other doctrine of the Trinity.

With this word on the meaning and the metaphysics of the doctrine, let us pass to consider its religious and practical significance. For it is not, as many have fancied, a barren curiosity of theological speculation, if not a grievous affront to reason; it is rather the power of God unto salvation, and the central truth of Christianity.

And, first, the incarnation contains the highest revelation of God. We have no call to consider what might be possible in worlds of which we know nothing; but in our human world God's highest manifestation of himself is made in the incarnation and humiliation of his Son. The revelation of power and intelligence is simple enough. A certain measure of goodness also may be shown in the beneficent arrangements of the natural world; but the highest revelation, the revelation of moral love in the highest degree, lies far beyond all these things and involves another order of manifestation altogether. Theology has said many things about the divine holiness, but it has been largely a negative and abstract thing. God has been conceived as governor, as promulgating and executing righteous laws; and his holiness would seem to be exhausted in these things. The old philosophies hardly conceived God as ethical at all. They thought of him as a kind of metaphysical perfection, and were careful to free him from much thought or care for his creatures as beneath his notice. God was made on the Epicurean model and sat apart,—

> Where never falls the least white star of snow,
> Where never lowest sound of thunder rolls,
> Nor sigh of human sorrow mounts to mar
> His sacred, everlasting calm.

And this philosophy, which was little but a reflection of human vulgarity and selfishness, infected theology. Again, a great deal of our theology was written when men believed in the divine right and irresponsibility of kings, and this conception also crept into and corrupted theological thinking, so that God was conceived less as a truly moral being than as a magnified and irresponsible despot; while the thought of affirming that God is under any kind of moral obligation to his creatures would have been shuddered at as

absurd, if not blasphemous. The God of that theology could not have been imitated by man without infamy. But Christian thought has moved
far away from this notion; and we have come
to see that God is the most deeply obligated being
in existence, and moral principles are as binding
for him as for us.

It was an awful responsibility that was taken
when our human race was launched with its fearful possibilities of good and evil. God thereby
put himself under infinite obligation to care for
his human family; and reflections on his position
as Creator and Ruler instead of removing, only
make this obligation more manifest. In particular,
the attempt to conceive God as love has compelled
the giving up of those absolutist notions of divine
sovereignty which formed the foundation of theology a hundred years ago. We that are strong
ought to bear the burdens of the weak, is seen
to be a principle of universal application. A God
of love must do works of love and be all that love
implies. Else love is not love.

It may be that there was a time when the
Jewish or even the Mohammedan conception of
God as simply Ruler and Master was more useful than the Christian view. Men needed to learn
the lesson of law; and for this stage of development possibly the conception of a Ruler issuing

commands, bestowing rewards, and inflicting
punishment, was the best. But there comes a
time in moral development when such a view is
seen in its inadequacy to moral demands; and
then only the gospel of divine self-sacrifice meets
the case.

We return now to the claim that the incarnation is the highest revelation of God. If God had
filled space and time with inanimate worlds, that
would have revealed only power and skill. If he
had filled the world with pleasure-giving contriv-
ances, that would have revealed benevolence. If
he had sent us prophets and teachers at no real
cost to himself, that too would be something;
but it would not greatly stir our hearts toward
God. Our love would go out to the prophets and
teachers themselves, for the toil and the pain would
fall on them. In all beneficence of this sort God
would appear simply as a rich man who out of
his abundance scatters bounty to the needy, but
at no cost to himself. A certain gratitude would
indeed be possible, but along this line God would
forever remain morally below the moral heroes
of our race. Their gifts cost. They put themselves and their hearts into their work. They
attain to the morality of self-sacrifice, and this is
infinitely beyond the morality of any giving that
does not cost. And there must ever be a higher

moral possibility until we reach the revelation of God in self-sacrifice, until God becomes the chief of burden-bearers and the leader of all in self-abnegation. Then the possibilities of grace are filled up. There is nothing beyond this. The heroic, the self-sacrificing God stands revealed, and God makes the highest revelation of himself.

And this is made possible in the incarnation. The Father loved the world and gave his Son for its redemption. The Son leaves the glory which he had with the Father and enters into the human lot and becomes obedient unto death that he may reveal the Father and reconcile men to God. There is great mystery here, but through it all we get the impression of boundless love issuing in mysterious self-sacrifice, a work of love at boundless cost and pain for the salvation of a perverse and sinful world.

Let me put the matter in another way. Suppose there were anywhere a human being who sat down to enjoy himself in the face of the world's misery and pain and sorrow, and looked indifferently on woe and suffering which he might relieve, yet did nothing. What should we think of him? And suppose we magnify this human being until he becomes very great and wise and powerful, would not his selfishness become all the more horrible? And suppose we

enlarge the conception until the being becomes
all-wise and all-powerful, what then? Plainly
such a being would be the monster of the moral
universe. His greatness in all other respects
would but emphasize the awful wickedness of his
selfishness; and every act of self-sacrificing love
on the part of men would be his condemnation.
Nor would it help the matter if we called this
being God. We that are strong ought to bear
the burdens of the weak; and the strongest
ought to be the greatest burden-bearer. In the
moral world he that is greatest of all should
be the servant of all. There is no exception from
this rule, not even for God himself. Of course it
is not a matter of legal obligation, but of moral
goodness. The courts know nothing of this matter, but love understands it. And love, with all
that love implies, is the highest and supreme duty
in a moral system. Moral goodness, whether in
man or God, does not consist in doing things
beyond requirement, but in meeting for love's
sake love's highest and supreme requirement. In
the highest sense there is no such thing possible
as transcending requirement; but there is such a
thing as divinely doing what divinely should be
done.

I know something of the arguments whereby
we seek to keep our faith in the divine goodness

in the presence of the world's pain and sorrow and the manifold sinister aspects of existence. I do not disparage them; upon occasion I use them; but I always feel that at best they are only palliatives and leave the great depths of the problem untouched. There is only one argument that touches the bottom, and that is Paul's question: "He that spared not his own Son, but delivered him up for us all, how shall he not with him also freely give us all things?" We look on the woes of the world. We hear the whole creation, to use Paul's language, groaning and laboring in pain. We see a few good men vainly striving to help the world into life and light; and in our sense of the awful magnitude of the problem and of our inability to do much, we cry out: "Where's God? How can he bear this? Why doesn't he do something?" And there is but one answer that satisfies; and that is the Incarnation and the Cross. God could not bear it. He has done something. He has done the utmost compatible with moral wisdom. He has entered into the fellowship of our suffering and misery and at infinite cost has taken the world upon his heart that he might raise it to himself. This is the highest revelation. Of course the order of life is still mysterious. The mystery of pain is not yet solved. But in the presence of this revelation we say, with the Apostle: What shall separate us from the love of God? For he that spared not his own Son for our sakes must with him give us all things; so that against all evils and distresses whatsoever we are more than conquerors through him that hath loved us.

In such a world as ours the incarnation contains the highest revelation of God. It is only a further specification of the same thought when I add that the incarnation is the great source of the power of Christianity. In illustration of this claim, consider the following facts: The chief value of the Christian revelation consists in its being a revelation of God. It is not primarily and essentially a series of verbal statements about God, but rather a description of what God has done and intends for men. And the things said and done get their chief significance from the one who said and did them. Apply this to Christ himself. He went far beyond Moses and the prophets in his insight into divine things; and if he were only a man like them, this would be all. He would reveal God as they did, by word only; and God himself would not come near enough for self-revelation. But assume that the incarnation is true, and the meaning and power of the whole are infinitely changed. Now we see God in act, in self-revelation. The Divine Son is living the ideal human life before men to reveal the heart of God, to show us God's thought of humanity, and the way God would have us live. The Divine Son is bearing the sins and sorrows of men, and is faithful unto death; that he may show the love and righteousness of God and redeem the world unto himself. The Divine Son identifies himself with the least of these his human brethren, so that whatever is done to them is done to him. These things are the essence of Christianity; but what becomes of them apart from the incarnation? It is one thing if only a Jewish peasant uttered these words; it is quite another if the speaker was the Lord of life and glory. It is one thing if he who hung on the cross was only a good young Jew of Nazareth, meeting an undeserved and shameful death — such things have happened before and since; but it is quite another if he was the Son of God who might have summoned twelve legions of angels, but who for love's sake endured the cross and the contradiction of sinners against himself. The power is gone if we are dealing with Jesus, the carpenter's son; for the power depends not on the words and deeds themselves, but on him who said and did them. The infinite poverty appears only as we contrast it with the infinite riches; and only in this contrast is the infinite love revealed. The life and character of Jesus acquire their supreme importance only through the incarnation.

The boldness of Christian thought at this point is a constant amazement and astonishment. Having ventured the great thought that God is love, it draws the appropriate conclusion. What shall a God of love do but works of love? And where shall love be found so surely as there where it is most needed? And where is the divine help so much needed as here in our human lives? And so Christianity with sublime audacity and logic recalls God from that far-off throne where our vulgar thought had placed him, and finds him present to every soul and to every need. In the exercise of his love God has sent us rain from heaven and fruitful seasons and daily bread. But this was not enough. He also sent us prophets and teachers to reveal his will. But this also was not enough. There was a still higher thought, and Christianity dared to think it. It was that God himself should come into humanity for his supreme self-manifestation and for the redemption of men. And when the way had been prepared, the Divine Son appears as the Divine Redeemer. There is nothing beyond this. The possibilities of grace are exhausted. God has made the highest moral revelation of himself. He is seen at the head of all those who love, and

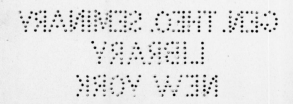

for love's sake bear burdens and sacrifice themselves.

A Divine Person working for love's sake a divine work for man's redemption is the centre of the Christian faith and the source of its power. Drop it out of our teaching, and, though the external form and facts may remain unchanged, the life is gone nevertheless. Men wonder that Christian faith should cling so pertinaciously to this mysterious doctrine, — mysterious to speculation, but clear to love, — but the reason is that it contains all that is distinctively Christian. The self-sacrificing love of God, and even the ethical perfection and moral grandeur of God, are all bound up in this doctrine. That which stirs men's hearts has always been the condescension, the grace of the Lord Jesus, the cross, that is, the self-renunciation, of Christ. " Herein is love, not that we loved God, but that he loved us, and sent his Son to be the propitiation for our sins." " He loved us and gave himself for us." Now the revelation of love and righteousness is complete. And now not merely gratitude, but adoring love and absolute self-surrender, become possible on our part. Now intellect and conscience and heart and will alike can come to God and say, " Thy kingdom come. Thy will be done." No wonder that Paul cried out : " God forbid that I should glory, save in the cross of our Lord Jesus Christ." No wonder that Peter declares that the angels desire to look into this grace of God. For surely in earth or heaven there is nothing great or divine besides.

Thus the power of God's revelation has its chief source in the incarnation. And we may be perfectly sure that no lower conception of God will permanently command the minds and hearts of men. We should not have reached the conception ourselves, but now that it has been revealed to us we see that something of the kind is a moral necessity if we are to think the highest thought of God. And there is a peculiar dialectic in human thought whereby we are compelled to think of God as perfect or not at all. An imperfect God is none. As soon as a higher conception emerges we must adopt it into our thought of God, or see our faith in him fade out until it vanishes altogether. A fairly good God we cannot abide. We can be satisfied with nothing less than the Supreme and Perfect. Hence it is that the Christian thought of God wins its way. It is the only one worthy of God or man. So far as speculation goes, it is as thinkable as any other; and it is the only one that is able to inspire and perfect our human life. History is the sufficient criticism of all others and the survival of the fittest must give the decision. Cavils can be raised against anything, and anything can be rejected if we see fit; but history clearly indicates the continuity of Christian thought in the past and enables us to forecast it for the future.

Thus we have considered the moral fitness and necessity and religious importance of the incarnation. We now pass to consider the atonement, of which the incarnation is the pre-condition.

This doctrine also has been the subject of much misunderstanding. The Church has always held that a great work of grace has been wrought for the salvation of men. "God so loved the world, that he gave his only begotten Son, that whosoever believeth in him should not perish, but have everlasting life." "The Son of man came not to be ministered unto, but to minister, and to give his life a ransom for many." Such passages set forth the work of love, and because of this work the forgiveness of sins is promised unto all those who turn to God in repentance and faith. But when it comes to the philosophy of this work we find a vast deal of confusion, owing partly to unclearness of thought, and more especially to a misunderstanding of the nature of language and its imperfection as an instrument of thought. We must first bring this fact out into clearness.

Assuming, then, the reality of a divine work of grace for the blessing of men, the question arises, How shall it be expressed and made accessible to our minds? A little reflection convinces us that there must always be something transcendental in the divine life and activity to which our earth-born thought, and especially our "matter-moulded" forms of speech can only approximate. Thought itself has its parallax with reality when dealing with these high themes; and even when we are sure we have the right conception, we see it vanishing into mystery on the farther side. Such conceptions are of the nature of limits, to which we must approximate but cannot fully attain. Approached from the side of experience we see their necessity; but when we take them abstractly and absolutely, and reflect upon them in their metaphysical possibility, we soon find ourselves wandering in "endless mazes lost." Conceptions of this type are clear only from the side of the facts; if we attempt to approach them from the farther side, or by the way of deductive speculation, we only delude and confuse ourselves.

We may illustrate our meaning by our conception of the divine life and consciousness. When we attempt to construe our experience of the inner and outer world, we are shut up to the affirmation of an absolute and intelligent cause as their only adequate source. But as soon as we seek to construe this cause in its inner life, we find mysteries thronging upon us. We have to affirm an unbegun life of tideless fullness, of unchanging self-possession, a life transcending time, and subject to no spatial limitations. How mysterious this is! Our own life of spatial and temporal limitation furnishes a very inadequate key, and we have to be constantly on our guard against transferring to that life conceptions born of our own limitations.

This illustrates what is meant by saying that thought itself has a parallax with reality which we must never forget. A further parallax is found in language, which is only an imperfect instrument for the expression of an already imperfect thought. All language for expressing spiritual things is necessarily based on metaphor. However spiritual the conception itself may be, it can find linguistic expression only through some physical image or experience. All such language is literally false, but we use it in the hope that it will be taken, not for what it says, but for what it means. The process by which the mind passes from the metaphor to the meaning is one of the dark places of psychology and epistemology; but it is fundamental to all intellectual communion through linguistic or any symbolic expression.

This use of the physical to express the spiritual is especially prominent in religion and theology. Here we perpetually use language which we know to be literally false in the hope that it will be rightly understood. Thus we ascribe form and place to God, and speak of Jesus as sitting at the right hand of God. "They shall see his face; and his name shall be in their foreheads." God has a sword and arrows, and flies upon the wings of the wind. Of course, no one would fancy that any objective fact corresponds to these utterances. Again, we often attribute psychological and even physiological experiences to God which are necessarily limited to the finite spirit. "He that sitteth in the heavens shall laugh: the Lord shall have them in derision." "And it repented the Lord that he had made man."

Of course, we do not object to the use of language of this kind. To be sure, there is a choice in metaphors, but metaphor of some sort is a necessity of religious speech. All that we can demand is that the metaphor, however impossible when literally taken, shall adumbrate a true conception or make a true impression. Nevertheless, these considerations show us that we must beware of taking our words as exact and literal statements of the truth, and we must even beware of taking our thoughts themselves as exhaustive and final conceptions of the truth. Thought has its element of relativity, and language needs more than the dictionary for its interpretation. Without a vital and spiritual process there is no possibility of understanding language, and there is hardly any absurdity which may not be evolved from language when the living soul is lacking. The letter always kills; only the spirit, the understanding, can profit.

So much for thought and language in general. It is further plain that, for setting forth the great truth of the divine grace, it was necessary to use the actual speech and conceptions of the time. Any revelation which might be made to men must be cast in the existing moulds of thought and expression; otherwise it would be unintelligible. Accordingly we find the great salvation set forth in the language of ancient life and custom. In particular the religious rites and traditions of the age had produced a great system of thought and speech, and in terms of this system the doctrine of grace was naturally cast. The language of the altar and temple, the customs of ransom and redemption, the legal usages of the time, all lent themselves to its expression. Accordingly, Christ is a sacrifice and propitiation for our sins. He is the Lamb of God which taketh away the sins of the world. He is our passover. He gives his life a ransom for many, and thus becomes the Redeemer of the world. This language was necessary. The religious thought and development of the time would have been inaccessible to any other. Exact theological and speculative statement would have been unintelligible, or confusing and misleading, just as exact scientific statement would have been in the field of nature. Thus the language of the time is used; and for that time and for all times it makes a true impression ; and Christian thought is left, under the guidance of the Spirit, to distinguish between the spirit and the letter, between the abiding truth and the changing form of its expression.

As children must think in pictures and spatial forms, and only slowly pass beyond images to conceptions, or beyond pictures to meanings, so the entire race necessarily began its religious thinking in the picture and dramatic form, and only slowly and very imperfectly reached the form of conception and rational significance. We must note the necessity of the early stages of this process, and also their temporary character. We must also note the practical nature of Scripture language, and its relativity to our present needs. It is becoming more and more apparent that the aim is to make a practically true and important impression, and that the language must not be taken in an absolute sense, as if it were the expression of a speculative finality. The truth is to be found in the impression rather than in any logical or dictionary analysis of the forms of speech ; and the expression and understanding will vary with the growth of thought and life and knowledge.

The language of Scripture, then, has its pictorial, dramatic, metaphorical, and relative elements ; but it is not to be set aside on that account. We must rather seek to understand it in a free and living way, neither allowing ourselves to be intimidated by the dictionary, nor rejecting the language as meaningless. Metaphor is metaphor, indeed ; but metaphor in all intelligent speech must have a meaning. How, then, is this language concerning the great salvation to be understood ?

First of all, we may consider the general impression it makes, apart from any question as to its literal truth. And the thing which clearly appears when the matter is thus considered is a divine work of condescending grace. We see the love of God in the gift of his Son, and the love of Christ in his work for us, and the gracious condition in which, as the result of that work, we find ourselves. The forgiveness of sins is proclaimed. The divine love is declared, and the divine help is proffered to all. This is the clear revelation which emerges from these forms of speech ; and this is a divine gospel which is worthy of all acceptance.

So long as the language is thus viewed as an instrument, as a mode of putting the truth and making a true impression concerning the grace of God, it is permissible and useful so far and so long as it makes that impression. As just suggested, it was originally necessary, and it is by no means antiquated now. We may then recognize its value as a form of expression, and at the same time hold its purely instrumental character. We may hold that in another stage of moral and religious development these modes of speech would not be the best possible because the forms and customs on which they rest have passed away. For instance, we may well believe that the biblical forms of speech, while expressive and necessary for the time when they originated, would not be employed if the Christian teaching were to be set forth for the first time to-day ; just as swords and arrows would not be used to

represent the divine weapons, or harps would not
be the chief musical instrument of the saints.
We cannot doubt that the doctrine would be cast
in modern moulds rather than in those of the
Jewish Church and the Roman law. There is no
good reason for thinking that those ancient forms
have an eternal fitness beyond all others for expressing the grace of God. We, then, who inherit
them have to consider not so much what was said
as what was meant, and to guard ourselves
against a worship of the letter which shall cause
us to miss the spirit.

The significance and expressiveness of these
ancient forms of thought and speech are allowed
when they are taken in a free and vital way,
and are not reduced to literal statements of fact.
But why may we not take them literally, and
view them as exact statements of an objective
process? For excellent reasons, which we now
proceed to discuss.

But, first of all, and for the sake of clearness,
we must make a distinction in order to avoid
confusion. We distinguish between the fact and
the philosophy of the atonement, or between the
atonement as a fact and the theories of the atonement. By the atonement as fact we understand
the gracious work of the Lord Jesus for the

blessing of men. All else is theory and mode of putting. And it is plain that one might well hold fast to the fact with all conviction and devotion, and at the same time find no acceptable theory. This is the case with many thoughtful Christians at present. In the religious life the fact is the effective thing and the abiding thing; the theory belongs to theology, and is by no means a constant quantity. The grace of the Lord Jesus and the love of God which Jesus revealed are what moves men's hearts and compels devotion. The cross of the Lord Jesus was that in which alone Paul would glory, not the governmental, or any other theory of the atonement. This acceptance of the fact is the sum of the matter with the great body of Christians, and it is all that is practically needed. It carries with it faith in the love of God, and the forgiveness of sins, and all other benefits of the Saviour's work. And it is conceivable that a Christian agnosticism should content itself with accepting the fact without any theory whatever. A Christian teacher who should simply proclaim the love of God and the self-sacrifice of the Lord Jesus on our behalf would proclaim the truth of the atonement far more effectively than another who should dwell on its philosophy. The former is intelligible even to the wayfaring man; the latter is not everybody's affair; indeed, in some of its forms, it would not seem to be anybody's affair.

The Scriptures themselves deal mainly with the fact, and give no single or consistent theory. The statements which seem theoretical are not harmonious with other statements by other writers or even by the same writer; and this shows that they are ways of putting rather than dogmatic finalties.

Let it, then, be clearly understood that the present discussion does not concern the fact of the atonement in the sense defined, but only the theory of it. The fact we affirm and insist upon; the theory, which is a matter mainly of theological speculation, remains uncertain until now. With this understanding we return to the question whether the Scripture expressions concerning the work of Christ are to be literally taken.

The answer to this question is, No. They are expressions of the truth in terms of the thought and speech of the time, and as such are significant and expressive; but when taken in any other sense they become incredible or immoral. This appears first in the fact that the Scriptures themselves have no single and consistent scheme of expression. This is sufficiently shown by the age-long debate among theologians on the subject. When such different theories can be held, all appealing to Scripture, it is plain that the language is not to be absolutely taken, or that the Scriptures themselves are not clear and decisive in their teaching. In particular, two incommensurable notions underlie the general New Testament exposition. One is the notion of substitution based on the sacrificial figures of the Old Testament, and the other is the notion of the imputed merits and righteousness of Christ whereby the believer is justified. These two conceptions are entirely disparate when taken literally, and can never be united in one homogeneous thought. They serve well to express the salvation wrought out by the Saviour, and the safety in which the disciple exists because of the redeeming work; but if we take them in strict literalness we are forthwith lost. In general the New Testament writers, and especially Paul, were laboring to express the great salvation and the glorious liberty of the children of God thence resulting; and they availed themselves, as we have said, of all the customs, religious and social, which might serve for expression. If sin be thought of as a debt, it is paid. If it be thought of as a slavery, we are redeemed or ransomed. If it be thought of as guilt demanding atonement and propitiation and expiation, there has been one supreme sacrifice for sin. If we think of the mediating high priest of the old Temple, we, too, have a Mediator and a High Priest, Jesus, the Son of God, who has passed into the heavens, where he ever liveth to make intercession for us. If we think of our guilt and unworthiness, we are clothed with the righteousness of Christ and are accepted in the Beloved. This language springs naturally out of the customs and modes of thought of the time; and it is striking and expressive when taken as the language of devout emotion and adoring gratitude; but it is full of embarrassment when taken in rigid literalness. Much of it also is foreign to our modes of thought, and has to be translated into modern forms of conception before we can make much out of it.

Yet many persons, with little insight into the way in which living language is used, find it hard to distinguish between such instrumental and adumbrative use of language and its falsehood. If the language does not mean what it says, they fancy it must be false. Yet how much of religious or other language means what it says? God is spoken of as a fortress, a dwelling-place of his people, as covering his saints with his feathers, as the shadow of a great rock in a weary land, while the righteous trust under his wings and abide under the shadow of the

Almighty. All of these statements are literally false, and the various conceptions are mutually contradictory. Even the dullest can see this. Even the dullest perceives that the truth of such language lies in the idea it conveys, and that contradictory or incommensurable figures may be used to express the same truth. But fancy the result if any one should insist on taking this language with mechanical literalness. We have similar absurdity or impossibility when we take with rigid literalness the Scripture language concerning the Saviour's work.

The same impossibility is further seen from the progress of theological discussion concerning the atonement. The language of satisfaction, payment of debt, etc., has been universally abandoned in theory, or else so modified that it means something else. The latter is the more common course. This makes it possible to retain the language of Scripture and restrict it to a permissible meaning, which reduces to a contention for words rather than for ideas. But Antinomianism was seen to be the immediate and unavoidable conclusion when the language was literally taken. The debt was paid or the penalty was exacted, and the sinner was, of course, free. The payment was demanded in the name of justice; and, payment once made, justice could never demand or even permit that it be paid twice. The same conclusion resulted from the suppositions of substitution and satisfaction. Supposing these to be psychologically or morally conceivable, which is far from evident, it resulted at once that the sinner was unconditionally free. The suggestion of conditions whereby some sought to elude this conclusion did credit to their moral sense, but not to their logic. Such substitution, in the nature of the case, was in the indicative mood, and either was or was not the fact. If it was the fact, nothing either great or small remained for the sinner to do. But if something did remain, then it was not a literal substitution or an absolute satisfaction, but something else, a substitution which did not substitute, a satisfaction which did not satisfy. With this result the doctrine became, as just said, a contention for words. It was thought necessary to *say* substitution and *say* satisfaction, but the meaning was left indefinite. The Antinomians, the holders of the unconditional perseverance of the saints, and the Calvinistic Universalists of the death-and-glory type, were the only logical defenders of the literal view; and even they did not duly consider the embarrassing fact that, in spite of the substitution, the saints are left to endure for themselves the visible consequences of sin; and this was well calculated to awaken the suspicion that perhaps the invisible consequences might come around to them also. But the progress of theological thought, and the loud protest of the moral reason have compelled the abandonment of this theory in any literal sense. It is seen in its non-literal character.

Methodist and other Arminian writers have generally succeeded in making this point clear; and, as a consequence, the view of the atonement most in favor with them is some form of the governmental theory, and that, in spite of the fact that the language of the Scriptures so largely lends itself to the abandoned views. This fact is interesting as showing the settled conviction that the language of Scripture must be interpreted in accordance with our moral reason, no matter what it seems to say. It also shows that, for Arminians at least, the problem is not one which can be solved by dictionaries alone; for the governmental theory is about the last thing the dictionary method would evolve from the text of Scripture. In fact, no theory departs more widely from the literal language of the Bible; and its lawyer-like devices appeal neither to the heart nor to the conscience. Its non-literal character will clearly appear if we take almost any of the leading texts on this subject and substitute the conceptions of the rectoral theory. Still it was a moral advance upon an immoral or impossible literalism. This general fact is especially commended to the consideration of all those who, not having mastered the distinction between the fact and the theory of the Saviour's redeeming work, are prone to mistake a departure from the latter for a rejection of the spirit. No Arminian who understands his own position can ever be a literalist in this matter. There is all the more need of emphasizing this point from the fact that popular religious speech, and especially popular hymns, are saturated with substitutional and sacrificial literalism, and thus the idea is easily formed that this is the very gist and essence of the gospel. This error is inevitable to all who interpret religious speech as the language of a dogma or a statute.

There is, then, no literal substitution of one person for another, no literal satisfaction of the claims of justice, no literal payment of a debt, no literal ransom or redemption, but a work of grace on our behalf which may be more or less well described in these terms. One who has been saved from sin and restored to righteousness and the divine favor may well think of himself as redeemed and ransomed, or as freed from debts he could never pay. And he might also well and

truly think of his Saviour as having offered himself up as a sacrifice for him, as having died for
him and redeemed him by his blood. But this is
the language of emotion, and devotion, and gratitude, and discipleship. It is the language of the
Christian heart and life, not the language of theological theory. To turn it into the mechanical letter
of theory is to lose the spirit which alone giveth
life. We have now to inquire into its theoretical
and theological meaning.

The theory of the atonement has largely been
vitiated by two prominent mistakes. First, it has
been discussed in terms of abstractions and in
very general oversight of the concrete facts of the
case; and, secondly, the relations of non-moral
things have been substituted for the relations of
moral persons.

The mass of the discussion illustrates the first
point. Abstract notions of justice and government
have been put forward as fundamental; and various statements have been made as to what they
demand. Much of this work was done *ad hoc*,
and represented no unsophisticated utterance of
the moral reason. It was the work of advocates
rather than of inquirers. The failure to understand the instrumental and adumbrative nature
of language led to the fancy that every bold and

striking metaphor was a literal fact; and the spec-
ulator had to conduct himself accordingly. This
led to unlimited sophistication of reason and conscience. Justice was defined as only a theologian
could define it. The final cause of the definition
was to work the theory and catch the sinner. The
moral nature had few rights which theology was
bound to respect. The claims of the Divine Sover-
eign were the supreme thing, and were determined
in accordance with the political absolutism of the
time. The Heavenly Father, the God of Love,
nowhere appears. In his place was a Being very
jealous for his own honor, and careful to exact the
uttermost farthing. To be sure, the atonement
was said to be the work of love, but in its philosophy love entirely disappeared. The entire operation was carried on in a fashion unpleasantly
suggestive of an almighty Shylock. In addition,
the makeshifts of human governments, which result solely from their imperfection, were taken as
models for our thought of the divine procedure.
Thus an indefinite amount of sophistication and
moral hocus-pocus was introduced into the theory.

A brief sketch of the history of the discussion
will illustrate this matter. Before the time of Anselm the theory of the atonement had not been elaborated. In the main, Scripture language was used,
and in the early Church many fruitful glimpses

of the positive and moral meaning of the Saviour's
work abound. Christ came not merely to remove
the curse, but also to give men power to become
the children of God. God became man that men
should become divine. But these truths were only
dimly seen, and were not freed from distorting
misconceptions and elaborated into systematic
expression before the collapse of the classical
civilization. There were some floating notions
that the need of the atonement rested on the
veracity of God ; and in cruder minds there was
a fancy that the devil was a party to the transac-
tion. He had acquired a right and title in man,
it seems, by virtue of our sin ; and the work of
redemption consisted in extinguishing this claim.
This was often done in a rather doubtful fashion,
which was excused, however, by the consideration
that the devil deserved to be defrauded. All of
this was definitely set aside by Anselm, who left
out the devil entirely, and brought forward the
justice of God as the divine attribute which
demanded a substitutional suffering for man, if
he were to be redeemed. On this basis the theory
was built up.

Sin, Anselm defines as the failure to give God
his due. By sin a debt of indefinite magnitude is
incurred. God is defrauded of his due, which is
especially the honor owed him by his creatures ;

and to be just to himself God must conserve this
honor. This can be done only by the punishment
of the sinner, or by a sufficient satisfaction for
sin. Satisfaction for sin consists in restoring
what the sinner has taken away, and in making
due recompense for the dishonor of God arising
from sin. Of course, man can never make this
satisfaction, and hence arises the need of the God-
man, who alone can bring salvation. Throughout
the discussion three things are confused: the fact
of the atonement, the theory of the atonement,
and the theory of the person of the Redeemer.
The subject is quantitatively and commercially
conceived ; and the entire discussion goes on so
abstractly that neither God nor man, as a moral
being with moral ends, has much interest in
the case. There is nothing in it that speaks
clearly and convincingly to the consciousness and
moral reason of any one. The abstract notions
of justice, sin, satisfaction are shuffled and
quantitatively measured against one another ; and
this is the true theory of the atonement.

In such crude notions the Christian philosophy
of the atonement began ; and it has been in unstable equilibrium ever since. How crudely it has
been managed is familiar to every one acquainted
with the history of Christian doctrine. Apart from
the crude and unworthy conceptions of God and

his government, borrowed from the undeveloped political and ethical philosophy of the time, justice was made into something abstract which demanded penalty or payment; and the penalty also was made something so abstract that justice was quite indifferent who paid it, provided it was paid. Thus the thought was reached that justice might be satisfied by the pain of a second party; and in this way the possibility of atonement was secured. But, then, in order to retain a hold on the sinner, it was further held by all but the most rigorous logicians that the penalty already once exacted from the Redeemer might justly be exacted again from the sinner. Without this drawback the theory fell into Antinomianism; and with it, it fell into contradiction with itself.

Thus the theory is full of internal inconsistency. The atonement is said to be necessary to the forgiveness of sins; but, in truth, when the atonement is thus conceived, there is no forgiveness. To demand satisfaction, whether by substitution, or otherwise, is to collect the debt or inflict the penalty which in forgiveness is forgiven. But if the debt is paid, or the penalty is exacted, there is nothing to forgive. If, after such satisfaction, payment or penalty is still demanded, we have no forgiveness, but simply a trick whereby the debtor and his surety are defrauded, while

the creditor gets paid twice. Not even faith could
be demanded of the sinner on this scheme ; for
either the lack of faith as a sin is atoned for, or
else something stands apart from the range of the
atonement ; and this, according to the theory,
would be a fatal admission.

Thus forgiveness and even love itself disappear
so far as the Father is concerned. The love is on
the part of the Son ; but the Father is simply
satisfied by paying the debt, and has no further
claims. A recent religious publication contains a
good illustration of this result. A preacher represents himself as having called on an old saint in
obscure life, and as having asked her if she did
not wonder at God's goodness in forgiving her
sins. To his surprise she replied, No. This seemed
to him to argue a great insensibility, and he set
forth the divine grace, and repeated his question.
But once more the answer was, No. God, she said,
was only just in forgiving her sins, since Jesus
had taken her place, and paid it all. Then the
preacher discerned, according to his own account,
that he had been the dull one, and that the old
saint had entered more deeply than he into the
meaning of the gospel. Such a ghastly travesty
of the doctrine of grace is possible only to profound mental and moral illiteracy.

Equally confused was the traditional theory as

to the relation of Christ to his work whereby he
became the Saviour of the world. Of course, there
was a strong tendency to fix attention on the physical fact of death and its physical attendants as
the supreme and essential thing; and this often
ran into hysterical excesses from which we are not
even yet entirely free. But, apart from these, we
find in the exposition a continual oscillation between Christ as literal substitute, whose sufferings
were a literal equivalent for the pains due from
us for our sins, and Christ as having infinite
merit, which makes us righteous by being transferred to us. The notions of merit and satisfaction
having been distinguished, it became a puzzle to
know how Christ could have any excess of merit
which might be transferred to another. The merit
was supposed to arise from his perfect obedience;
but then the query arose whether this obedience
was not his duty, so that, after all, Christ did no
more than his duty, and, hence, had no excess of
merit to transfer. This scruple was met by the distinction of active and passive obedience. In the
former Christ remained within the bounds of his
obligation; but in the latter he transcended requirement, and this provided a store of merit
which might be transferred. But the interpretation
was not constant. Sometimes the passive obedience
did away with our sin and guilt, and the active

obedience secured for us the necessary merit. The
double obedience became quite a labyrinth of barren subtleties. What the transfer of moral merit
or moral character would mean in any case is, of
course, an insoluble question; but these mechanical thinkers gave little attention to this phase of
the problem.

And just as little was the theory thought
through with reference to God the Father. The
theorists largely tended to make him the incarnation of justice, and as needing to be propitiated
by sacrifice and suffering of some kind. This, as
said, was often carried so far as to miss the love
of God altogether, in the most flagrant contradiction of Scripture. The Father was full of wrath
and vengeance, from which he was turned away
only by the suffering and supplication of the Son.
This notion crept into the creeds and popular
hymns, and still appears in the cruder utterances
of the pulpit. Thus the true order is inverted.
The love of God to man is made the effect of the
atonement, whereas the Scriptures represent the
atonement as the effect of the Father's love. God
so loved the world that he gave his Son; God
was in Christ reconciling the world to himself;
and God in Christ, not God for Christ's sake, for-
gives us.

But when this error was avoided, and the

Saviour's work was seen to root and rise in the Father's love, it was exceedingly difficult to say in what the propitiation for sin consisted, or what necessity existed for it as any objective fact. Certainly the father of the prodigal son did not need to propitiate himself or to have any one else propitiate him when the repentant prodigal came home; and it is impossible to see any greater difficulty in God's pardon of men.

Equally obscure was the objective meaning of the propitiation made by the Son to the Father. No one could tell what it meant when the matter was analyzed and clarified. Phrases and terms, some Scriptural and some not, abounded; but few cared to take them in strict literalness. They had to be explained or turned into mysteries before they could be adopted. On account of these difficulties the holders of the governmental theory abandoned the notion of a personal propitiation, and made it rectoral. But propitiation was a poor term for such a regent's device. It satisfied neither the language of Scripture nor the mind and conscience of the disciple. The truth is, the theorists were bent on saving the language, and failed to note its figurative and non-absolute character. To persons living in the midst of sacrificial customs and conceptions, the figure of propitiation would well set forth the repentance and submission of the sinner, and the gracious disposition on the part of God; and this was the underlying truth, and the only truth we can find. If we insist on more, we must content ourselves with *saying* propitiation, without *meaning* anything beyond, possibly, the affirmation of an inscrutable and ineffable mystery; and that could be more directly expressed.

And, then, when the theory was at last adjusted, it still would not work. For the theory, such as it was, seemed to imply the removal of all the consequences of sin; and, unluckily, many of these visibly remained. In spite of the substitution, or satisfaction, or expiation, as we have said before, the saints, and even the elect, are left to endure for themselves the visible consequences of sin; and this is well calculated to awaken the suspicion that the invisible consequences also may come around to them in the course of time. Thus the theory is seen to be mal-adjusted to reality. We may still insist on substitution and expiation; but we have to admit that it is a substitution which, so far as experience goes, does not substitute, and an expiation which does not expiate.

Thus the dialectic of these unrhymed notions appears. They are a tissue of inconsistencies arising from taking the free and living language of

Scripture in a hard, mechanical fashion. And the notions themselves are taken in a non-natural sense. The abstract justice of this theory exists only in the theory. If justice demands anything, it is the punishment of the sinner himself. Only a mind debauched by theology would ever dream of calling anything justice which contented itself with penalty, no matter who paid it; and only the same type of mind could tolerate a justice which demanded or permitted double payment. The worthy doctors who speculated in this way were in great straits. They thought that they must take Scripture language as dogma, and interpret it like a statute; and they felt that they must save their scheme from its immoral implications. This they sought to do by introducing the contradictory notion of a conditional satisfaction; which satisfaction became such by being called satisfaction.

Something of the same abstract and fictitious character appears in the governmental theory, inaugurated by Grotius and variously elaborated since his time. According to this view the difficulty in forgiving sin does not lie in God himself as moral being, but in his rectoral relations as governor of the universe. These complicate the matter and form the problem. God himself, as moral person, needs no propitiation, and justice is not incompatible with forgiveness. But as ruler

God must magnify the law and make it honorable. Hence the need of the atonement.

If we take this view abstractly, and interpret it in its own terms, we are still in the midst of confusion. The law must indeed be magnified and made honorable; but this cannot be done in the forensic fashion which this theory proposes. In what way is the law magnified and made honorable by the suffering of an innocent person instead of the transgressor? In what way would such suffering reveal God's hatred of sin or his love for sinners? Unless the problem be treated from the standpoint of vicarious love, such suffering would argue a blindness or indifference to moral distinctions which would be a source of terror rather than of confidence. Besides, the rectoral difficulty itself, when inspected, is found to be imaginary. It has been the rule to point out that human rulers cannot forgive on simple repentance, and this has been thought decisive. But this is very superficial. Human governors must proceed by crude methods because of the impossibility of surely knowing the heart; but even here we are rapidly coming to see that when true reform is reached, neither government, nor society, nor morality has any interest in further punishment. The indeterminate sentence embodies this principle or rests upon it. If a community

were able to make its unrighteous members righteous, justice would be satisfied to let them go free.
The real difficulty is not rectoral, but dynamic.
Forgiveness upon repentance, with the limitations hereafter to be mentioned, is entirely in
order. How to produce true moral repentance is
the real problem.

Equally misinterpreted were the vicarious features of human life. The innocent suffer on account of the guilty, especially in rescuing them
from the evil case into which they have fallen
through the transgression of the laws of their
being. But there is nothing in this of the nature
of satisfaction, or substitution, or of an example
which magnifies the law and makes it honorable.

Vicarious suffering and vicarious sacrifice
abound in life, owing to the solidarity of life and
especially to the solidarity of love, but there is
a world-wide difference between them and *vicarious punishment*. The former we all accept as
love's greatest manifestation; the latter is the
caricature by mechanical minds of love's supreme
manifestation, so as to turn God's grace itself
into one of the great stumbling-blocks to its acceptance. The facts of vicarious sacrifice fit only
into the moral view of the atonement. Indeed,
it is clear that unless this question be transferred
from the field of judicial abstractions to that of

concrete moral relations this rectoral theory also is hopelessly bad ; and with this transfer it passes over into the moral theory. Vicarious suffering of the kind just mentioned would be moral; but in any other sense it would reveal neither love, nor justice, nor morality of any permissible kind.

This notion of an " example " for the sake of the law is even worse than that of a substitute. There is a kind of gloomy, tragic grandeur about the latter ; but the former is merely a regent's device. It provides no satisfaction for sins committed or to be committed; it is only a kind of police measure to frighten off future transgression. The value of this theory consists in its revolt against the moral scandals and impossibilities of the satisfaction doctrine whereby it became a step in theological progress. But in itself it is a halfway measure both exegetically and morally. Professor A. A. Hodge speaks of it as " a theatrical inculcation of principles which were not truly involved in the case." [1] If grammars and lexicons are to settle the question, the rectoral theory is a heresy ; and it was long so considered, and is so considered even now by a large part of the Christian world. A theory for whose enunciation we had to wait sixteen hundred years, and which is now rejected by great bodies of Christian think-

[1] Quoted by Dr. Munger in *Horace Bushnell*, p. 242, note.

ers, can hardly be reached by simply reading off
the text. The language of Scripture is sacrificial,
substitutional, and satisfactional, and would sound
strange enough if it were translated into the
terms of the rectoral theory. Not grammatical
exegesis but the moral reason is the great source
of the theory, and to satisfy this reason the theory
must go farther than it has gone. The reasons
which produced it are carrying us beyond it.

These things illustrate the abstract method of
discussing the atonement, and also warn us
against it. By that method we reach only confusion, and lose sight of reason and conscience and
reality altogether. It is equally dangerous to discuss it in terms of things, and not from the standpoint of moral persons. The difference is well
illustrated by the following quotation from Coleridge : —

" A sum of £1000 is due from James to Peter,
for which James has given a bond. He is insolvent, and the bond is on the point of being put in
suit against him, to James's utter ruin. At this
point Matthew steps in, pays Peter the thousand
pounds, and discharges the bond. In this case
no man would hesitate to admit that a complete
satisfaction had been made to Peter. Matthew's
£1000 is a perfect equivalent for the sum which
James was bound to have paid, and which Peter

had lent. It is the same thing, and this is altogether a question of things. Now, instead of
James being indebted to Peter in a sum of money
which (he having become insolvent) Matthew
pays for him, let me put the case that James had
been guilty of the basest and most hard-hearted
ingratitude to a most worthy and affectionate
mother, who had not only performed all the
duties and tender offices of a mother, but whose
whole heart was bound up in this her only child,
. . . all which he had repaid by neglect, deser-
tion, and open profligacy. Here the mother
stands in the relation of the creditor ; and here,
too, I will suppose the same generous friend to
interfere, and to perform with the greatest tenderness and constancy all those duties of a grate-
ful and affectionate son which James ought to
have performed. Will this satisfy the mother's
claims on James, or entitle him to her esteem,
approbation, and blessing ? Or what if Matthew,
the vicarious son, should at length address her
in words to this purpose : 'Now I trust you are
appeased, and will be henceforward reconciled to
James. I have satisfied all your claims on him. I
have paid his debt in full ; and you are too just
to require the same debt to be paid twice over.
You will, therefore, regard him with the same
complacency, receive him into your presence with

the same love, as if there had been no difference
between him and you. For I have made it up.'
What other reply could the swelling heart of the
mother dictate than this : ' O, misery ! and is it
possible that you are in league with my unnatural
son to insult me ? Must not the very necessity of
your abandonment of your proper sphere form
an additional evidence of his guilt? Must not the
sense of your goodness teach me more fully to
comprehend, more vividly to feel, the evil in
him? Must not the contrast of your merits magnify his demerits in his mother's eye, and at once
recall and embitter the conviction of the canker-
worm in his soul?' " [1]

This passage is decisive. It shows how odious
and abominable are the results when we discuss
this doctrine in terms of things and apply them
to the relations of moral persons ; and also how
utterly impossible it is that any one should ever
take another's place in his moral relations. It
would be playing hide-and-seek with intelligence
and conscience, a series of make-believes and false
pretenses, a calling of black white, and a pretend-
ing that it is white when all the while it is black, and
we know it is black. Turning a black man into a
white man by putting a white robe on him would
not be more fictitious. Such is the case with all

[1] *Aids to Reflection*, Aphorism XIV.

notions of substitution, transfer of moral quali-
ties, imputed righteousness, etc., when they are
literally taken. Thus we see the necessity of considering the question from the standpoint of the
moral personality. Abstractions are illusory and
fictitious ; and the relations of things are incommensurable with the relations of persons.

After so much of abstract and negative criticism it seems well to remind ourselves of the distinction between the atonement as fact and the
atonement as theory. We still believe and maintain that a great work of grace has been wrought
for man ; that the Father gave the Son to be the
Saviour of the world ; that the Son loved us and
gave himself for us ; and that God was in Christ
reconciling the world unto himself. Neither do we
desire to do away with the sacrificial and substitutional language of the Scriptures, which will
always have its value for Christian speech. " Rock
of Ages, cleft for me." " O Sacred Head now
wounded." " O Haupt voll Blut und Wunden."
There is no sign that the Church will ever outgrow this speech. But there is need that we
understand this speech and do not caricature the
vicarious suffering of Divine Love by turning it
into the *vicarious punishment* of theological
theory.

Our discussion, then, concerns only the theory

of our Lord's redeeming work, and here we find much to be desired. The traditional theories have been an incongruous compound of inconsistent speculation and halting exegesis. The speculation was never rigorous, but was helped out by the exegesis; and the exegesis rested on the fancy that Scripture language is that of dogma, and must be interpreted like the words of a statute. Moreover, a good part of the exegesis consisted in reading the Scriptures in the light of the traditional dogma, thus often reading into them doctrines undreamed of by the Scripture writers themselves. A sufficient illustration is found in the fact already mentioned, the making God's love the effect of the atonement instead of its cause.

The total result was something about equally obnoxious to reason and conscience on the one hand, and to the Scriptures themselves on the other. The living revelation of the love of God, and the grace of the Lord Jesus, and the sanctifying work of the Holy Spirit, which illumine the Scriptures, was replaced by frigid juristic speculations, lifeless and life-destroying, the despair of reason and the opprobrium of faith. And because of the failure to distinguish between the fact and the theory of the Saviour's work, these speculations were thought to be the gospel itself. The only saving feature of the case was that, in spite

of these obscuring mists of theory, the love of
God nevertheless gleamed through the words of
Scripture, and a wholesome moral instinct generally prevented the theory from working its logical
results. The same moral instinct enforced the demand for righteousness, and thus supplemented
the most grievous lack of the speculation. Meanwhile, and on the other hand, the critics of the
traditional theory have often dissolved away both
the love and righteousness of God into a hazy
good-nature, with no power to awe or to attract.
Both extremes are about equally far from the
truth.

The necessity of transferring the discussion of
this doctrine from the realm of juristic abstractions to the realm of life and conscience has already appeared. Many hints of such a view appear in the writings of St. Paul, and since the time
of Abélard there have been more or less definite
attempts to construe the atonement as a moral
process, having for its aim less the canceling of
debts supposed to be due to justice than the positive lifting of men into the life of righteousness.
This is certainly an aspect of the problem which
Christian thought will never again consent to lose
sight of. It is the stone which the traditional
builders have commonly rejected, whereas in the

gradual moralizing of theology which Christian
progress is bringing about, it is becoming the
head of the corner. We have now to consider
whether reflective criticism will allow us to rest in
this view, or whether it must go along with the
others.

And, first of all, it is plain that we must not
only keep clear of abstractions, but we must also
discuss the question with regard to our human conditions. We have no call to consider the relation
of abstract government to abstract subjects, or
what might be demanded in the government of
angels, of whose nature and conditions we know
nothing, or what penalty should be exacted for
disobedience wrought in the full light of knowledge, and because of pleasure in the evil. Discussing the subject on that abstract basis, we
should most probably come to the conclusion that
there can be no forgiveness of sins, and that justice could never rest without exacting the full
penalty from the sinner. But all such questions
we set aside ; for we really have neither the mental nor the moral insight needed for such discussion. What would be abstractly just in general
is beyond us ; we must confine ourselves to considering concrete cases. The atonement seems
intelligible only in connection with a developing
moral world, and would appear to be inadmissible
in a completely developed moral order.

Moreover, our human life is not lived on the abstract plane of abstract moral agency. It is a life of ignorance and weakness ; a life of crude beginnings and shadowy incipiencies ; a life without insight into itself and without foresight of the end ; a life in which power and faculty and knowledge and moral sensibility and self-control have to be developed ; a life rooted in the animal out of which we only slowly and by much trial and error emerge; a life largely moulded by heredity and environment, and solicited by temptations from without and within, from above and beneath and around. Now, the application of abstract rectoral and forensic notions to such a life is as absurd as it would be in the case of the family. Manifestly the only possibility of getting any conception of the case which will not revolt the moral reason lies in replacing the conception of the Divine Governor by that of the Heavenly Father, and the conception of the divine government by that of the divine family. If the dearest and deepest thought of God be that he is our Father, then our deepest and truest thought of his dealings with us must be determined by this conception ; and all other conceptions of whatever kind that will not harmonize with this must be cast out. Whatever notions of government and justice we may form must be subordinated to the thought of this Divine Father-hood of which every other fatherhood in heaven or in earth is named. Instead, then, of a Divine Ruler anxious mainly for his own claims and laws, we have a Divine Father in the midst of his human family, bearing with his children and seeking by all the discipline of love and law to build them into likeness to and fellowship with himself.

The primal demand for the economy of grace lies in the form and nature of human development. These constitute a claim for fatherly patience, for-bearance, and discipline. There could be no more ghastly travesty of justice and goodness than any abstract forensic procedure would offer. The-ology, as we have said, long echoed the political absolutism of the time, and regarded God as an irresponsible ruler, whereas, from an ethical point of view, he is the most deeply obligated being in the universe. And having started a race under human conditions he is bound to treat it in accord-ance with those conditions. God is bound to be the great Burden-bearer of our world because of his relations to men. We that are strong ought to bear the burdens of the weak, is a principle of unlimited application. All dealing with the moral problem of humanity must regard our hu-man circumstances.

Further, our development begins on a submoral plane. That was not first which was spiritual, but that which was animal (psychical), and afterward that which was spiritual. Whatever may have been true of the first man, this word of Paul's is true of his descendants; and the reported performances of even the first man would not seem to set him very high in the scale of development. By consequence, sin itself in many of its aspects is a relic of the animal not yet outgrown, a resultant of the mechanism of appetite and impulse and reflex action for which the proper inhibitions are not yet developed; and only slowly does it grow into a conciousness of itself as evil. Thus sin is born; that is, human beings become willful and selfish, and willing to do wrong. This may, indeed, go to any extreme of malignity, but it would be hysteria to regard the common life of men as rooting in a conscious choice of unrighteousness.

Now, given sin in the sense defined, what is to be done? As said, it is conceivable that there should be orders of being, say first-born sons of light, with whom any sin would be fatal. But we need not concern ourselves about them. With us human beings the case is otherwise. Unless we suppose God to have made the world in the dark, we must allow that he foreknew and intended to have just this developing human world with its necessity for struggling out of the animal into the spiritual, out of the mechanical into the free, out of the selfish into the loving, out of the earthly into the divine. It must be dealt with, therefore, under the law of development, and under the law of love. Hard-and-fast laws, mechanically imposed and mechanically applied, would be unspeakably absurd or unspeakably unjust in such an order. Tendencies, direction, outcomes, are the important thing; and judgment must come not at the beginning but at the end.

This is something which formal ethics finds difficult; for this science delights in categorical imperatives and abstract relations, and finds it hard to adjust itself to a moving moral world just as formal logic finds it hard to adjust itself to a moving physical world. In both cases, however, the adjustment has to be made. The human moral world does not exist as something fixed and complete; it is rather becoming. The saints are not saved; they are being saved. The whereabouts of a developing being is not so important as the direction of his movement; and his moral standing depends not on single and isolated deeds, but on the character which he develops. And this admits of no mechanical and quantitative measure in any case.

We abandon, then, all theories of an abstract

atonement based on abstract considerations of abstract moral agents and abstract transgression, and confine our attention to the concrete and living human world. Closet theories have no application or value. We are not concerned to find something which might be consistent as an abstract ethical speculation, but something which will commend itself to our moral reason when applied to this imperfect, developing, ignorant, and sinful human world. Such a doctrine must be sought in life and experience and the moral personality.

The primal attitude of God toward the human world, we have said, must be that of love in all the manifold expressions which our human life requires. But as this life develops into the moral form, the moral nature makes its demands. It is conceivable that God should have made a world capable only of sentient and non-moral satisfactions. The animal world seems to be of this kind. In such a world it suffices to furnish the conditions of animal development and comfort. But if a moral world is to exist, the moral nature must prescribe its form and imperative conditions. And one thing on which the moral nature is categorical and unyielding is that moral good and moral evil shall not be treated alike. It would be the overthrow of the moral universe to hold that moral evil could ever be ignored as indifferent or treated as if it

were good. Now, we are in the world of moral
persons, and here we come upon a real moral difficulty which demands consideration, one which
has formed the real strength of the theories of
the atonement that have demanded some sort
of satisfaction as a condition of forgiveness, although they failed rightly to apprehend the nature of the demand.

The essential moral fact in this matter is that
if God is to forgive unrighteous men some way
must be found of making them righteous. This
difficulty is not forensic but moral. It does not
spring from rectoral complications, but from the
moral nature itself. To forgive wicked men while
they remain wicked would be immoral. The fundamental problem is to find a way whereby the
righteous God can make righteous the ungodly;
and this cannot be secured by calling or declaring them righteous, but only by a spiritual transformation. Some dim insight into this fact underlies the highly obscure traditional conceptions of
the relation of justification to regeneration; and
this fact misunderstood has been the real strength
of the demand for some kind of satisfaction as a
condition of forgiveness. With the tendency of
uncritical thought to mistake distinctions for divisions, the several aspects of salvation have been
made into separate processes, and an "order of

salvation " has been laid down, to depart from
which would be heresy. Much of this trouble
arises from viewing the subject from the judicial
rather than the moral and vital standpoint. From
the former, penalties are externally attached, and
might be externally remitted; but from the latter,
penalties are organically connected with life and
conscience, and demand regeneration as well as
absolution.

The problem, then, must be concretely considered, and from the human standpoint. And here,
again, in order not to lose ourselves in abstractions, we must recur to the concrete life once
more. We cannot too resolutely keep to the
world of actual experience. We observe, then,
that our moral life is not something going on in
a vacuum by itself and without relation to the
system of law and reality. It is conceivable that
there should be a life with only abstract moral
contents and adapted to an abstract moral probation. This is the kind of life which the abstract
theorists seem to have in mind when they make
theories of the atonement. But our life is altogether different. It roots in and grows out of the
natural life of sense and impulse and desire ; and
it is geared throughout with the world of natural
law and uniform sequence. The moral life abstractly considered deals only with will and mo-

tive; but the moral life concretely considered deals with the whole system of law and consequence besides. And the concrete moral life is the only reality; and its aim is not simply to be formally good, but to attain unto largeness and richness and fullness of life itself. The abstract moral form is but the form; the contents are life, ever more abundant and glad and blessed.

This order of law and consequence exists as the foundation of our life. And this fact compels us to transfer the whole question of salvation from the realm of fictitious forensic abstractions and barren legalities to the realm of living natural and moral law. It is not a question of courts, but of life; not a question of abstract rules, but of the solid structure of reality. We have not to deal with arbitrary enactments, with penalties arbitrarily attached, but rather with constitutional law; that is, with law wrought into the constitution of things, and executing itself with the inevitability of gravitation. Any real solution of the problem must be sought from this point of view. We exchange, then, the forensic standpoint of external enactments for that of organic law.

And this fact enables us to make another distinction of great importance for the understanding of this matter of forgiveness and salvation. The moral life is now seen to involve two elements: relations

of will, and a set of organic consequences. The
two interpenetrate, but are nevertheless distinct.
The former represents the attitude of the will;
the latter is independent of volition, and represents the stored-up and incarnated outcome of
conduct in the world of law. The existence and
continuity of this order of law are absolutely
necessary to any rational and moral system; and
any tenable doctrine of forgiveness must be adjusted to it.

There is a great deal in this order of consequence which is mysterious to us. Why the consequences of physical wrong-doing should be
what they are is quite beyond us. The special
forms and intensity of discord introduced into
our faculties by sin, the peculiar weakening and
depolarization of the moral nature itself resulting
from conscious wickedness — all these points are
involved in great obscurity. We must believe,
however, that they are no random effects, but
represent the moral judgment and wisdom of the
Almighty.

We now return to the question of forgiveness.
In the personal field evil-doing is followed by the
displacence of moral beings, whether the deed be
against ourselves or others. The attitude of the
moral will is this personal displacence toward the
offender.   Forgiveness would mean the removal

of this displacence and the restoration of the offender to harmonious relations of will again. The condition of such forgiveness would be true repentance, that is, a heartfelt repudiation and condemnation of the deed, and a purpose to rectify the wrong done so far as possible. With God and man alike such repentance should remove personal displacence and restore the offender to harmonious relations of will with the one sinned against. There is nothing now in the attitude of his will which calls for condemnation. But this would not end the matter; for in the other field of law and outcome forgiveness does not cancel consequences. The spendthrift may be forgiven, but his property is gone. The abuse of health may be forgiven, but the broken constitution remains. No forgiveness, no pardon, can recall the wasted years, or bring back the vanished opportunity, or make the past never to have been, or escape its entail of evil. Experience gives no hint of pardon such as this.

In this realm of constitutional law the utmost we may hope for is that consequences may be eliminated by bringing in other laws, as health eliminates disease. And in order to any effective forgiveness it is necessary that the system of law shall be such that restorative or countervailing agencies shall exist whereby the evil tendency may be prevented from becoming fatal, or from continuing forever. As provision is made in the physical system for restoring equilibrium when the disturbance is not too great, or as provision is made in the living organism for the elimination of disease within certain limits, so provision must be made in the moral system for moral recovery. Otherwise there can be no moral system under human conditions. Without such provision the system would be in unstable equilibrium, and would be hopelessly overthrown at the first disturbance of its balance. In a forensic system, where penalty is externally attached, forgiveness might end the matter, but in an organic and vital system forgiveness is nothing without cure. What would the forgiveness of a self-induced fever mean?

We have, then, an unchangeable system of law, not forensic, but expressed in the nature of things, as the precondition of any moral and intelligible order. And this system must be looked upon as an expression of the divine goodness and righteousness; and being such, it must be without variableness or shadow of turning. No arbitrariness can be admitted here. Thus we come in sight of a fixed system of law to which all our conceptions of forgiveness have to be adjusted. And it would be more tolerable to the moral nature to deny outright the possibility of forgiveness than to allow this system to be tampered with in such a way as to treat good and evil alike, or to introduce arbitrariness into the divine procedure.

And here is the truth, and the only truth, in the traditional philosophies of the atonement, the claim that sin itself can never be treated as a matter of indifference, and that its forgiveness can never be a subject of arbitrary volition. There are moral conditions to be regarded which are of absolute obligation. But while these philosophies have rightly held this truth, they have by no means succeeded in rationally satisfying the demands in question. They have insisted that the consequences of sin cannot be canceled without an atonement, but have signally failed to see that they are not canceled even with an atonement. Their occupation with fictitious forensic consequences has prevented their seeing the world of concrete consequences.

An opposite error of the sentimentalists must be noticed at this point as resting upon the same oversight of the system of organic consequences. We might well fancy, in some moment of moral deliquescence or of half vision, that there ought to be absolute forgiveness upon repentance, with relaxation of all penalty. This notion would root in the nervous sensibility rather than in the moral

reason. In the root sense of the word, it would
be pathological rather than moral. Its plausibility
rests upon oversight of the distinction between
forgiveness as the removal of personal displacence,
and forgiveness as the canceling of natural organic consequences. The sentimentalist fails to
see that consequences are not forgiven. He also
fails to see that as God's laws are founded in love
and wisdom, there can be no departure from them.
There are conditions for everything in the divine
order, and a road to every place. If we wish the
thing, we must fulfill the conditions. If we would
reach the place, we must travel the road. We
shall never get wheat by planting weeds; and
just as little shall we reap to the spirit if we sow
to the flesh. Imagine the folly of one who should
say, "I sowed weeds, but I expect wheat; for I
have repented since then, and I trust I shall have
wheat when the time comes." Such is his folly
who in a world of law expects to reap what he
has not sown, or to escape from reaping what he
has sown. It is God's purpose to have and to bless
only a world wherein dwelleth righteousness. However inconvenient we may find it, and however
strong our desire for sport may be, the unrighteous must come to grief; and God will never depart from his moral laws to make it otherwise.
And let all the people say, Amen. It would be

insufferable to suppose that God, having desired a holy world and failed to reach it, should then content himself with making the unholy happy.

Furthermore, the sentimentalist conceives repentance very superficially. In fact, true repentance is so difficult and takes such deep hold on the moral nature that not without reason is repentance itself spoken of as the gift of God. Mere regret, especially in the face of penalty, is not moral at all; least of all is it any ground for forgiveness. The fear that haunts every thoughtful mind at this point is, that there will never be any truly moral repentance. The sorrow of the world is easy enough, but the godly sorrow that worketh a change of mind is not so easy nor so common. We may well believe that true repentance is followed by forgiveness, but the problem how to produce such repentance remains unsolved; and this is one of the greatest practical difficulties in the case.

This distinction between forgiveness as the removal of personal displacence and forgiveness as the canceling of natural consequences deserves emphasis; for there are many crude and immoral notions in popular religious thought respecting what forgiveness does. These are illustrated by that odious fancy which one often comes upon

in religious circles, that the best adjustment between this world and the next would be to sin as
long as possible and repent just in time to escape
the penalty. Such a notion has no warrant in
experience, is hateful to conscience, and is most
unseemly in the face of unchanging law; and
one holding this notion should consider that true
repentance is thereby made impossible, and that
forgiveness does not cancel consequences.

Notions of this kind spring from the abstract
conception of the atonement. Sin is supposed to
constitute an abstract debt to abstract justice;
and this debt is canceled by the atonement. The
necessity of personal righteousness and the world
of inflexible law are lost sight of; and these immoral fancies result. But they vanish forever
when we view the subject from the concrete, ethical standpoint. So long as any one wishes to be
saved not from sin but from the penalty of sin
there can be no salvation for him. He knows neither the Scriptures nor the moral reason. True
salvation is from sin, not from penalty. It means
deliverance from the sinful life and establishment
in the life of active righteousness, which is the
only possible condition of fellowship with the
Holy God. Only the pure in heart can see God
or have fellowship with him. Yet so inverted are
our notions on this matter that a large part of

religious effort seems to be directed to saving men from hell rather than from sinning, and to getting men to heaven instead of recovering them to holiness of heart and life — a frightful heresy in both faith and practice. It is even to be suspected that not a little of popular zeal for the traditional views of the atonement rests at bottom on the secret fancy that in some way the atonement enables us to escape the stringent necessity of personal righteousness. In some way we are to be "let off," and Christ's "finished work" is to pass as a substitute for our own effort. In that case it is only a specification of the general mechanical tendency in religion, whereby men seek to avoid the narrow way of spiritual life. Men are ready to believe and do anything which promises to absolve them from girding themselves for strenuous and holy living. To detect the presence of this tendency in this matter we need only ask ourselves what we really desire from God. Is it the forgiveness of sins, restoration to the divine favor, and God's help in holy living? All of this is provided for by the gospel. But if it be anything else, as escape from consequences or relaxation of moral demands, we are using the grace of God as a cloak for iniquity and an incitement to sin. This is the heresy of heresies. The love of God, like parental love, takes the will for the deed, bears with weakness and imperfection, avails itself of all the resources of discipline, and waits for development; but if any one regardeth iniquity in his heart, the wrath of God abideth on him; and any doctrine to the contrary is a heresy.

The sins of the world, then, may not be ignored; neither may they be taken away by mere sovereignty. The problem is a moral one and must receive a moral solution. And the solution must be sought in accordance with God's fundamental purpose in our human world. That purpose is to have a family of spiritual children, made in his image and likeness, who shall know him and love him, and upon whom he may bestow himself in blessing for ever and ever. And the method of procedure is that of growth and development. There are animal beginnings with moral endings. Love and law are omnipresent throughout the whole of the work; and judgment is possible only at the end.

God's supreme aim is to secure the love and obedience and sympathy and filial confidence of his children. On the human side the response is slow. As in the earthly family, there is a long period of irresponsiveness, ignorance, willfulness, and even of rebellion; and as the earthly father bears with this, waits for development, and seeks by all the resources of love and correction and

discipline to bring the child to the filial insight
and the filial spirit, so the Heavenly Father bears
with his children and seeks to bring them to a
recognition of his presence and purpose in their
lives, and to a filial acceptance of, and coöpera-
tion with, his purpose. They must be recovered
from their willful and evil ways, from their distrust and alienation also, and given power to
become the children of the Highest. Any work
which did not secure this, which left men in their
alienation and rebellion, might conceivably satisfy
a fictitious justice; but it would never satisfy the
Father's heart. To treat men as righteous when
they are not righteous would involve the deepest
depths of mental and moral confusion. The only
effective atonement for sin must consist in salvation from sin and restoration to righteousness.
Nothing else could satisfy God or man.

How, then, are the sins of the world to be
taken away? This question in a forensic sense
we dismiss altogether as being fictitious. In the
practical sense the meaning is better expressed in
another form: How are ignorant, weak, willful,
sinful men to be recovered from unrighteousness
and developed into the life of God? This is the
real problem for which we must seek a concrete
moral solution. Mere power can do nothing. Mere
volition is inadmissible. It is either a moral solu-

tion or none. It is a question of moral goodness
and of moral dynamics with which juristic abstractions have nothing to do.

Here comes in the work of Christ as a necessary part of the work of grace. God's supreme
resource must lie in himself and in the revelation
of himself. God must be revealed as a moral
being and in such a way as to make forever sure
both his love and his holiness, and to furnish the
supreme incentive to repentance and righteousness and love on the part of men. This is done
by the incarnation of the Divine Son, who reveals
the heart of the Father, not in word but in deed,
so that God is manifest in the flesh for the salvation of men. And in the fullness of his devotion
the Divine Son enters into human limitations,
lives the perfect life before men, shows God's
thought for men, comes into contact with our sin
also, submits to its outrage and violence, and becomes obedient unto death, even the death of the
cross.

Now, two things are forever clear for all who
receive this faith : First, that God will never depart from his moral laws in order to make men
happy or to save men in their sins. They must
be saved morally if saved at all. Secondly, the
love and grace of God are set on high forever ;
and now every one that thirsteth may take of the

water of life. This is the specific meaning of the
Redeemer's work. It was not a fictitious haggling with abstract and fictitious justice. It was
Infinite Love going forth to seek and to save the
lost. It was the father of the prodigal going in
search of his boy. It was the Good Shepherd
giving his life for the sheep ; not, of course, at
the demand of justice, but at the instance of divine love. This is the true vicariousness of love,
of sympathy, of the living moral reason, not an
abstract and fictitious vicariousness which no one
can understand or find any place for in an unsophisticated conscience.

Thus the righteousness of God is set forth and
forever demonstrated. If God were simply a being
of good nature, and without interest in the righteousness of his creatures, he could easily make
them happy by mere power and at no cost to
himself or any one else. This is the sentimentalist's notion of what ought to be. This notion
is forever vacated by the cross of Christ. God
will be at infinite cost to save men, but he will
save them morally or not at all. It is a moral
world in which we live ; and we are under the
inexorable law of righteousness. There is no provision made for relaxing moral demands, or for
"letting sinners off." The promised land is only
for those who attain unto the spirit of righteous-

ness. The willful and disobedient may wander in the desert forever; they cannot enter in. The only hope for sinners consists in their being saved from sinning, and in being recovered from their alienation from God and righteousness, which is the essence of sin and perdition. There is and can be no other salvation which the moral reason will accept. The work of Christ, as thus morally conceived, demonstrates, we repeat, the righteousness of God.

And not only is the righteous God thus revealed, but we also see God's great method for making righteous the ungodly. We see the revelation of righteousness, and we also see divine love in divine condescension and sacrifice in order to win men from unrighteousness and raise them to the righteous life, to do away with their estrangement and misunderstanding, and bring them into filial fellowship with their God and Father. This is the great meaning of the work of Christ. In this way the righteousness of God is declared, and the just God becomes the justifier of the ungodly; that is, the righteous God helps the ungodly to become righteous. Thus God was and is in Christ reconciling the world unto himself. And the work of Christ himself, so far as it was an historical event, must be viewed not merely as a piece of history, but also as a manifestation of that cross which was hidden in the divine love from the foundation of the world, and which is involved in the existence of the human world at all.

And is this all there is in the atonement? In reply, we say we no longer care to use the word atonement, as it has become misleading or uncertain through long association with doubtful theological theories. But this is all there is in the work of Christ to which we can give articulate and tenable expression. If any one chooses or feels a need for something more, it is open to him to say that there are back-lying mysteries in the divine nature which transcend this view. To this we should have no objection, if we were allowed to add that they also transcend all the traditional views. These transcendental mysteries cannot be expressed in terms of the satisfaction and substitution theories without contradicting our moral reason. They cannot be expressed in terms of the governmental theory without impressing us with a sense of fiction. As we have before pointed out, all these views oscillate between an untenable literalism in exegesis and a freer interpretation of the language of Scripture. Whoever departs from any of these views is reproached with departing from the teachings of Scripture. Thus the holder of the governmental view is charged with ignoring the teachings of the word; and he in turn makes the same charge upon the holder of the moral and vital theory of the atonement. But in fact this only shows their failure to grasp their own position. No one holds to a strictly literal interpretation of Scripture language, except when he has a polemic on hand, or wishes to make a charge of heresy. The satisfaction of the satisfactionist is one which does not satisfy. The substitution of the substitutionist is one which does not substitute. The justice of the rectoral theory is unlike any justice recognized by the unsophisticated moral reason. The satisfaction and the substitution and the justice have to be manipulated until they mean what they may be allowed to mean according to the exigencies of the theory, but what no one would ever think they meant who relied solely on the ordinary usage of language.

It is, then, open to any one, as we have said, to hold that there are back-lying mysteries in the divine nature which transcend the view we have set forth. Such a claim would be quite in line with our own insistence on the relative and adumbrative character of all our thinking on things divine. But we must insist also, and once more, that these mysteries equally transcend all the traditional views. They must be left unexpressed, therefore, beyond the point to which the view set forth carries us; and in any case this view must be included in any theory of the subject. It may be inadequate, but it is true as far as it goes. Whatever we may believe concerning superethical necessities in the case, they will never justify us in contradicting ethics. Theology may conceivably transcend the intuitions of conscience, but it may never contradict the enlightened conscience. The doctrine of the atonement, then, must lie at least partially in the moral field, and all of it must be harmonious with the moral reason. No conception of God in this matter will do which puts him below the moral heroes of humanity, and even below the daily self-sacrifice of the family. No theory will do which views God as without obligation, or as needing propitiation, or as being propitiated by a quantum of suffering. No abstract theory of the relation of abstract attributes, resulting in an abstract righteousness which leaves the living man as unrighteous as ever, with the necessity on the part of God either of letting man fall helplessly back into unrighteousness or of treating men as righteous when they are not — no such theory will longer command the thought and conscience of men; and for the sufficient reason that every such theory is at bottom irrational and immoral.

It must be noted, too, that the conception set forth has become practically the working view of the Church, so far as it is alive. We have come to see that the important thing is to save men from sin, and we are sure that consequences will take care of themselves if this can be done. And in doing this we fall back on Christ's revelation of the Father, on his summons to repentance and discipleship and his promises of forgiveness and divine renewal.

And if one should say, " Well, if that is all; if the sole work of Christ was to reveal the Father and bring men to God, what need was there for his life and sufferings and death?" the answer would be: How otherwise could the Father be effectively and dynamically revealed? Love is poorly revealed in words; it demands deeds for its true revelation. No proclamation of words, though attended by never so many miracles, no writing spread across the sky, could make any such living revelation of God and his character as is made in the incarnation and life of our Lord. And the revelation which he made derives its deep significance, not from what he said, nor from what he did, but from what he was. The incarnation is the central truth of Christianity ; and the incarnation is the essential fact of the atonement. But instead of saying that this is all there is in the work of Christ, we should rather say, *All this* is in the work of Christ. And where, in earth or in heaven, is there anything great besides?

But where are our sins in the mean time? All that has been said at best seems to point only to the possibility of reformation, and does not look to the atonement for our past sins; yet this is the most important matter of all. This difficulty is partly fictitious, and in so far results from considering the subject from an abstract forensic standpoint. The law claims our perfect obedience at all times, it is said ; and hence no later obedience can possibly atone for earlier disobedience. This, then, must always remain against us on the books of justice. How artificial all this is appears when we apply it to the case of the family. The father of the prodigal son, for instance, did not, after the feast was over, distress himself about the debt of filial duty which remained unpaid. And we may be sure that the Father in heaven will not unduly concern himself about the debt of the past when his prodigals return to their Father's house. To entertain such a notion is to leave the category of moral persons for that of things again. Love has no difficulty with the problem and only love can solve it.

But still, we may say, there is a debt which remains even after forgiveness. This is true. Some-

thing indeed remains, but it is not well conceived
as a debt to be paid in any commercial sense. It
would be more exact to say that sinners, rather
than sins, are forgiven. It is inverted and mechanical to fix our thought on the sin instead of
the sinner. Nothing would be gained if all sins
were forgiven and the evil will remained. This
recalls our distinction between the moral displacence which must be visited upon the evil will
and the natural consequences which result from
its indulgence. The forgiveness of the sinner involves the removal of the former, but not of the
latter. They are never forgiven so far as experience shows, and never ought to be forgiven. Of
course, they do not remain as a set of legal and
forensic liabilities; but they remain as effects in
a system of natural law. They can only be eliminated, as we have said, by bringing restorative
influences into play. When the moral displacence
of the Holy God is removed in the case of the
repentant sinner, a great deal of work still remains to be done with reference to the past.
And God presents himself as ready to coöperate
with the sinner in working out a better future
which shall in some measure undo the past and
cut off its entail of evil. The utmost we can hope
for is, that the system may be so ordered as to provide for recovery, and for our undoing or elim-

inating the wrong and mischief that have gone
forth from us. And this we ought supremely to
desire. What sort of a moral being would he
be who could rest content, even in Abraham's
bosom, if he knew there was anywhere any one
suffering a hard and bitter lot because of his evil-
doing? And what sort of a moral being would he
be whose deepest desire was not to have a chance
anywhere and anyhow to remedy every evil which
had gone forth from him? Any permissible doctrine of forgiveness must be construed in accordance with these considerations. Otherwise,
forgiveness itself becomes immoral, and the desire
for forgiveness becomes an expression of that
very selfishness which Christ came to destroy.

Am I, then, never to get clear of my past?
That depends on the meaning. Through the grace
and gracious help of God I may get clear of the
sinful life and emerge into the life of the spirit.
The healing and restoring resources of God are
great, and thus I may hope at last to remove the
scars and undo the evil. But that the past should
be made nonexistent, or memory blotted out, or
the entail of consequences arbitrarily cut off, this
is not to be hoped for, because it ought not to be.
We can make new departures, but we must start
from where we are. We can begin again, but
never at the beginning. The past always has a

mortgage on the future. This is self-evident as soon as we transfer the problem from the realm of fictitious or abstract forensic claims to the concrete world of organic law and consequence. And as this is the real world, we must adjust our theories and our hopes to it. Certainly, as we have said before, visible and experienced consequences are not forgiven; how, then, can we claim that any consequences will be forgiven, except in the sense of overcoming and eliminating them? Long, long regret must haunt many a forgiven soul; and there are sins against love and trust so dark and base that only the sight of him of the pierced hands and the bleeding side persuades us they ever can be forgiven. Paul remembered his persecution of the Church unto the end of his life, calling himself the chief of sinners on that account, and saying that he obtained mercy because he did it ignorantly in unbelief.

We reach then the following conclusions: All thought of literal substitution, satisfaction, payment of debt is morally impossible. Forensic and governmental difficulties are fictitious except as modes of expression. Abstractions throw no light upon the real problem. The venue must be changed from supposed enactments to natural laws; and from the evolutional form of the moral life judgment must be put at the end and not at the beginning. Then every one goes to his own place, to the place which he has chosen, and for which he has fitted himself. In this matter, also, there can be no arbitrary volition. What the eternal moral reason prescribes, that is what must finally be. Some of the earlier theorizers about justice, meaning thereby the moral reason, were not so much wrong in their contention as to its inexorable demands, as they were in ignoring the fact of development and putting the demand at the wrong end. Meanwhile God has revealed himself in his Son as our Father, as bearing us upon his heart, and as supremely desirous of saving us from the sinful life which must end in death if persisted in, and recovering us to righteousness and the filial spirit. For this the Divine Son has given himself; for this the Holy Spirit came and comes; and the work of both the Son and the Spirit roots in the Father's love. But in all this the aim is not to satisfy the demands of justice, nor yet to save men from penalty, but to save men from sinning, to lift them Godward, and to bring them to that spiritual attitude which will make it possible for God to bestow himself upon them in infinite and eternal blessing. As we have so often said, it is not a problem in forensic technicalities, but in spiritual dynamics.

Now, what shall we call this view? It is really
no matter what we call it, provided the thing be
understood; but the proper title is the moral view;
that is, the view which seeks to understand the
Saviour's work by the principles and analogies
of the ethical realm rather than by those of the
governmental and juristic realm. There is considerable criticism of what is called the " moral-in-
fluence theory " of the atonement scattered about
in theological treatises, but it is superficial and
unsatisfactory. The title itself is a bad one, as
failing to suggest the eternal love and eternal
working which underlie the life and salvation of
men, and of which the earthly work of the Redeemer is only a part and as it were a sample.
The Father worketh hitherto and I work, is as
valid now as when it was first uttered. No theory
which exhausts itself in anything so impersonal
as an " influence " or an " example " will be very
effective. But the title and the criticism alike fail
to grasp or express the depth and breadth of the
true moral theory.

In the work of Christ the love and righteousness of God find their supreme revelation. Here
we have the final illustration and demonstration
of what God is and what he means for men. But
here again it is easy for us to fall back once more
into mechanical and juridical thinking. We may

think of a store of merit acquired for men, in
which they are to share, so that nothing now remains but to bestow this merit upon men, puzzling ourselves meanwhile how the bestowment is
made, and how it is conferred upon infants and
imbeciles, and invincible ignorance, and those who
never had a chance. The attempt to answer these
questions has led to some highly artificial fancies
and some very doubtful inferences. First of all,
we have the mechanical or magical application of
this merit through the performance of some rite
or utterance of some formula. Or we have a
highly artificial scheme for saving the babies from
the wrath of God and making them sharers in the
benefits of the atonement. Or we have a set of
doubtful inferences concerning future probation
and what will take place there. Such notions are
mainly mechanical solutions of mechanical difficulties generated by mechanical thinking; and
they disappear when we think of the love of God
and the grace of the Lord Jesus, and remember
that it is this God and this Saviour with whom
we have to do. We need no theory to assure us
that our race in all its members is safe in their
hands. Jesus' revelation of the Father puts this
beyond doubt forever, and we must not allow
mechanical theorizers to obscure the fact.

In this ethical and spiritual way the work of

Christ which we call the atonement is to be understood. However much more we may put into it, in the way of ineffable mysteries, the features dwelt upon must not be left out. As an intelligible working theory they must form the gist of the doctrine. We must take the work of grace as a whole, and must note that its essential aim is to save men from sinning and to lift them into the life of the Spirit. With this understanding, we may retain the traditional language as a mode of expression, or as much of it as is adapted to modern Christian thought; but we must not turn it into a theological theory. This is the letter that has killed, and still killeth. We must also note that in the better view the divine love is not denied or diminished, but rather freed from obscuring misconceptions. Again, we must note that the way of life is the same it always has been. We must repent and forsake our sins, and become the disciples of the Lord Jesus, if we would enter into life. He is still our Redeemer and the way by which we come to God. Whatever mystery there may be in the Saviour's work, trust and discipleship are all that is needed for securing its benefits. This must be borne in mind in our preaching. Neither philosophy nor theology can save us. We must proclaim the love of God the Father, the gracious work of Christ the Son, the forgiveness of sins, and the sanctifying work of the Holy Spirit which Christ has made known; and we must summon men to discipleship and obedience in his name. To do this is to preach the atonement in its practical significance, and to escape the intellectual and moral scandals with which theory has long burdened it.

These abstract and mechanical conceptions of the atonement have led to correspondingly abstract and mechanical conceptions of the closely allied topics of salvation and faith, and especially of salvation by faith. For the full clearing up of our thought, it seems well to consider these subjects also, in the hope of reaching a concrete moral conception in line with our previous study and in harmony with the moral reason.

Grace, not faith, is the deepest factor in our salvation. It is the grace of God on which everything else depends, and which gives value to everything else. Hence the formula given by St. Paul, "By grace are ye saved, through faith." Here grace is made fundamental, and faith is only instrumental or conditional. The salvation is not of ourselves; it is the gift of God. It is not of our good and meritorious works, lest any man should boast. Grace, then, is the source of our salvation, and by faith we enter into it. This is a wholesome doctrine and very full of comfort; but this doctrine also, when mechanically understood, may become an intellectual and moral scandal.

First of all, it is clear that all finite beings, even the first-born sons of light, stand only in the grace of God. They have nothing which has not been given them; they depend continuously upon God for their life and all their powers; and if they should estimate their value to God from the low standpoint of quantitative profit and loss, they could only say, "We are unprofitable servants." And that which is true of the first-born sons of light is truer still of the children of men. If we had kept all the commandments, we should still be unprofitable servants. And when to this we add our record of unfaithfulness, waywardness, wickedness, we see that we are not only unprofitable servants, but sinners also, whose only hope must lie in the divine grace.

Any value, then, which the world of finite spirits may have depends primarily and essentially, not on the merit and worth of their service, but on the divine love, in which they live and move and have their being. All we can do is to love and trust and obey; and the love of God does all the rest. It takes the will for the deed, and finds the sufficient service in love itself.

Such a relation is quite unintelligible on the

plane of profit and loss, when coarsely estimated by the standard of things; but we understand it readily from the side of the family life. Profit and loss have no place here, but only the incommensurable relation of parental and filial love.

A father does not value his child for what he can make out of it considered as a financial investment or speculation; he values it as his child. We are struck with horror and filled with indignation when we see the parental relation degraded to the level of pecuniary standards. And the child, on the other hand, does not have its standing in the family because of the money value of its services, but because it is a child. It belongs to the family, and its great value is determined by its relation to parental affection. It is saved by love, not by works. And that which parental love supremely demands is filial love in return. The child may show forth the filial spirit and live in answering affection, and parental love does all the rest. Nothing could be more odious than this relation when measured by pecuniary standards — a father wondering whether he will ever get back the money spent on the child, and a child unwilling to do anything unless it be paid; but nothing is more beautiful when interpreted in the light of love. Then parental love takes the will for the deed, and thus gives all its value to

the child's imperfect service; and then, in turn,
finds in the answering filial love its own supreme
and exceeding great reward.

This is the general form in which we must
conceive the relation of God to all created spirits.
Infinite love bestows, and finite love answers
back. This relation is caricatured or degraded as
soon as the element of profit and loss is introduced into it. The finite may never boast, for it
receives everything from God. And the gifts of
God are not rewards of merit, but expressions of
fatherly affection.

And this which is true even of the highest
orders of created spirits is preëminently true of
men. For, as we have before pointed out, our
life is one of development. It is not a conscious
moral life from the start, but a sub-moral, subrational, even animal life, which is to develop
into moral and spiritual forms. The individual
in his personal life develops slowly into intelligence, knowledge, and self-control; and the social
development, which has such significance for the
mental and moral life of the individual, is an
age-long process. Account has to be taken of
both orders of development in estimating the
moral life of men. And in this upward movement,
as in the family, there are long periods of irresponsiveness, ignorance, waywardness, thought-

lessness, with which love must bear, and out of
which love must seek to bring its objects by all
its resources of discipline and law and chastise-
ment and self-revelation. And throughout this
process men manifestly stand, not in the value of
their works, but in the great love wherewith God
has loved them. To boast of their merits would
be like an infant declaiming on the value of its
services, or a learner of the alphabet priding
himself on the greatness of his knowledge.

If there be any salvation, then, it must necessarily be of grace and not of debt. But salvation
itself has often been mechanically, and even
magically, conceived. The juristic and abstract
conception of the atonement has led to a corresponding conception of salvation which still
haunts much of our thinking. The divine law is
supposed to have a claim upon the individual or
the whole race. This claim stands unsatisfied in
the court of divine justice, much as a judgment
stands on the books of an earthly court; and
salvation consists in the satisfaction and cancel-
lation of this claim. But Christian thought is
fast outgrowing this conception of a legal and
forensic relation, and replacing it by the thought
of a vital, personal, and moral relation. The ideal
relation between God and man is love from God

above, and answering love and trust and obedience from man below. And if this relation does not exist or has been disturbed, man is so far forth lost. And the establishment or restoration of this relation is salvation. It is not a thing of abstract forensic or judicial character which may be mechanically secured, but a personal and moral relation. Its essence consists in the development or restoration of the filial spirit, the subordination of our lives to the will of God, the loving recognition of God's loving will and presence in our lives. Any salvation which comes short of this is an abstract and non-moral thing which could satisfy neither God nor man.

The failure to grasp this fact of the moral nature and aim of salvation has led to a great many abstract or mechanical schemes. To begin with, the atonement was conceived as having furnished a satisfaction for sin, absolute or conditional; and individual salvation consisted in securing the juristic advantages of a share in this satisfaction. Or, and this was the more common conception of the matter, the atonement was conceived as having furnished a store of merit or righteousness which might be applied to the extinction of our demerit or unrighteousness; and individual salvation consists in having a due share of this merit transferred to the individual account.

With this mechanical conception of the atonement and of salvation, it was only natural that correspondingly mechanical conceptions of the mode of securing salvation should arise. As salvation did not involve the personal love and loyalty of the spirit, but was only a quantitative balancing of claims in a court of abstract justice, it was entirely credible that it might be secured by almost any sort of mechanical rites or ceremonies performed by us, or for us or upon us. Hence arose the scheme of sacerdotal proxyism, sacramentalism, and religious mechanism in general. The priest had mystical powers and the keys of heaven and hell. The sacraments were made saving ordinances, thus degenerating from a beautiful symbolism to the level of magical incantations. Then men betook themselves to meats and drinks and divers washings and carnal ordinances, to all manner of external rites and ceremonies and mechanical exercises, and supposed that their due performance would secure salvation. And this was entirely logical. Salvation itself being external and mechanical, it might well be mechanically secured. Thus spiritual religion lost itself in unspiritual exercises which hid God from men, and kept men from God. From these aberrations Christian thought is returning only as it discovers the spiritual nature of salvation and the worthlessness of mechanism and proxies of whatever kind.

That salvation must be of grace is manifest. We have now to consider the meaning and function of faith in the matter.

The doctrine of salvation by faith has played a great part in Christian history; and it is not entirely intelligible apart from the history. What gave it such epochal significance at the time of the Protestant Reformation was the errors against which it protested. The mechanical and external development of religion in the Christian Church had reached its climax at that time. The system of rites and ceremonies, of fasts and penances, which began innocently enough, had become a yoke which the people were unable to bear. The priestly class also claimed to have the keys of heaven and hell, and by this means was enabled to exercise a dreadful tyranny over the minds of men. The system of indulgences debauched the Christian conscience, and purgatory with its allied doctrines made it possible to keep the living in abject terror concerning the dead. Good works, too, were largely mechanically conceived, and as such were without any spiritual character. Against all this the doctrine of salvation by faith was a revolt. It proclaimed the worthless-

ness of good works, and good works of the kind
meant were worthless. Salvation, then, was not
of works, but of God's grace through faith.

The doctrine also equally meant the direct
access of the soul to God. No man or set of men
or institution has the keys of heaven or hell.
The moral relation between God and the soul is
purely personal, and no third party may interfere. This doctrine meant the overthrow of sacerdotalism with all that depended upon it. Thereafter the priest was no person with mystical
powers for blessing or condemning men, but
simply a person appointed by the Christian body
for the proper administration of the spiritual
services of the Church. On all these accounts the
doctrine had epochal significance in the history
and progress of Christian thought and life. Over
against all mechanical good works, it proclaimed
that salvation is by faith only. Over against all
spiritual pride and self-sufficiency, it proclaimed
that salvation is of grace. Over against all
priestly or ecclesiastical assumption and usurpa-
tion, it proclaimed the direct access of the soul
to God.

But it rarely happens that a great truth is
clearly apprehended in its essential meaning and
just limitations from the start, and it certainly
did not happen in this case. Both faith and good

works were misconceived, and much confusion resulted. Owing partly to the quantitative and juristic conception of the atonement, faith was often viewed as mere intellectual assent to a doctrine, and was finally identified with dogmatic orthodoxy. We find this error even in the apostles' time; and St. James sharply criticises it by saying the devils have this faith. "Thou believest that there is one God; thou doest well: the devils also believe and tremble." Later on the error became still more pronounced and general, and constituted one of the great aberrations of theology, and a fruitful source of persecution. Of course there is nothing morally saving in mere intellectual assent; and this conception made salvation by faith an absurdity. What is there to save any one, or to transform character, in assenting to any dogmatic creed? Even if one understood them, which is not always the case, assenting to all the articles of the Athanasian Creed would save as little as assenting to the multiplication-table or a book of logarithms. As thus conceived, salvation by faith would be scarcely more than an idle fiction or meaningless hocus-pocus of words.

But all of this mistakes the doctrine. The faith that saves is no mere assent of the understanding; it is the practical surrender of ourselves to the revealed grace and will of God, according to the commands and promises of our Lord. Our trust in this divine grace, our yielding ourselves up to it in obedience and submission, is our faith. It is a moral act which includes trust, submission, obedience; and only as it includes them all is it saving faith. And that we can be truly saved — that is, lifted Godward — only in this way, is manifest. No mechanical rite or round can lift us, or has merit. We must trust in the grace above us, and submit ourselves to it, and we must struggle toward the ideal that grace holds out. The object of our trust may never be sought in ourselves, but only in the grace revealed from on high. However we stumble or fall, we must not abandon this trust and devotion. We can rise only as our eyes are fixed on the Infinite Goodness above us.

Understood in this way, salvation by faith is one of the deepest truths of religion. The faith merits nothing; for it is grace which gives faith its value. But this faith is all we have, and indeed it is all that any finite spirit can have. And where this faith is, God can bestow himself upon us. We open our hearts and bid him come in. We bring ourselves to him to be made the temples for a divine indwelling; and he receives us according to his word. To as many as thus receive him he gives power to become the children of God in the spirit. When faith is thus conceived we see that there can really be no other ethical and spiritual condition of salvation. All other conditions are mechanical and non-spiritual, and can never lift any soul Godward. But when faith is conceived as bare assent to any dogma whatever, instead of a living surrender to God in reliance upon his grace, then it becomes unfruitful, if not immoral and pernicious.

The rejection of good works was likewise not clearly conceived, and this led to some disparagement of the doctrine. The one thing perfectly clear was that good works by machinery were worthless; that is, all performance of rite and ceremony of whatever kind which did not include, or which might be separated from, the living and loving surrender of heart and will to the love and service of God. All such works remain external to the soul, and count for nothing. They could never please God or lift a soul toward God. " My son, give me thine heart," is the supreme and all-inclusive demand from the divine side, and the supreme and central duty from the human side. The rejection of mechanical good works is the first condition of spiritual religion.

But the doctrine was not so clear when it passed out of the mechanical into the moral field;

and here misunderstanding arose. The desire to emphasize the opposition to Roman Catholic teaching was itself a source of aberration. Again, good works themselves in an ethical sense were superficially conceived, as if they might exist without any inner loyalty and devotion of heart. This was to confound morality with legality, and led to those dreary denunciations of "mere morality" and natural goodness as "filthy rags," which formed the staple of so much preaching a century ago. But, on the other hand, much that was passed off for morality was only external conformity to outward law and custom, and was spiritually worthless. This difficulty disappears before a deeper insight into the true nature of morality. When it is seen that the supreme condition of true morality is the loyalty of heart and will to righteousness, it is plain that we need have no fear of good works in the moral sense; indeed, the more of them the better.

This difficulty arose partly from a fear of agreeing with the Catholic doctrine, partly from a superficial ethics, and partly from a fear of recognizing human goodness, lest the necessity of grace should seem to be diminished. A deeper and more rational source of the confusion in this matter lies in confounding the ethical side of life, which is based on our freedom, with the religious side, which is based on our dependence; and thus either the moral sense or the religious sense was violated. The religious sense in its feeling of reverence and dependence would ascribe everything good to God, and feels as irreverent any assumption of merit on the part of man. But the moral nature in its experience of freedom and responsibility insists on vindicating a place for virtue and merit in man also. The former by itself would find its limit in a powerless passivity, which would cancel humanity altogether. The latter by itself would easily pass into Pharisaism and spiritual pride. Out of the failure to recognize the existence and equal legitimacy of these opposite aspects of the spiritual life has arisen a great deal of unwisdom concerning the value of our good works.

The moral nature itself has a double aspect which, in a measure, runs parallel with these two antitheses. We may judge men by a double standard. If they are faithful to their light and possibility, we call them good on that account. Or we may compare them with our ideal of perfection, and then we find them imperfect, and hence condemned by the ideal. There is a similar dualism in our judgment of knowledge. If we judge a man's attainments by the standard of his time, by the acquirements of his fellows, by reference to his practical needs, we may well call him a wise man. But if we should judge with reference to perfect and completed knowledge, we should be unable to distinguish him from the fool, as all finite values and differences disappear when compared with the infinite. In like manner, when we judge men morally by the standard which obtains in their social environment and by the expectations which men justly form, we may accord them a high standard of goodness; and they might, as Job, maintain their integrity against all charges. But when we hold up our lives against the background of infinite holiness and perfection, the matter is altogether different; and the language which comes spontaneously to our lips is the prayer of the publican, "God, be merciful to us sinners." But these are only apparent contradictions. Both views are true according to our standpoint. There is such a thing as human merit, but all boasting is excluded before God.

In judging of human goodness we must always bear in mind this double point of view, not denying the reality of human virtue on the one hand, nor falling into a shallow spiritual pride and self-conceit on the other. Language here is not to be viewed as the formulas of logic, but as the expression of life, emotion, religion; and it is to be understood only from that standpoint. The moral will must always assert itself, and thus distinguish between the good man and the bad. And the religious nature, in its sense of dependence and reverence, will always delight in viewing all our virtues and graces as the gift of God.

And this double need of our nature is best met by the doctrine of grace and faith. Our salvation is of grace, and not of debt. It is a gift of God, and not a reward of our meritorious works. But this salvation is through our faith, which is an active principle, and which must issue in obedience, or it is not faith at all. We show and verify our faith by our works, and neither can exist in any moral sense without the other.

This is that salvation by faith which is the glory of the gospel, and which is a most wholesome doctrine, and very full of comfort. It is only the morally dull and blind who can be self-satisfied, as it is only the deeply ignorant who can boast of the greatness of their knowledge. In both realms the ideal grows faster than the actual, and ever condemns our utmost attainment. No strenuous conscientiousness, no faithfulness of service, can give us peace. For this we must be taken out of ourselves, and away from the contemplation of our own works, and made to gaze upon the infinite grace of God in which alone we trust and by which alone we stand.

Thus I have sought to relieve the doctrines of divine grace from the verbal and mechanical misunderstandings which infest popular religious thought, and make the gospel itself a stumbling-block to many. In concluding, I emphasize several points: —

1. We must distinguish between the fact of the Saviour's work and the theological theory of it. The latter is not of faith, but of speculation. Moreover, the fact is the essential thing; and the religious teacher must never allow any one to think he has abandoned the fact because he is dissatisfied with the theory.

2. We must note the instrumental and undogmatic character of Scripture language on this subject, and the resulting necessity of taking it in a free and living way rather than as the language of a dogma or a statute. A person who reads the Scriptures with no aid but the dictionary, and without knowledge of ancient life and custom, and without diligently comparing Scripture with Scripture, will certainly go astray in this matter.

3. The doctrine itself must be brought out of the desert of abstract speculation, and be con-

structed and interpreted in the light of life and human experience. The ethical aim and aspect of the doctrine must be emphasized; and whatever conflicts therewith must be set aside. It is God's aim to save men from sin, not in sin; to save men from sin, not from penalty; to recover men to righteousness, not to plant them in heaven. Forgiveness and salvation must be interpreted in accordance with this fundamental fact.

4. In religious instruction the teacher must put supreme emphasis on the fact of the Saviour's work. He must proclaim the love of God, the grace of the Lord Jesus, the forgiveness of sins, and must summon men to discipleship in his name. This is practically the gist of the matter, and whatever attention we give to theory, we must never allow it to obscure this simple fact.

5. For practical purposes all we need is to become the disciples of our Lord, trusting in his promises and the Father whom he revealed. With this practical discipleship we shall receive all the benefits of the Saviour's work without any theory; and without this discipleship we are lost, whatever our theory.

III

THE CHRISTIAN LIFE

III

THE CHRISTIAN LIFE

My purpose in writing, and the scope of the discussion, will best appear from some facts of experience: —

Not long ago a most worthy minister of my acquaintance, one who had been preaching more than fifty years and who was a model of saintly living, came to another minister, also a friend of mine, to talk about the witness of the Spirit. And his trouble was that he could not feel sure that he had ever had this witness. The expectation awakened by the phrase had never been satisfied. And the good man's heart was disturbed; and he sought counsel of his brother.

My professional life has largely been spent in contact with thoughtful young men and women; and I have frequently observed an uneasy feeling on their part that the traditional phrases of religious speech do not set forth with unstrained naturalness and transparent sincerity the facts of their religious life. Often they have formed a conception of what the religious life should be by reflection on the customary and inherited phrases;

and thus they have been led to entertain unwarranted expectations. Then the failure to realize
them has led to an uncomfortable sense of artificiality and unreality in all religious experience.

In addition, I may say that I have been listen-
ing intelligently to preaching for over forty years.
Of course I have heard a great many good sermons, but in all that time I have heard very few
sermons on conversion and the beginnings of the
religious life which were not both confused and
confusing. Theological expositions have been
plentiful enough; vague, verbal exhortations have
abounded; but there has been a grievous lack of
clear statement of what the seeking soul is to
expect, or of what is expected from it.

Such facts suggest, what every thoughtful and
observant person must recognize, that there is
need of revising popular religious phraseology,
and also of clarifying popular conceptions concerning the religious life itself, and especially
concerning its beginnings in conversion. This
study is intended as a contribution to this desirable end.

The popular confusion on this subject in our
individualistic churches has several leading sources,
and our first work must be to indicate them. The
first is the confounding the language of theology

with the language of experience. The second is the mistaking of the abstract classifications of theological discussion for concrete classifications of living men. The third is an exaggerated individualism. We consider them in their order.

On the first point we must note that a great many things may be theologically true which are not psychologically true. We may express and explain the experience in terms of doctrine, and in so doing we may have the truth; nevertheless, the doctrine is not a fact of consciousness, but a theory about the fact.

Thus, when some brother of picturesque habit of speech says in the social meeting, "The devil told me not to come here to-night," we are not to think that he has had an infernal interview. The fact of experience is that he was disinclined to come, and this disinclination he attributes to the devil. But however correct this may be as a theory of the hidden source of the temptation, it would be highly infelicitous to suppose that anything of the sort occurred within the consciousness of the individual himself. The experience as he states it is not the experience as lying within the range of consciousness, but rather the experience as theologized or, more properly, diabolized by this infernal reference.

A less distasteful illustration of the difference

between the language of theology and that of conscious experience may be found in our speech concerning the divine providence in our lives. We believe and teach that our times are in God's hand; but this does not imply that we have any preception of the divine presence, or even that we can clearly trace the way in which God is working out his will concerning us. The life of experience is the familiar life of question, uncertainty, forethought, calculation, and venture, in all of which, moreover, we commonly seem left at our own risk to find the way; and not infrequently we miss it, and go astray. We still retain the doctrine as an article of faith; but we see that we must work out our own salvation nevertheless. We may indeed be profoundly convinced that we have been divinely guided, but this is more generally a later inference than a present revelation. The doctrine then expresses a theory of life rather than a conscious experience; and unless we bear this distinction in mind, it is more likely to be a source of doubt than of comfort.

This is self-evident to every thoughtful person; but what is not so plain to every one is that there is a vast amount of language concerning the inner life which is of the same sort. It is not the language of experience, but of theological theory. A great many things are said about the work of the Lord in the soul, the operations of the Spirit, his presence with us, — and all this may be true theologically, but it is not true psychologically. Moreover, a person who holds the theology in question may very naturally use it for expressing his experience; yet even that does not make it a fact of experience. It is an object of belief, not a fact of consciousness; an accepted doctrine, not a conscious datum. Nevertheless, this language of theory is put forward as the language of experience, and then confusion arises. By consequence a great many try to experience theology instead of experiencing religion.

Two classes of persons escape this confusion. The first class consists of those persons, unskilled in reflection, whose language has only an accidental connection with their ideas. They hear and inherit phrases, and they have a measure of religious life. They also use the phrases upon occasion; but no one could ever discover from a reflection on the phrases, and the ordinary secular use of language, what the corresponding experience might be. One must gather this from an acquaintance with the subject-matter, and with the peculiar forms of speech in this field. Here again we find illustration in the brother who says the devil tells him to do this or that. No exegesis of the utterance, according to the recognized usage of secular speech, would ever reveal that this means only that the person feels an inclination to some evil deed, and ascribes it to the devil as its source. Persons in this stage of development are not harmed by speech which would be misleading to one who sought to understand it in the ordinary way. They do not get any ideas from language, but they express the ideas they have in the phrases which have become conventional upon the subject.

The second class of persons who suffer no harm from such language consists of those who have learned to take the language, not for what it seems to say, but for what they know it means. They understand the picturesque phrase, or discount the extravagant metaphor, or penetrate to the meaning behind some grotesque or distasteful image, and thus escape the illusion which might otherwise arise.

But there is a third class less fortunate. This consists of persons who have attained to some measure of reflective consciousness, but who have not learned to distinguish the language of theology from the language of experience. By consequence they seek to tell what the religious fact should be by reflecting on the language they hear used to describe it. Only such or such an experience would come up to the demands of the language, and then they seek to have the experience. But somehow or other the appropriate experience does not come; and then comes either an attempt to believe the actual experience is the one desired, or else a suspicion that the whole matter is fictitious. Not a few good Christians have lived on uneasy terms with their religious experience on this account. They have taken the language of theology for the language of consciousness, and thus have been led to form unwarranted expectations. My friend who was troubled about the witness of the Spirit had the root of his difficulty right here. The phrase had led him to expect some sort of celestial manifestation, a testimony from without, and standing so clearly apart from the ordinary laws of mental movement as to be undeniably produced by the manifest God. In lack of any such experience, he doubted whether he had had the witness of the Spirit. This class comprises the great mass of thoughtful young persons in the churches. And for this class the religious teacher needs to bear in mind the distinction between theology and consciousness, in order to escape misleading and dangerous confusion.

The language of theology must often be used, indeed, but it should be used in such a way as not to mislead the inexperienced hearer or reader into an attempt to experience theology. And in general we must remember that all language about the inner life must be misleading to any one who interprets it only by the dictionary. Commonly the language is a metaphor, or it has a fixity and definiteness which do not belong to the fact; or it may express an ideal toward which we strive, but which we never fully attain. There is much religious speech of this sort. It indicates a direction or sets forth an ideal, to which we can only approximate. The fact itself, however, can be learned only in life; and the language is only an imperfect instrument for expressing the life. The religious teacher cannot be too careful and discriminating at this point, for really there is no language on this matter that does not need to be carefully guarded to prevent confusion.

The second great source of our confusion is the mistaking of the hard-and-fast lines and antitheses of theological ethics for concrete facts among living men. Ethics in general tends to fall into this error. We speak of the moral agent and of responsibility, and have fairly clear ideas as to our meaning so long as we remain in the field of abstraction. But the matter becomes indefinitely more complex when we look at actual human beings. Then we find that we have to deal, not with hypothetical and abstract moral agents, but with beings in an order of development where the intellectual insight, the volitional energy and self-control, and the moral sensibility have to be developed, and where the development is never complete. This complicates the matter indefinitely; and while our abstract ideas are still true as abstractions, we see that they have to be greatly modified in application. Every thoughtful person knows how difficult it is to determine the measure of merit or demerit in a concrete case. Environment, heredity, and the inscrutable personal equation have to be taken into account; and these are all beyond us.

The fact appears even more prominently in theology. We form such antithetical classes as saints and sinners, the saved and the unsaved; and we fancy that living human beings admit of being classified in this hard-and-fast way. Of course these abstractions are necessary in theoretical discussion, and the opposed classes are mutually exclusive and contradictory; nevertheless, concrete men, women, and children cannot be divided off so easily. This is a world of growth from irresponsible ignorance and weakness toward responsible power and insight; it is a world of development from sub-moral and subrational beginnings toward moral and rational endings. And in such a world we must view great masses of men as neither saved nor lost, but as developing towards these conditions. They are neither good nor bad, in a strictly moral sense, but are becoming good or bad. An academic ethics and an artificial theology find no place for them, yet they form the bulk of the human race. And we shall never reach any theory which will satisfy the developed moral judgment of men until this fact has been recognized. The human world is less a world in which moral classes exist than one in which moral classes are forming.

The difference between the abstract and the concrete standpoint appears with startling vividness when we are dealing with our dead. Damning the abstract sinner is an easy matter and seems to be meet and right and a bounden duty, but it looks different when it is our own flesh and blood. Then in one way or another we leave open some door of hope. The Church wisely makes no distinction in its liturgy for the burial of the dead and refuses to pass judgment. A letter of Fénelon's well illustrates the difference between the abstract austerity of the theologian and the human heart of the man. He writes to a father whose son had lived a reckless life and died gallantly in battle: "You must not give way too much to distressing thoughts. The frailty of such early youth in a life so full of diversion is not so poisonous as some sensual vices which are refined into the disguise of virtues in later life. God sees the clay of which he has moulded us, and has pity on his poor children. Besides, although the force of nature and example may lead a young man in some degree astray, we can, notwithstanding, say what the Church says in the prayers of the dying, 'Nevertheless, O God, his hope and trust were in thee.' A foundation of faith and religious principles which has been overwhelmed by the excitement of passions is stirred in a moment by imminent danger. Such an extremity as this routs all life's illusions, lifts a sort of veil, reveals eternity, and recalls the realities that have become shrouded. However little God may seem to be working in that moment, the first instinct of a heart that has ever been accustomed to him is to throw itself upon his mercy. Neither time nor exhortations are needed for him to be felt and heard. To Magdalene he said but the one word, 'Mary,' and she replied to him but that other word, 'Master'; and no more was needed. He called his child by her name, and she was already returned to him. That ineffable appeal is all-powerful; a new heart and a new soul are born in the inmost being. Weak men who can see only the surface desire preparation, definite ritual, spoken resolves. God needs only a moment wherein he can do all and see that it is done."

This passage is quoted not for the sake of expressing approval or disapproval, but solely to show that even the most orthodox may draw back from the abstract theory in concrete application. But in our closet speculation we commonly overlook this fact and divide men into antithetical classes, as the saved and the unsaved. This has generally been an abstract division, and abstract law and abstract justice and abstract holiness and abstract sin have played their abstract part. But after we have adopted this division, it becomes an important matter to fix the standard of distinction. If one is not saved, it is a matter of serious concern to know the ground of the exclusion, particularly as the traditional classification by no means always runs parallel with our unsophisticated moral judgments. In response to this need, theologians have given a great variety of answers. Those who have lost themselves in theological and ritual mechanism have found the mark of being saved in the due performance of some rite or pronunciation of some formula; but this removes the matter from the moral and rational field alto-

gether. The churches which insist on personal
piety tend to fix attention on conversion, or a
change of heart, or the new birth, as the distinc-
tive mark of the saved; and because of the failure to grasp the fact of development, this is commonly supposed to have a definite date in time.
And in order that there be no mistake about a
matter so important, these churches have sought
for unmistakable signs of grace which should
leave no question. This has led to certain conceptions of these things to which experience must
conform, on pain of being distrusted, if not rejected as spurious; and this in turn has led to an
indefinite amount of distortion of experience in
order to bring it up to the assumed standard.

In the imperfect conditions of undeveloped
men, every good thing has its attendant evil, or
at least a tendency to develop into mistaken
forms. A very general tendency, even in the
Christian religion, has been to develop into mechanical externalism, in which the spirit is missed
altogether. Ancient Pharisaism is a monumental
example. The same thing is seen in the mediæval
Church; and modern church history is not lacking
in illustration. There is a tendency to substitute
a mechanical performance of mechanical rites
for the love and loyalty of the heart. Hence, reli-

gious reformers have commonly had to protest against this tendency, and to recall men to the worship of the spirit. The Lord looketh at the heart. They that worship God must worship him in spirit and in truth. The prophets of the Old Testament had for one of their chief burdens the worthlessness of rites and ceremonies, and the necessity of the pure heart, if we would secure the divine favor. God, who looketh at the heart, can never compound for spiritual obedience by accepting anything less. And this has been the tone of all succeeding reformers and reformations. Away with all salvation by machinery, by hearsay, by proxy, and let the soul come face to face with God in repentance and humility and faith! Only thus can it hope to obtain the remission of sins.

This view certainly represents the ideal of spiritual religion; and religious development must be looked upon as imperfect, even formally, until this stage has been reached. And if we were dealing with human beings ready-made and finished from the start, we might conceive that this is the only conception to be allowed. But the matter is complicated by the fact and form of human development. This spiritual attitude may be demanded of those who have developed far enough to understand it; but what of those who have not? Are they saved or unsaved?

This question has been the source of some extraordinary notions in theology. The question itself arose from a failure to observe that development is the law of human life; and the notions held rested upon factitious ethical difficulties, based upon considering the problem in an abstract, forensic way, instead of a concrete and truly ethical manner. Some theologians of rigor and vigor taught the damnation of infants, but humanity generally protested at this ultra rigor. But how to save them was a problem which received no single solution. The great body of Christians turned baptism into a regenerating rite which insured the safety of its subjects. One cannot make much out of this on ethical and rational grounds; but it is interesting as showing the well-nigh universal conviction of the Christian world that some way must be found of saving the children. Those who did not accept this device found or invented others; and the same fact was true of these — they testified to a good disposition and to the recognition of a moral necessity; but it was exceedingly hard to adjust them to any ethical and rational scheme.

In general, here was a problem which the religious reformer did not always sufficiently consider. In assuming responsibility for the immature, the Church had made some provision for comprehending the race as a whole in the scheme of salvation ; but in so doing, it had also exposed itself to a variety of dangers. The Church easily came to be looked upon as having complete power of attorney in the case, so that the individual need not appear at all. This readily passed into a mechanical conception of religion, and a magical conception of salvation, in which all spirituality disappeared. The individual had nothing to do but to make arrangements with the Church, and the Church would do the rest.

Against such a conception the religious reformer rightly revolted. What does baptism amount to without the spirit ? What does anything in religion amount to without the pure heart ? And this cannot be secured by proxy or machinery of any kind. Away then, once more, with all such matters ! for salvation is a strictly individual thing. State churches were abominations, as their fruits clearly showed. The truly spiritual were to come out from among them, and be separate, and thus build up a peculiar people, zealous of good works.

All of this was well-meant, and all of this had its historical reasons, if not its justification. But none the less was it one-sided. Of course we must reject the mechanism of rite and ceremony as anything in which to trust, or which can dispense with the devotion of the heart; but we can do this and still recognize that this mechanism may be a valuable instrument in forming the thought and training the feeling of developing men. Of course we must reject the notion that the Church can forgive sins; but still we may believe that it can declare the forgiveness of sins which of itself it cannot confer. We must remember that the mass of human beings must live by hearsay, in religion as well as in most other matters; and thus the authoritative teaching of the Church acquires profound significance for the religious life of the individual. The religious reformer was right, but the churchman was right too. The reformer emphasized individualism; and the churchman emphasized solidarity. The reformer rightly held that the individual must for himself recognize and accept the divine will, and that all below this was vain if this result was not reached; but the churchman rightly held that the preparatory steps, while making nothing perfect, still had their religious significance in the development of the individual. Both views are needed for the full expression of the truth; and if the historic circumstances of the time had permitted the reforms to go on within the Church, the result would have been better for all concerned. And this is true alike for the great Protestant Refor-

mation and for minor reformations before and
since. That both views are needed especially appears from the struggles of the extreme individ-
ualists in fixing the beginning of responsibility. One considerable body, which would hear of
nothing but conscious choice and self-initiative
in religion, officially fixed the tender age of eight
years as the date when adult life begins! Of
course, back of both views, as the only thing that
gives either of them any standing, is the simple
grace of God, who is not working a scheme of
technical salvation, but who is developing men
into his image as his spiritual children.

But in their determination to have a holy
church, our Nonconformist ancestors decided to
have only the best; and this made it necessary
to draw a sharp line between the Church and the
world. It was heresy to find this in baptism or
any such thing. They knew only too well that
baptized persons could hold full membership in
the synagogue of Satan. And as spirituality was
their aim, they naturally fixed their attention
on the religious life, and more especially on its
assumed beginning in conversion. And, in order
that there might be no mistake about the matter, a deal of attention was directed to the signs
of grace, whereby a sheep might infallibly be
known and separated from common goats. This

led, in New England, under Edwards's influence, to much fictitious psychology and ethics, and to a general browbeating of human nature. The early Methodists tended to test conversion by its emotional attendants. Other things being equal, these will vary with the measure of the break between the new life and the old. An outbreaking sinner, who has been living in violation of all the laws of God and man, could not begin the new life without a break with about all there was in his old life. In such a case the fountains of the great deep would be broken up within him, and there would be an intensity of feeling and a manifest new departure which would be lacking, or less obvious, in the case of a better man. And as Methodism, in its original work, dealt largely with persons of this class, conversions were largely of this type, and they came to be the standard to which conversions should conform. Such conversions were said to be clear or powerful; while others, less marked, though admitted, were still open to the suspicion of being less thorough. Every one familiar with Methodist revival services knows how common such views have been.

Thus we have seen the origin and justification of the ideal of the individualistic churches in regard to personal religion; and we have also seen how much confusion and uncertainty exist in popular thought respecting the matter. And the only way out of this confusion seems to be to get back to our fundamental religious conceptions, and from them seek to find our way to some clearer views of the religious life.

Religious truth can be expressed only by figures borrowed from the relations of the life that now is. All religious speech, then, is based on metaphor, and must be taken, not for what it says, but for what it means. The task of religious thought is to find the meaning in the metaphor, and also to find the metaphor which shall best express the meaning. There is a choice in metaphors.

The traditional theological doctrine concerning sin and salvation has been largely built on metaphors, taken partly from the rites of the ancient temple service and partly from governmental, legal, and criminal relations. God's relation to men was generally conceived, in the obsolescent theology of the past, as that of an irresponsible governor. Men were by nature criminals, and the theory of the mutual relations of God and men was based mainly on this conception. The notion of the governor and his rights was determined largely by the political absolutism of the time, and the standing of men was determined by the

forms of criminal law and criminal procedure.
The two together produced a most incongruous
compound. The theology was bad, and the ethics
was worse. God, like the king, could do no wrong,
and the clay was forbidden to protest at anything
the potter might do. The infinite ill-desert of a
sin against an infinite being was a favorite contention. Guilt was artificial, justice was artificial,
penalty was artificial, salvation was artificial, perdition was artificial. There was very little in the
doctrine concerning any of these things that
spoke clearly and convincingly to the reason and
conscience of men. This general view resulted in
conceiving men as rebels, apostates, traitors, and
as all deserving immediate perdition at the hands
of God. They were by nature children of wrath,
and of course unsaved. A great many texts, interpreted according to the fashion of that time,
readily lent themselves to such notions.

But the entire Church has grown away from
this view, except as a very imperfect and inadequate representation of the truth. God may be
represented as governor, but never with the limitations of a human governor, and still less with
the irresponsibility of an Oriental ruler. The
crude devices of criminal law, also, which are
mainly makeshifts for doing as little injustice as
possible, are never to be appealed to as models of

divine procedure. We are fast displacing the entire conception of God as governor by the conception of God as father; and the conception of the divine government is giving place to the conception of the divine family. The deepest thought of God is not that of ruler, but of father; and the deepest thought of men is not that of subjects, but of children. And the deepest thought concerning God's purpose in our life is not salvation from threatening danger, but the training and development of souls as the children of God. Salvation or redemption is but an incident or implication of this deeper purpose, and must be interpreted accordingly. The entire subject must be studied as a relation of living moral persons rather than of ethical and juristic abstractions.

This new conception of the fatherhood and the family contains all that was true in the old conception of governor and subject; but it is deeper and more comprehensive, and hence truer, than the old. And in so far as the older view conflicts with this, it must be modified or set aside. It may be retained as a partial view, or as one aspect of the subject, but it must always be interpreted in accordance with the larger view. But, on the other hand, the new conception is not to be viewed as a sentimental one, or as involving a relaxation of the rigor of moral demands.

The training and development of souls as the children of God, then, is God's essential purpose in the creation of men; and we must understand our human life from this point of view. And we must also bear in mind that it is an order of development. That was not first which was spiritual, but that which was natural, and afterward that which was spiritual. The development has a natural root as well as a spiritual goal. The development also involves the unfolding of the constitutional powers of man as well as his abstract spiritual capacities. For a long time the development remains on the plane of the natural without attaining to the consciously spiritual; but all the while it is the development of man in a divinely ordered scheme ; and all the phases and factors of this scheme have their place and function in the divine plan for men.

Of course, in such a scheme our traditional categories of the saved and the unsaved cannot be applied in any hard-and-fast manner, but must be limited to a relative significance. They have a value in abstract theory, and they may express a limit toward which men are tending, but they cannot be rigorously applied to the rank and file of the race. As said before, men are not so much saved as they are becoming saved ; and men are not so much lost as they are becoming lost. The process is going on ; the classes are forming ; but we are totally unable to form any fixed classification of these living men and women about us. The various traditional tests are grotesque in their inadequacy, when they are not purely mechanical and non-moral.

Human beings are carried on in the beginnings of their existence as unconsciously as nature itself. They are borne along like the rocks and the trees, the earth and the stars, without any sense of the will and the purpose which underlie their motion. But it is God's thought for men that they shall not always be borne along thus unconsciously, but shall become aware of God's presence and purpose in their lives, and shall reverently recognize the presence, and filially accept and coöperate with the purpose. They are to pass from the unconsciousness of nature and the ignorance of childhood to the conscious recognition and acceptance of the divine will; and then they are to go on with God in deepening sympathy and growing fellowship forever.

This is God's eternal thought for men, and it is not modified in any way in its essential nature by the fact of sin. Of course, much of what we call sin is error and mistake, arising from the ignorance of men who have to feel their way. And sin itself, as we find it among men, is largely the willfulness of freedom which has not learned self-control, rather than any deliberate choice of evil. Ignorance and untrained willfulness abound, and both alike must be removed, or they will increase and lead to disaster. Ignorance must be enlightened if men are ever to find the way. The unchastened will must learn self-restraint if it is to run at large. But during the process we must not indulge in extravagant condemnation by bringing in the categories of abstract theological ethics. These have as little application to the case as they would have to the judgment of the family life.

This reference to the family gives us a hint of how developing beings are to be judged. The father's desire is that the children shall come to recognize his love and filially to accept his commands. He desires that they shall develop into sympathy and fellowship with himself; and not until this stage is reached is the development complete. But in the mean time the children belong to the family, and have immeasurable value for the father's heart. They know little or nothing of the love that is lavished upon them; but it is there, nevertheless, and by it they are upborne and carried along. The parents have patience with the ignorance, the irresponsiveness, the willfulness, knowing that time and discipline

and some experience of life are necessary to
bring the children to any proper knowledge of
themselves and of their duties. Meanwhile the
wise parent is not unduly distressed at childish
imperfection. He knows it is to be expected and
must be borne with. He knows, too, that it is
nothing very serious in itself—it is serious only
in its tendencies; and he avails himself of all the
means of discipline, of instruction, of correction,
to prevent the evil tendencies from being realized.
But he would regard it as in the highest degree
false and abominable if one should claim that
the little rebellions of childhood forfeit membership in the family. Children cannot rebel to this
extent. Their ignorance and general lack of
insight make it impossible. What might be possible with angels, we cannot tell. What doom
should follow rebellion committed in the full
light of knowledge and with full insight into its
evil nature, might be hard to say. But human
life is not of this sort, and cannot be treated in
this way. Such discussion must be limited to
treatises on the sin of the devil and his angels;
it has no application to human conditions.

But we are sinners. Yes, but not outcasts. But
we are rebels. No, we are prodigal sons. And
God's grace is such that his essential will for us
remains unchanged, that we should become aware

of his loving purpose for us, and should accept it in filial submission, and work together with him in building up his kingdom among men. And this, too, we understand from the side of the family again. The supreme desire of the prodigal's father was that the prodigal should come home to him, the father; and the supreme duty of the prodigal was to go home in the spirit of penitence, and devote himself to doing his father's will. And we, as prodigal sons of our Heavenly Father, have the same all-inclusive duty.

How the forgiveness of sin is made possible has been the subject of much theory, largely abstract and often unedifying. In fact, there is no completely satisfactory theory on the subject, supposing any theory is needed. We find various conceptions given in the Scriptures, which are mutually inconsistent when taken in strict literalness, and some of which would be immoral. This shows that they are not to be taken literally, but must be viewed as adumbrations of the truth; not the truth itself, but ways of putting it. And these views are to be understood psychologically rather than logically; as expressions of life rather than as statutory enactments. Taken in the former way, they are full of significance and truth; taken in the latter way, they become mechanical, irrational, and pernicious. But in any case this question belongs to theology and not to religious experience. However it may be brought about, or whatever hidden mystery there may lie in the divine nature, the one thing we have to proclaim is the grace of God, the forgiveness of sins, the divine help for all those who truly seek it. The revelation of God in Christ is essentially a revelation of his grace and his gracious disposition toward us. He has sent his Son to proclaim this, and to put it beyond all doubt forever. The Father's heart yearns after the prodigal children; and all that we have to do is to come home in penitence and humility, trusting in his mercy and seeking to do his will. Whatever is more than this belongs to theology, and may possibly be important in that field. But the prodigal's duty is to go home; and for this he needs no theory of the atonement, no doctrine of substitution, or of imputed righteousness, or of ransom paid to the devil, or of governmental exigencies happily provided for; but solely the desire to find the Father's help and favor and forgiveness. And this conception of God, as full of grace and compassion, as ready to forgive the penitent soul, and to give it power to become the child of God in the spirit, is the central idea of the gospel.

If these things are so, then the essential matter of Christian teaching is simplified. God's aim is to bring men to the recognition of his presence and purpose in their lives and to a filial acceptance of that purpose in all their conduct. If men are ignorant of that purpose, we must teach them. If they ignore it, or turn away from it, we must warn them. If they seek after God, we must declare his infinite nearness and his gracious condescension. If they turn from their evil ways, we must proclaim the forgiveness of sins. The whole matter will be clear if we bear in mind what God's purpose is for men. And the duty of the inquirer is equally plain. Let him at once begin to do the will of God so far as he knows it, trusting in the divine mercy for the forgiveness of sin and for all needed help. "Let the wicked forsake his way, and the unrighteous man his thoughts: and let him return unto the Lord, and he will have mercy upon him; and to our God, for he will abundantly pardon." But, on the other hand, "if I regard iniquity in my heart, the Lord will not hear me"; and he ought not to hear me.

What, then, does God require of us? Various answers are given, all of which come to the same thing. An old prophet found the requirement in doing justly, loving mercy, and walking humbly with God. Loving submission and active obedience to the will of God is another formula. Seek

to live so as to please God in all things is still
another. Believe on the Lord Jesus Christ— that
is, become his disciple and follower — is another.
But they all mean the same thing. We are not
required to have affecting views of our sins, or a
sense of our deep unworthiness, or an insight
into theology of any sort, but we are required to
surrender ourselves to God to do his will, and
then at once set about our Father's business.

But we are not yet converted, or born again,
or saved. What has been said thus far smacks
of legality and good works, and seems to make
nothing of faith and the new birth and the witness of the Spirit; and these things are the very
gist of spiritual religion.

In this objection we have an almost complete
list of the confusion and misunderstandings
which have darkened the discussion of this subject. We must consider them singly.

Underlying this objection there is a secret
reference to the theology of abstraction. Abstract
law and abstract justice are supposed to have
claims upon us which must be met before we can
become children of God; and surely our thought
of conversion must largely concern itself with
these. But here we must again remind ourselves
that these questions belong to speculative theo-

logy and not to experience. If we were giving a
philosophy of Christian doctrine, these questions
might come up; but they are out of place when
we are preaching the gospel. And we must further remind ourselves that the claims, whatever
they may be, have been met; and the difficulties,
whatever they may be, have been removed; so
that we have to consider only the practical
aspects of Christian doctrine. We turn over the
speculative and philosophical questions to the
theologian, and continue to occupy ourselves
with the practical life.

There are many important theological terms
and phrases which, from long use and thoughtlessness, have worn so smooth as to have lost
most of their meaning; and the only way to
restore them to significance seems to be to look
directly at the facts from which the terms arise.
Proceeding in this way, we discover that there is
a vast deal of wrong thinking in the world, not
merely erroneous thinking as in speculative matters, but wrong practical thinking. Men see
things out of their right relations. They misjudge
values and invert their relative importance. They
have their minds full of these misconceptions,
and practical confusion and misdirection result.
Hence, the first condition of a new and better
life is to repent; that is, men must change their

minds or their ways of thinking about things. The word translated "repentance" means just this, to change one's mind. This is the Christian, or New Testament, idea of repentance; and this is the first condition for entering into the kingdom of God. It is not a question of getting to heaven, but of entering into that kingdom which is righteousness and peace and joy in the Holy Ghost; and, of course, no one can enter this kingdom except by attaining to the spirit, the temper, the way of thinking, in which the kingdom consists.

Again, men are traveling the wrong road or in the wrong direction. They are moving away from life and from the highest things. They are on the downward grade. Hence they must be converted, that is, must turn around, if they would enter into life. This is the New Testament idea of conversion. In the authorized version the translation makes it appear as a passive process in which we are acted upon: for instance, repent and be converted; whereas the Greek verb is active, and is so rendered in the revised version. Conversion, then, is a turning from the wrong road into the right one. It is not to be understood in a metaphysical sense, as implying some change in the substance of the soul; nor in a theological sense, as implying some difficult forensic adjustment in the court of heaven whereby the antithesis of justice and mercy is happily mediated. It is to be understood solely as implying the opposition between the contents and direction of the new life and those of the old.

In the same way the new birth is to be understood. If we consider the contents of the earthly life, its low aims and maxims, — and hence its opposition to the life of the Spirit, — we see that the change required for passing into the spiritual life is very strikingly called a new birth, or a birth from above. St. Paul called it a resurrection from the dead. Both expressions mean the same thing, and both are equally metaphorical. They are to be understood from the side of life, and not from the side of theology. When thus understood they are striking and expressive ; but when they are taken for a hidden metaphysical process they lose all intelligible meaning, and become an opaque theological wonder. Without doubt the Holy Spirit must assist us in our efforts. The weak will must be strengthened, the dull conscience must be enlightened, the wayward affections must be fixed ; and in all this we need the co-working of God. But we always need this. And whatever mystery may attach thereto, its effect for us, and the only intelligible meaning we can ascribe to it, must consist in the turning of heart and will toward God, in the set purpose to please and to serve him.

The same thing must be said of salvation or being saved. This also is to be ethically understood. What may be possible in the way of a forensic understanding, we leave to theologians to decide; but in any case salvation must be ethically understood, or we are landed in artificial hocus-pocus, if not in downright immorality. To be sure, St. Paul used the terms of the Roman law very freely to set forth the great salvation, and in this he has generally been followed by Protestant theologians. But it has long been apparent that these terms are not to be taken in a rigid literal sense. They must be seen as metaphors or ways of putting, and must be interpreted from the side of the moral life, and not by the dictionary alone. To love God and to seek to serve and please him is the sum of human duty, and it is forever incredible that God should demand any more or be satisfied with any less. The divine aim is to bring men into the loving recognition and acceptance of the divine will. Forgiveness by the Heavenly Father is no more difficult than forgiveness by an earthly father, and in both cases what is desired is the establishment of the filial spirit in the heart and will of the wayward child. And this is salvation in the ethical sense, and the only salvation with which we have any practical concern. Salvation conceived as something possessed by one and not possessed by another of similar spirit and life, or conceived as depending on some device of celestial bookkeeping, or as depending on the performance of some rite or the utterance of some formula, has no moral contents at all, but sinks to the level of magical incantations.

The importance of conversion in the Christian sense of the term cannot be overestimated. But the popular thought is not Christian. For it the test of conversion is about this: Have they had some rhapsodic experience or some great emotional rapture? Have strange and extraordinary psychological events taken place in their consciousness? If not, then they may be " moral," but they are not converted. Probably even yet many churches could be found where the serious purpose to lead a religious life in reverent dependence on God for help would be a far more doubtful proof of conversion than would be furnished by some emotional ecstasy; and apparently little suspicion of the dismal blunder would be aroused even if the person should fail to manifest in daily life any real love for God and righteousness. But in this popular sense no one is under any obligation to be converted; neither in this sense does it matter in the least whether one be converted or not. Dr. Cuyler, in his autobiography, "Recollections of a Long Life," says that he cannot fix the time or place of his conversion. He was led gradually along, and grew into a religious life by the power of the Holy Spirit working through his mother's influence. And Dr. Washington Gladden has this to say of Phillips Brooks : —

When Dr. Vinton was spoken to about this plan of studying for the ministry, he answered that confirmation was supposed to precede theological study, and that conversion was regarded as a requisite for confirmation. Phillips Brooks answered that he did not know what conversion meant. The reply is somewhat startling. Probably, the conventional notion of conversion which had been enforced upon him was one that he did not then understand, and, perhaps, never did. But if conversion means the resolute turning of the soul to God with the purpose of obedience, he had, beyond a doubt, already experienced it. Dr. Vinton knew the young man too well to be troubled by this frank confession, and he counseled him to go at once to the Seminary of the Episcopal Church at Alexandria, Virginia. Thither he betook himself, and there, for three memorable years, he devoted himself to the work of preparing himself for his chosen calling.

Such cases make manifest how ignorant both of the Scriptures and of the religious life those persons are who insist on dates and " frames " as marks of conversion. In that sense neither of these good and great men was ever converted. But in the true Christian sense of turning toward God they were converted; and they remained converted in the sense of ever facing toward God and working with him. Such cases, indeed, are the rule with the non-revival churches. It is said that not one in ten members of the Moravian communion can fix on any date when he became a Christian; and the same is true for the large majority of the members of the German churches, who still are living lives of faith and trust in God.

The emphasis on conversion as a turning toward God on the part of those who are turned away from him in lives of wickedness cannot be overdone; but the emphasis on conversion as a special emotional experience with striking psychological attendants is illiteracy, both Scriptural and religious. It is a narrow provincialism rather than a feature of universal Christianity, and it is increasingly confusing to an increasing number of thoughtful persons. The manifest remedy is to return to the truth of the gospel and insist on obedience as the test of discipleship, and reject all others. Thus, on the one hand, we shall escape those non-ethical conversions which are the product of neuropathology or social contagion; and, on the other, we shall no longer con-

fuse honest inquirers by sending them to grope
in the labyrinths of obscure emotional psychology
which has been mistaken for religion.

But what of the supernatural in the religious
life? We have spoken of men changing their
minds and converting themselves, whereas they
supremely need the aid of the Holy Spirit in this
work. These reflections will naturally occur to
those who fail to distinguish between the theological standpoint and that of conscious experience. But what we have said involves no denial
of the supernatural. Without doubt men need
help from above in effecting these changes, but
no more than they need it in the spiritual life in
general. And however much supernatural assist-
ance may be needed, the thing to be reached is
the changed mind and heart, or the change of
thought and feeling and direction of life. And
the supernatural reveals itself in this power to
become the children of God, and not at all in
any scenic or hippodromic manifestations. In
the former sense we affirm the supernatural with
all conviction. Of course we cannot effectively
turn to God without divine help, and we cannot persevere in righteousness without divine
help. The saintliest souls know this best. Without
our knowing precisely when or how, the Pelagian
controversy has become obsolete. The Pelagians

no longer even " vainly talk." But while we
maintain with all strenuousness that God must
work in us, we find the marks of his presence
not in signs and wonders of any sort, but in the
renewed life and the fruits of the Spirit. And
the religious teacher must not allow ignorant and
excitable persons to mistake neurological disturb-
ances, without any ethical contents, for divine
manifestation. Untrained persons, of wonder-lov-
ing mental habit, easily fall into this mistake,
and they must be guarded against it.

And from this concrete ethical standpoint,
again, the meaning of sin and the sinful life is
equally clear. The gist of the sinful life consists
in the willingness to do wrong and the unwillingness to do right. Some dealers in abstractions have
thought to find something deeper than this, and
they have proclaimed that sin is a nature, and
that its nature is guilt. With such notions nothing but a web of abstract fictions can be woven.
And others, who have rejected this view, have
often been so occupied with denying the existence of any abstract sin that they have overlooked
the undeniable fact that there is a good deal of
concrete wrong-doing among men, and that this
wrong-doing must be done away with if men are
to enter into life. It would tend to real progress
if religious teachers would postpone the study of

sin in the abstract until we have overcome this willingness to do wrong and this unwillingness to do right, from which both society and the individual so grievously suffer. If this state of mind could be replaced by the love and practice of righteousness, we should have no practical concern about abstract sin.

We have made this excursion into theology because the phrases examined constantly recur in the language of experience, and give it a peculiar form. Our conviction is that these phrases are largely misunderstood from taking the implied metaphor for a literal fact, or from interpreting them by the dictionary instead of by life. But however this may be, it is clear that the theological doctrine concerning these matters must not be confused with the data of conscious experience. Whatever mysterious Godward relations these doctrines may have is no practical concern of ours, and will doubtless be arranged for without our aid. This is a happy circumstance for most of us. A reputable work on theology lies on my table, in which ninety-seven octavo pages are devoted to "Theories of Salvation"! But for the consciousness of the disciple, nothing is to be demanded or expected beyond the surrender, the devotion, the obedience, of the filial spirit. Theology is good, important, and even necessary in its place; but we do not bring men to God by means of theology. Nor should we confuse the mind of any seeker after God by trying to cast his thought and experience in any dogmatic mould; as if one could not find God without setting forth a scheme of evangelical theology, duly recognizing the several persons of the Trinity and their respective offices, specifying the provisions of the atonement, and going in order through the programme of repentance, faith, justification, regeneration, adoption, and sanctification. Whatever value such a programme may have is theological, not psychological; it represents abstractions of theory rather than facts of consciousness. The two points of view should never be confounded. The life of trust and obedience is not to be secured by an examination in the catechism; and for bringing sinners into the kingdom of God we need no more theology than is contained in the Parable of the Prodigal Son. Let the prodigals come home, trusting in the Father's love and mercy, and take their places as penitent and obedient children in their Father's house. This is the invitation of the gospel.

Thus far we have warned against confounding experience and theology, but we have said little about the contents of experience itself. We come now to consider this question, for here also there has been much confusion. A good many worthy people, instead of seeking to keep the commandments of God and walk in his holy ways, are trying to have an experience of some sort as the test and verification of their religion. Here the trouble is due, not to a confusion of experience with theology, but to the setting up of a type of experience as alone truly religious, so that the inner life must conform to it, or be rejected as spurious.

This error is not without some foundation. The reaction against the mechanical religion of external rite and sacerdotal proxy could not fail to emphasize the religion of the inner life. Besides, it is quite incredible, if God is our Father and we are his children, that this relation should find no expression in our spiritual experience. Otherwise, in prayer there is no communion, in holy living there is no support, and the soul is without any contact with the divine. In that case religion can only become a mechanical ritual again. Here, then, is a real foundation for the demand for a self-evidencing inner life, in which the soul shall become aware of divine help and shall know that it is not alone, because the Father is with it.

But this well-founded demand has often been so misunderstood and misinterpreted as to become a source of great confusion and error. Various subjective tests of a purely psychological and non-ethical type have been constructed, to which the genuine religious life must conform; and these have often wrought no small confusion. We now seek to clear up this subject.

Among the doctrines of this kind which have a large factor of truth but which are often twisted into error is the witness of the Spirit, held in some form by all churches, but especially elaborated and insisted upon by my ecclesiastical clansmen, the Methodists.

It is hard to get along without this doctrine, in order to express the conviction of the saints of all ages of the indwelling God. Religion is not all on one side, as if we prayed into the empty air with not even an echo in response. But, at the same time, how easily the doctrine can be distorted. The words are more definite than the experience, and readily awaken false expectations when interpreted by the dictionary. Thus it is said to be a fact of experience, and not merely a doctrine of theology. And it is further said by many that no one may count himself a true disciple, or member of the divine household, until he has received this witness. And many good persons — some of the best, indeed — have been greatly troubled thereby. The phrase seems to call for a miraculous manifestation, in which some external power stands manifestly apart from ourselves, and testifies that we are received into the divine favor. And many persons, like the minister before mentioned, have watched and waited for some such manifestation, and as nothing has ever happened to them which contained any such psychological break, or which revealed any such apparition of another personality within the field of consciousness, they are left to doubt whether they ever had the witness of the Spirit. And as this witness is supposed to be a necessary mark of discipleship, they are left in doubt whether they are members of the divine family at all. There is special need of clearing up our thought on this subject, lest the truth in the doctrine be lost and only destructive error be left in its stead.

Two considerations must be premised: One is, that the doctrine, whatever it may be, must not be held in such a way as to make void the gospel. The other is, that the experience, whatever it may be, cannot be confined to any single religious body.

The first point is by no means always regarded. That one should commit himself in faith and obedience to the keeping and service of the Lord Jesus, is not thought to be enough. That one should enter upon the life of discipleship, trusting in the promises of the gospel and seeking to do God's will, would not suffice. One might do all this, and still have no right to assume the place of a son in the Father's house. For this he must wait until he receives the witness; and the result often is that the object of faith and trust is not Christ and the Father whom he revealed, but rather and only certain feelings in the disciple. If these are present, he has confidence; if absent, he has not found the Lord, or the Lord has hidden his face. Thus the gospel itself is made void by thrusting some subjective test between the soul and its Saviour, the only object of faith and trust.

And that this is no fictitious danger appears from the recent utterance of a distinguished Methodist ecclesiastic: "John Wesley was sent out to preach a knowable religion — that a man might know that his sins are forgiven. There is only one way for him to learn that. Pardon is a change in the divine mind concerning the sinner; whereas God regarded him as a guilty sinner, he now regards him as a pardoned sinner. No one but God knows this change till he tells it. This is the old doctrine of the witness of the Spirit. When we get a man down before the altar, we do not tell him his sins are forgiven. We do not know. We simply hold him to it till God tells him; then the sinner knows it."

According to this master in Israel, then, it would seem that we may not venture on or rest in the promises of God without this special experience. We may indeed commit ourselves to his service in faith and obedience, trusting in his mercy; but we may not have any confidence that our Heavenly Father accepts us even then, because we cannot tell what takes place in the divine mind. This is a heresy from every standpoint, Scriptural and Methodistic alike. Wesley himself expressly rejected this interpretation of the doctrine.

Since I began writing, I have had a concrete illustration of the mischief of such undiscriminating teaching. A ministerial correspondent tells me of a woman of more than ordinary intelligence in his congregation, who for nineteen years wandered in a horror of great darkness because of such erroneous teaching. She had been told: "Don't take anybody's word. When you are forgiven, you will know it. God will tell you." Almost the exact language, it will be observed, of the dignitary before mentioned.

How completely such an interpretation makes void the gospel is manifest. Faith and trust in Christ and obedience to the commandments of

God count for nothing, apart from this special manifestation. In opposition to such heresy let the Church continue to proclaim the forgiveness of sins to all who truly and earnestly repent of their sins, and intend to lead a new life, following the commandments of God and walking from henceforth in his holy ways.

And the second point mentioned must also be borne in mind. The witness of the Spirit as an experience of the Christian cannot be limited to any religious body. Conceived as a doctrine, it might well be held by a single body; but conceived as an experience, it must be the common property of all saints, so far as it is necessary to saintship. It would be grotesque and fantastic to the last degree to suppose that God does something for Methodist saints which he does not do for Baptist, or Congregational, or Presbyterian, or Catholic saints; and it would be an impossible lack of charity to hold that only Methodists are saints. Most religious bodies have a few disciples of rigor and vigor who work out a sort of high-churchism for their own people, and question the discipleship of other bodies; but no sane Methodist would venture to construct his high-churchism on this line of the witness. And this fact shows either that the doctrine must be a theological one and not a datum of experience, or else that the expe-

rience itself, whatever it may be, is not so definite as to exclude varying interpretations.

Returning now to the doctrine, we find theologians very uncertain about it. There is general
agreement that it is most important, but there is
little agreement as to what it means. That the
phrase itself is not to be taken in strict literalness
is manifest. No outside being appears within the
disciple's consciousness and literally testifies to a
celestial fact concerning his standing in the court
of heaven. This is what our traditional language
would lead us to expect, but there is no warrant for
such expectation. The phrase itself as used by Paul
in the classical passage, Romans viii, 16, seems
to grow out of the ancient custom of adoption.
Paul is trying to make his readers know the grace
and wonder of the great salvation, and avails
himself of all the aids which familiar customs of
society furnish. Among others he hits upon the
custom of adoption familiar to the ancient world,
and says : We are not aliens and strangers, but
we are adopted into the divine family. God has
sent forth into our hearts the Spirit of adoption
whereby the filial spirit is wrought in us and we
are enabled to look up to God as our Father. And
having taken up this striking and suggestive figure, his thought runs on to complete it. For this
act of adoption was not done in a corner and out

of sight, but in public and before witnesses, that there might be no question about it forever after. And with this thought he adds: And the Spirit itself, that same Spirit of adoption, is a fellow witness with our spirits, not to our spirits, but a fellow witness of the fact that we are children of God. If Paul had not been familiar with Roman law, there would have been no doctrine of adoption and no doctrine of the witness.

It is not now a question of what the work of the Spirit within or upon the soul may be, or what the function of the Spirit may be in the regeneration and sanctification of men. It may be the Spirit which works in us the filial mind and heart, which is the essential meaning of adoption. But these are theological questions, with which we have no present concern. We inquire only what the witness of the Spirit may mean as an event in the conscious experience of believers. And it is plain that this can be decided only by experience, and not by lexicons and dictionaries. No etymological analysis of a metaphor will reveal its meaning.

The uncertainty of theological thought on this subject is largely due to the perennial confusion of the standpoints of theology and consciousness; and the aberrations are due to the attempt to construct the doctrine as a matter of experience by analyzing the metaphor. The distinction between the direct and the indirect witness illustrates the uncertainty. The latter is an inference from the discerned presence of the fruits of the Spirit; but this is not thought to exhaust the doctrine. According to Wesley, the direct witness of the Spirit is "an inward impression upon the souls of believers whereby the Spirit of God directly testifies to their spirits that they are children of God." This seems to be clear, but it is not. If the "inward impression" is produced by God, yet so that God himself does not appear in any supernatural manifestation, then we have a theological doctrine concerning the source of the impression ; but the witness is indirect. We have no supernal manifestation, but the heart is "strangely warmed." But Mr. Wesley does not seem to have been willing to affirm any miraculous appearance, but only the conviction wrought in us by the Spirit that we are the children of God; and this leaves us, so far as the Spirit is concerned, with a theological doctrine rather than a fact of consciousness. An experience wrought in us by the Spirit is one thing. An experience in which the Spirit is a factor of our consciousness may be quite another.

Wesley's uncertainty on this point comes out clearly in the series of letters to Mr. John Smith where this question is discussed. The person who writes under the name of John Smith presses for a definition of the doctrine, and especially seeks to know whether the experience involves any supernatural or miraculous manifestation. Wesley is embarrassed by the insistence, and finally falls back on the statement that he holds the doctrine because it is revealed in the Scriptures — a fact which shows that he had not clearly distinguished between the doctrine as a truth of theology and as a fact of consciousness. There is no need to fall back on the Scriptures for proof of anything which we immediately experience. He also admits elsewhere that he has known a few good persons who do not seem to have had the witness. Nevertheless, it is a doctrine of Scripture, and must be maintained on that ground. But by this time we have a phrase which we feel bound to use rather than a doctrine which we understand. At all events, it is not an experience which can be made a test of discipleship ; for good persons exist who have not had it.

In fact, this doctrine of the witness of the Spirit, as held in the Methodist church, is to be historically rather than exegetically or psychologically understood. We gather its historical meaning from the errors against which the founders of Methodism aimed their protest. These were twofold. On the one hand, the State Church had largely fallen a prey to sacerdotalism and religious mechanism. What with baptismal regeneration and sacramentarianism, the masses of its adherents had fallen into the notion that the Church would look after their salvation; and thus they failed to attain to any personal piety. In opposition to all this, the Methodist fathers summoned men to heart religion, setting forth the worthlessness of forms, rites, proxies, and insisting that every one should for himself experience the grace of God in the soul. To the hearsay and magic of baptismal regeneration, and the mechanism of rites and institutions, they opposed the self-evidencing life of the Spirit.

Again, at that time both the State and the Nonconforming churches were largely under the influence of Calvinistic doctrine, and also of the notion that religion is preëminently a matter of orthodox belief. The Calvinistic teaching concerning the perseverance of the saints made it morally unsafe to teach a doctrine of assurance ; and the heresy of orthodoxy tended to reduce religion to a barren intellectual assent to notional dogmas. In addition, God's goodness was so limited in any case, and the outlook for man was so grim, that there was little room or reason for joy in religion.

Against all these errors the Methodist fathers

protested. For them, religion must be more than a machinery of rites and sacraments, and more than correctness of belief. It was no hearsay matter, but a conscious life, which found its great witness in itself. They also denied with all vehemence the Calvinistic conception of God and his government, and thus made love and joy possible once more. And to express this conviction of life at first hand, and this joy in the Lord, they very naturally fell back on the witness of the Spirit. In the circumstances of the time it was practically a new doctrine, or a rediscovery of an old one. But the essential thing in it was the denial of the Calvinistic nightmare, the emphasis on personal religion, and the spiritual assurance which arises in the life of faith and obedience. This was historically the essential meaning and strength of the doctrine, and this it was that kept it sane and sweet. It was mainly a practical doctrine, and it was only under polemical stress that it ran off into doubtful exegesis and into theological and metaphysical interpretations. Thus the doctrine became prominent, and while thus practically held, it was true and fundamental. The attempt to give it a theoretical standing was rather confusing than otherwise. The multitudinous experiences of joy, and even of emotional excitement, were gathered up into the doctrine; and all these were accepted as the witness of the Spirit, because that was the way in which we regarded the matter. Nowadays more discrimination is needed; but the essential contention of the fathers must never be lost sight of, that religion is the ideal of religious training and development, and that this personal life must justify itself as true and divine within the consciousness of the disciple himself.

Now looking away from the form this doctrine has had in Methodist teaching, the general fact of Christian experience is this: The sincere and continued attempt to be disciples of Christ results in the conviction that we are in the right way, that we are on the Lord's side and he is on our side; and this conviction grows from more to more as the life broadens and deepens. The new life takes firmer hold and strikes deeper root; and as the soul grows in grace and the knowledge of the truth, this life becomes more and more rooted in the conviction of its divine origin. Under the influence of Christian teaching, the believer will adjust his experience to the forms of Christian thought and doctrine; and as we view the Spirit as the immediate agent in the purification, sanctification, and upbuilding of the soul, we naturally come to regard our graces, or strength, or joy, our peace, our rest in God, as wrought in us by the Spirit, as the marks of his presence, as the witness he perpetually bears in us to our being children of God. And this is all the witness of the Spirit means in general. What peculiar manifestations it may please God to make in certain crises of life or moments of spiritual exaltation, or what revelations he may make to particular persons, we may not decide; but such things are not to be demanded of any one as conditions or marks of sonship. For the great body of believers the fact of experience will be what we have described. If any claim that they have had more abundant manifestations, we do not deny that it may be so. At the same time we reserve the right to apply to all such claims the supreme test: By their fruits ye shall know them. If, as often happens, these alleged manifestations are accompanied by no increase of moral and religious effectiveness, they will have no practical significance; and if, as is sometimes the case, the receivers of the alleged manifestations are not remarkable for mental force and moral character, there will be good ground for thinking that they have misheard the voices.

If it be said that the witness as thus described is no witness but only an inference, the answer is that the meaning of a doctrine cannot be fixed by analyzing a metaphor, and that this is the only witness which it pleases God to give to most of his children. But when the doctrine is so understood as to subordinate even our faith in Christ and his gospel to some form of emotional experience, it becomes a pestilent heresy. We are not called to have experiences, or witnesses, or manifestations of any sort, but to be followers of Jesus. Whatever experiences of joy or peace or aspiration may come in this life of discipleship are to be welcomed, but they are never to be erected into tests of salvation.

Historically, the doctrine of the inner life as held in the Church has been confused and ambiguous. The one feature that is forever true and important is the emphasis on personal and spiritual religion, in distinction from all proxy and mechanical religion. This cannot be too much emphasized as the religious ideal. But along with this has often appeared a tendency to erect some form of psychological experience into religion itself. This has given rise to much misdirection and confusion which we now consider.

The training and development of souls as the children of God is God's essential purpose in the creation of men. Our human life is to be dealt with from this point of view; and the religious teacher must fashion his instruction and direct his effort in accordance with this fundamental truth. His aim must be to help men to a consciousness of the divine purpose, and to bring them into obedience to it. This recognition of the divine will, this filial trust and obedience, are the heart of religion and the central meaning of salvation. But the attainment of this end is often hindered, and even thwarted, by misconceptions against which we must be on our guard.

The emphasis which some churches have placed upon the emotional aspects of religion has not infrequently led to grave distortions of the truth. Emotion is good; and an emotionless religion would be a very questionable affair. Nevertheless it is easy to invert the true order, and this has often been done. Attention has been withdrawn from the solemn surrender of the will and life to God in order to engage in a barren hunt after emotions. This is inverted in every way, both religiously and psychologically. We must make clear to the inquirer that he is to consider himself as no longer his own, but as being in all things the disciple of the Lord Jesus and the servant of God. The exceeding breadth and depth and height of the commandment must be made plain, so that he may see how all-inclusive is the service of God. And, on the other hand, emotions are never to be aimed at as things by themselves at all. In order to be wholesome and rational, emotions must spring from ideas; and religious emotions must spring from religious ideas. When sought by themselves and for themselves they have neither rational nor moral significance, but are purely neurological or pathological. Religious emotions of this sort differ in nothing from the excitement of the howling or whirling dervishes. This is the source of the marked ethical weakness of popular revival services, and of the lack of moral fibre in so many alleged conversions.

It follows from this that religious emotions are not to be directly sought. They are to come as the unforced attendants of our religious faith and devotion and obedience. When thus coming, they are wholesome, helpful, and natural. In every other case they are unwholesome, harmful, and unnatural. Indeed, emotions, as an affection of the sensibility, have so complex a root, and are so complicated with physical conditions, that they are generally worthless as a test of will and character. Even those relations in daily life which are founded on affection, as the relations of the family, admit of no test of the emotional sort. Devotion shows itself chiefly in service; and it is only at special times, in some crisis perhaps, that the emotional sensibility is deeply stirred. Love itself abides in the will rather than in the feeling, and its distinguishing mark consists in the set purpose to please and to serve. And this is true of our love for God. It is to be found in the consecration of the life and the devotion of the will; not in ebullitions of the sensibilities, but in the fixed purpose to please and to serve. If, along with this, the heart should be "strangely warmed," there is no objection ; but, after all, the root of the matter must be found in the life of devotion and service. "If ye love me, keep my commandments." "Not every one that saith unto me, Lord, Lord, shall enter into the kingdom of heaven ; but he that doeth the will of my Father which is in heaven." "And hereby we do know that we know him, if we keep his commandments. He that saith, I know him, and keepth not his commandments, is a liar, and the truth is not in him." "Ye are my friends, if ye do whatsoever I command you." Such passages as these show that the essential test of discipleship is ethical and volitional, not emotional; and their frequent occurrence shows a purpose to ward off the very error in question.

Obedience, then, is the only test of discipleship recognized by the Master ; and he spoke very sharply of eloquent divines who prophesied in his name and did many wonderful works, yet were workers of iniquity. Though we should speak with the tongues of men and of angels, and had not obedience, we should be but sounding brass and clanging cymbals. And though we spoke in the social meeting, and were eloquent in public prayer, and bore testimony to wonderful outpourings and upliftings and spiritual manifestations far beyond those of common Christians, and had not obedience, it would profit us nothing. And though we had a wonderful conversion and became quite unconscious through the exceeding abundance of the outpouring, and had not obedience, we should be nothing. The Master mentions none of these things as conditions or tests of discipleship; but he was very particular about obedience. When he called Simon and Andrew and James and John, they left all and followed him, and thus became his disciples; and the same rule holds still.

A frequent consequence of this error concerning emotion is that the attention of the inquirer is diverted from the central and essential thing, the surrender of the will and life to God, and fixed upon having an experience. This experience is crudely conceived as a striking emotional event, which must be of extraordinary character in order to meet the expectation. Thus the volitional and ethical element, which is essential, is subordinated to a passive and emotional element, which in any case is only a non-essential attendant of religious consecration, and which, in many cases, is purely pathological. That it is such in a great many cases appears from the fearful disproportion between the number of reported converts and the number of those received into church membership. Who can believe that such disproportion would exist, if the inquirer had been rightly instructed, and had solemnly, intelligently, ethically devoted and consecrated himself to do the will of God? Emotional effervescence may subside in this way, but intelligent and moral self-consecration does not. There is so much confusion on this point that the majority of inquirers are aiming to have an experience rather than to surrender themselves to God in faith and obedience. And with this false aim they fail to " get through," or to " come out into the light." They are seeking after some sign, instead of fixing their thought on the surrender of themselves in faith to the Lord Jesus to be his disciples. Often enough the sign is not given them, and then comes the familiar sense of uncertainty and artificiality in religion.

In opposition to this error, our attention should always be directed to securing filial submission to the will of God. The inquirer must be instructed, if need be, in Christian truth. His thought must be made familiar with the grace of God and the gracious provisions of the gospel. Peace and joy will naturally arise in the penitent soul as it contemplates this grace and yields itself to it in trust and obedience. But their form and measure will vary very greatly with different persons according to education, temperament, and many other circumstances. But the disciple must not concern himself about them. Loving submission and active obedience to the will of God in accordance with the promises of Christ are the supreme and only mark of Christian discipleship. We are not called upon to have experiences, or emotional upheavals, or witnesses of the Spirit; but we are called upon to surrender ourselves in faith and humility to do the will of God. Cease to do evil, learn to do well, is the only infallible test of conversion.

The attitude of the will, then, is the central thing in the Christian life. But in applying this truth we must guard against an extravagance, often amounting to positive error, which may arise at this point. We are often told that we must be willing to do whatsoever God may require, to give up all for Christ, etc.; and this admits of easy exaggeration. Formally, the statement is correct; but the concrete meaning is not always plain. Negatively, the meaning is simple.

We must cease to do evil; any recognized iniquity, impiety, unrighteousness, wickedness, must be put away unhesitatingly, irrevocably, forever. That one should call himself the child of God while working the works of the devil is not to be thought of for a moment.

But the positive contents of the idea are very crudely conceived. We often fall a prey to mere abstractions of theory without duly regarding the realities of life. Error here may take a double direction. We may fall into an abstract conception of renunciation, and we may misconceive the relation of God's will to the great every-day life of work and social relations. The former error is illustrated by the fancy of some of the older New England theologians, that no one could be saved who was not willing to be damned for the glory of God. Of course, a good closet argument could be made for this abomination. One might say that, so long as anything was preferred to the divine glory, one had not fully submitted to the will of God; was keeping back a part of the price therefore, like Ananias; or, like Achan, had a wedge of gold and a Babylonish garment concealed in one's tent. Thorough work, then, could be made only by insisting upon willingness to be damned for the divine glory. This was the only sure test of selfishness. The purely

fictitious and inhuman character of this demand
is apparent. The only good thing that ever came
out of it is the reported reply of an applicant to
the examining committee which pressed the question, that he was willing the committee should
be damned if need be.

We have escaped such excesses; but a great
deal of unwisdom is still current on this point.
Vague general remarks abound about taking up
the cross, the surrender of this and that, the willingness to do a variety of disagreeable things;
and these are often made the test of discipleship.
Religious exhortation is full of matter of this
sort; and inquirers are left to torment themselves
with the fancy that anything which revolts their
taste or sensibility, or some purely imaginary
thing, as a willingness to go as a missionary to
Van Diemen's Land, or to address some stranger
on the street concerning his soul, is a part of the
cross which must be taken up, if one would enter
into life. They are also led to think that an
unwillingness to speak in public when they have
nothing to say is to be ashamed of Jesus, or to
do despite to the spirit of grace. And, on the
other hand, an unbecoming and unedifying vol-
ubility is often encouraged from the idea that
thus the power of grace is triumphantly dis-
played. The following quotation from a religious

paper of recent publication illustrates the former
error : —

Then the Lord God said to me : " David, are you
willing to consecrate yourself ? " " Yes, Lord. Everything, everything." And he brought one thing after
another in this way : " Are you willing to leave your
situation if I ask you ? " I was quite willing. " Would
you go to Africa to be eaten by cannibals ? " I was
willing to do even that. Then the Lord said : " Would
you leave your wife at home and go anywhere ? " Oh,
I was n't willing ! It was very hard to leave my dear
wife behind and go anywhere. Then a fight went on in
my heart. I did n't want to yield that ; but the Lord
brought Christ very prominently before me, and he
said that he must be first and my wife in the second
place. Then he brought before me the responsibility
of heathen souls, Mohammedans, Buddhists, and others.
" David, are you willing to leave all to win souls ? "
Then it came to me : " What am I to do ? The Lord
will take care of my wife " ; and I said, " O Lord, I
am willing to leave my wife behind and go anywhere."
Then the struggle ceased. " Would you like to become
as the dust of Colombo for my sake ? " Yes, I was willing. The Lord searched me through and through.

All this is purely fictitious. The Lord said
none of these things ; they were suggested solely
by the author's own misguided mind. The Lord
often calls us to sacrifice and renunciation, but
never in any such artificial fashion as this. The
person simply had in his mind the abstract notion

of complete surrender to God, and then proceeded to determine the concrete contents of the duty by calling up a miscellaneous collection of things to which he might be disinclined. Meanwhile reason and good sense were in complete abeyance, because of the fancy that all of these things were directly suggested by God as tests of the person's sincerity. The reference to leaving his wife is paralleled only by the testimony of a brother in class-meeting who reported that his wife had died, and that he had been so wonderfully supported by divine grace that he had not missed her at all or felt any sorrow. The leader had the grace and good sense to tell him never to repeat that story again, as it revealed inhuman insensibility rather than divine support.

But with the uninstructed and sensitive conscience, misconceptions of this sort are likely to arise when one is testing his willingness to do the will of God. And it is not to be wondered at that many good Christians have been unwilling to have their children exposed to such crude and undiscriminating teaching. Of course the intellectually and morally pachydermatous are unharmed, but with the sensitive and uninstructed conscience the danger is great. And the danger is double. On the one hand there is danger of falling into fictitious sacrifices and mortifications;

and on the other there is danger of a permanent revolt against religion when at last the fiction is seen through. I have had ample experience of both results.

There is great need at this point for the wise Christian teacher, in order to save the untaught or inexperienced from these dangers. He must distinguish between the positive and negative aspects of this surrender to the divine will. Its negative meaning, we have said, is clear; it involves the utter and final abandonment or avoidance of all unrighteousness and iniquity. On the positive side we must emphasize the central and primal duties about which there is no question. We must teach the inquirer to relate his life, internal and external, to the divine will, and especially to comprehend the daily round of routine life and of social relations, the round of work and rest, of neighborly intercourse and civic duties, within the divine thought and purpose, and thus within the scope of religion. But we must resolutely defend the inquirer from all this unwholesome casuistry concerning cross-bearing, and testifying, and fictitious self-crucifixions, and imaginary duties, and trumped-up sacrifices. Ignorant conscientiousness can settle none of these questions. We must fall back on good sense, that general sense of reality and soundness

without which the moral life becomes a series of
snares and loses itself in silliness or fanaticism.
We must point out that the essence of religion
lies in the filial spirit, in the desire to serve and
please God; and then we must point out that
our all-inclusive religious duty is to offer up the
daily life, pervaded and sanctified by the filial
spirit, as our spiritual service and worship of God.

But how shall we know when we have done
enough? This is a question which roots partly in
the unwholesome casuistry referred to, and partly
in a desire to get off as cheaply as possible. In
the latter case it shows that we have neither part
nor lot in the matter. We are trying to conceive
a spiritual relation mechanically, and we miss the
spiritual element altogether. By consequence we
assume that salvation may be something external,
and we desire to get it at the best bargain. Such
notions arise from our non-ethical conceptions of
the subject, and disappear forever when we see
that salvation must consist in establishing or restoring the filial spirit in the heart.

The question, as rooted in casuistry, overlooks
the essential truth of the gospel. The question
for the Christian to raise is, not whether he has
done enough, but whether he is seeking to live
in the filial spirit. The latter question no one can
answer for him, and he needs no one to answer

it for him. As to doing enough, no one does enough. There is no satisfaction in doing. We are at best unprofitable servants. We can always wonder whether we might not have done more, strained a little harder, reached a greater intensity of effort. That way madness lies. On such a view one's salvation is a sort of Rupert's drop, and is likely to fly into flinders at any moment.

To all such questions we reply by falling back on the gospel itself. We are not members of the divine family because we are profitable servants, but because God has declared us to be his children. We stand not in the value of our services, but in the divine love. And that love bears with our imperfect, halting service, and takes the will for the deed. This is the gist and glory of the gospel. It cannot be understood in forensic and mechanical terms, but it is perfectly intelligible through the life of the family or the gratitude of a penitent heart. No child has its place in the family because of the value and merit of its services, but because it is a child. It is saved by grace, not by works. But being a child, it can show forth the filial spirit in word and deed, and parental love does all the rest. Membership in the divine family is similarly conditioned.

We must, then, declare the forgiveness of sins to all those who do truly and earnestly repent of their sins and intend to lead a new life, following the commandments of God, and walking from henceforth in his holy ways. And this we do in the name and on the authority of the Lord Jesus, who has revealed the Father. And we must allow nothing to interfere with the simplicity of this revelation. Mechanical conditions of mechanical works, and subjective conditions framed from emotional states, are alike and equally departures from the truth of the gospel.

The religious life in its idea is altogether independent of the existence of sin. We are not, then, to think of it as a device for overcoming sin or for saving sinners. This work, indeed, has to be done; but it is only incidental to the deeper, more inclusive aim of religion. Religion has to do with the relation of man to God, and would exist if there were no sin in the world or in the heart. Indeed, it is only in the sinless life that the ideal of religion can be perfectly realized ; for only there can we find the filial spirit perfectly realized and perfectly expressed.

In what we have now to say, some readers of theological tendencies will miss a good deal of traditional matter concerning the relation of the sinner to God's law, etc. ; but we have once more to remind them that this, in its best estate, is matter of theology and not of experience. Whatever mysteries there may be in that direction, we have no practical concern with them. We have only to accept our place as children in our Father's house; and we must not confuse this simple truth of the gospel with matter drawn from theology.

If human development were normal, there would be no need of conversion, that is, of a turning around, or a turning toward God; for we should never have turned away from him. We should simply pass from the unconsciousness and passivity of dawning life to the distinct consciousness and volitional attitude of mature life. And this transition would be made slowly, and without break or jar, something as the dawn comes up. As in the family life no one can tell, in the child's unfolding, when love and obedience begin, so in the normal development of the religious life no one can tell when it begins. The inner life has none of the sharp divisions of our speech; and consciousness fades away from clear apprehension and distinct volition into incipiencies, and uncertain dawnings, and shadowy beginnings, where directions may possibly be discerned, but no fixed lines can be drawn. In such normal unfolding there might be great individual differences of experience, owing to differences of temperament and mental habit. With the more reflective the recognition and acceptance of the divine will might be a matter of more definite date, but they would be no more real on that account than they would be in a life of less sharply marked transitions. And with such reflective person such a date might well be a time forever to be remembered unto the Lord; but it would not mark a conversion, but only a conscious affirmation and ratification of what had already been unconsciously done.

In actual life the nearest approximation to such normal religious development is found in the Christian family. Here, too, the aim should be, not conversion, but to bring the children up in the nurture and admonition of the Lord; and the necessity of conversion, or a turning from sin to God and righteousness, hints strongly at parental failure, either to grasp the truth of the gospel or to realize it in the family life. The ideal form of the Christian life is that which never experienced conversion, and which cannot date its beginning. And if one says, But there must be a time of distinct choice between God and the world, etc., the answer would be that at best this only fixes the beginning of self-consciousness in religion and not the beginning of religion itself. And indeed self-consciousness can rarely be thus accu-

rately dated; but religion in the properly trained
Christian child has complex and untraceable beginnings in the spirit and atmosphere of the home,
in childhood's prayers, in participation in religious
rites and customs, in imitation of those about him,
in wise parental instruction and discipline, and
in the hidden influence of the Holy Spirit. These
things cannot be dated. The date of self-consciousness in choice and consecration might conceivably be fixed in the case of the Christian child;
but even this is rarely possible and it is unimportant in any case. When does filial affection begin
in the growing child, or patriotism in the developing youth? The important thing is not to know
when the day begins, but to have the day actually here.

Divine grace and help are always needed and
by all alike; but conversion as an event in conscious experience is needed only for those who,
from evil training or from willful transgression,
have turned away from God. All such persons
must convert themselves; that is, must turn around
and turn towards God and righteousness. But in
all cases the thing aimed at is the same, the establishment of the filial spirit as the ruling principle of life and action. Where the filial spirit is
consciously present we have the children of the
kingdom. Where it is consciously absent we have

the children of disobedience. Where there is no
consciousness as yet of the higher goods and relations of life we have simply the sub-religious
state in which so many human beings exist, and
out of which they are to develop through the
multiform discipline and experience of life. Meanwhile they are the objects of the divine grace, and
are comprised in an order divinely appointed for
their development and unfolding into deeper and
higher life. Hard-and-fast divisions and classifications are impossible in such an order; and forensic distinctions are as grotesquely impossible as
they would be in the life of the family. Meanwhile it is the task of the Christian teacher and
of the mature disciple to coöperate with the divine
love by setting forth and revealing the higher
life by precept and example, both personally and
through the organized institutions of the Christian
family and the Church.

And in doing this work it is important to remember that the religious life, except in its central factor of the filial and obedient spirit, is no
simple and single thing which is present always
and all at once and to all alike. On the contrary,
the contents of religious experience vary with the
disciple's age, temperament, mental type, and nature of his previous life. The Christian life is one
in principle, but in form and contents it is as
varied as humanity itself.

This truth has not been duly regarded by the churches which emphasize conversion and personal experience. The tendency has been to construct a pattern to which all should conform; and this pattern has largely been built out of subjective emotional states and various marks of grace which only, it was thought, clearly distinguish the work of the Spirit from spurious imitations. This was generally harmless when we were dealing with hardened sinners, but it became mischievous when applied to the religion of childhood and to the religious life that should develop under the influence of a Christian home and in a Christian community. Owing to the confusion of theology with experience, or to the undue estimate of emotional factors, the popular ideal of the religious life in our individualistic churches has little application to the larger part of the community.

In order to escape the confusion and inadequacy of traditional thought on this general subject, we must observe that the religious life is manifold in content and manifestation according to the age, the mental type, and one's experience of life.

Apart from the variations dependent upon age, temperament, and the vicissitudes of the individual lot, there are distinct types of religious thought and feeling, all of which are equally founded in human nature, and no one of which may set itself up as the norm or ideal by which the others may be tested.

The first type is the ethical. Religion consists in righteousness; but it is more than abstract ethics, because the moral law, from being an impersonal principle, is elevated into the expression of a supreme and holy will. The regard for impersonal abstractions is replaced by enthusiasm for the kingdom of God. Christianity summons us to be members of this kingdom and co-workers with God in its establishment. Under the lead of the Captain of our salvation, and relying on his word and promises, we become conscious subjects of the kingdom. In quiet times, and with persons of wholesome training and habits, or with persons of unemotional type, and especially with children, this is the prevailing type of Christian experience. It is not markedly emotional. It is not given to fervors, whether of joy or remorse. It has no deep distress over the depravity of our nature, and no flaming raptures over our deliverance. But it is founded in conscience; and a very large part of the work of the Church is done by the Christians of this type. This is the Christianity of the Synoptic Gospels, and of the epistles of James and Peter.

But this is not the only type. It is fundamental, indeed, and any type which does not include it is false. But it does not include the whole of Christian experience. There are souls which can be satisfied with their obedience to God's law. They hear the commandment, and they obey; and the joy of a good conscience is theirs. But there are other souls which can never find peace in this way. For them the commandment is exceedingly broad. It is not a matter of detached duties, but takes account of the heart. They hold their lives up against the keen, still splendor of the divine perfection, and they are overwhelmed by the revelation. For such persons there is no peace in doing. The more they do the worse they feel. For the ideal grows with obedience and thus condemns them more and more. For this state of mind there is only one prescription. They must be taken out of themselves and away from the contemplation of their own efforts, and must be taught that we are saved by grace, not works. Then their distress is removed by the vision of that condescending grace from above which saves us through itself. This is the Pauline type of Christian experience. It is not more truly Christian than the purely ethical type, but it is different. It is more intense, and touches the moral life at deeper depths.

With persons of a mechanical type it may pass over into Antinomianism, and thus, in revolting from bondage to rules, become the extreme of immorality. But when rightly understood, when interpreted vitally and ethically, it includes the obedience of the ethical type, but transcends it by a higher moral ideal and insight.

Another type of Christian experience arises from the desire for direct personal communion with God. If God indeed dwell within us, there must be some other way of reaching him than by hearsay, whether of the Bible, or of theology, or of the Church. And if we are his children, there must be some way of direct communion with our Father. Besides, the life of work is only part of experience. There is also the life of contemplation, of secret aspiration, of adoration and worship. And this certainly cannot all be on one side, as if we prayed into the empty air with no answer but the echo of our own voices. Here the mystical element of religion reveals itself. And this, too, is a real aspect of the religious life; not equally recognized by all, and scarcely realized at all by many, but important nevertheless. It is represented by the writings of St. John in the New Testament, by the various bodies of mystics in church history, and by multitudes of individual saints. As said, it belongs to the contemplative rather than the active side of religion; but it is important, even for practice, by furnishing the living water, without which life loses its deepest spring.

The perfect Christian life would involve all of these forms of experience; but in our one-sided life, one form or another predominates, and then we have to be on our guard against the short-comings of that form. For each form has tendencies to error, which will surely develop unless proper precaution be taken. The ethical form by itself may easily issue in Pharisaism and spiritual pride. When the spiritual nature is not deep, duty is exhausted in commandments; and if anything more be suspected, it is simply another commandment. The young man who had kept the law from his youth up, or the Pharisee who recited his good deeds in his prayers, furnishes a fair specimen of the tendency and the danger. And this can be averted only by enlarging the moral insight, and replacing a code of isolated good works by the law of perfect purity and perfect love. This only can cause the self-satisfied Pharisee to exchange his vainglorious prayers for the cry of the publican, " God be merciful to me a sinner ! " The ethical type, also, from its pre-eminent attention to conduct and action, tends to become dry and thin, and to lose itself in ineffectual bustle, while the spiritual life withers. This, too, can be avoided only by the deepening and enriching influences of prayer and meditation, and of spiritual communion with the Father of our spirits. Thus the ethical type of religious life always needs to be combined with the other types, in order to save it from its own short-comings.

But they equally need to be combined with the ethical type to save them from their own shortcomings. When one has sought in vain for peace through mechanical good works or strenu-ous conscientiousness, there is no more glorious truth than this, that we are saved by grace through faith ; but this becomes a pernicious and immoral doctrine unless it be ethically appre-hended and applied. How often this danger has been realized is familiar to every student of church history. The contemplative life also easily loses itself in quietistic indifference to the work of the world, or in a barren cultivation of emo-tions, in which all moral quality and moral strenuousness disappear altogether. Now, while the ethical view needs to be deepened by the others, they, in turn, need the ethical view to give them fibre and substance, and to furnish the active nature of man a worthy task. And this can be found only in recalling the mind from painful inspection of its own states, and from quietistic dreaming and contemplation, and setting it upon the positive task of realizing the kingdom of God in the world. The ethical view is fundamental and central; and however far we may go in religious fervor and aspiration, we must never lose sight of the ethical aim. All truly religious growth and insight must be based on this. And one of the promising features of the present religious outlook is the tendency to pay less attention to subjective states and more to the objective aim of building up the kingdom of God, which is the kingdom of righteousness and good-will.

Even at the expense of some repetition it is desirable further to insist on righteousness and obedience as the central thing in religion. It is well known that the non-Christian religions have largely ignored righteousness as a religious factor; and even in the Christian Church it has been no uncommon thing to find something else made fundamental. Apart from the coarser errors of this kind, which need no condemnation, there are others of a more refined sort, which also arise from the failure to make righteousness the central thing. There are feelings which gather around the æsthetic and contemplative side of religion, and which are easily mistaken for religion. For any fairly developed mind of normal character, religion must be a profoundly interesting subject of reflection. It takes hold on the unseen and the eternal. It holds a philosophy of existence — the key to the puzzles of life, the solution of its problems, the harmony of its discords, the meaning of all finite being. We are thrown back upon it when we contemplate the tragedy of human life. Art and poetry cry out for it. Our sense of dependence and incompleteness forces us upon it. Nameless longings and voiceless aspirations find in religion their expression. Under these and similar influences the human mind has developed its great religious forms.

The spirit of reverence demands that all things shall be fittingly done, and naturally seeks to body forth the feelings of awe and aspiration and worship in rite and ceremony and music and symbol and architecture, which thus become the visible speech of the otherwise dumb souls of men. In this way were produced the great church buildings, the religious music, the splendid rituals and liturgies, and the whole system of religious symbolism. Much of this is needed for the full expression of man's religious nature ; and when that which is perfect is come we shall have these things also in perfection.

But these things, though connected with religion, are not religion in God's sight. They are simply the æsthetic or contemplative side or aspect of religion. Persons of taste and culture, or of contemplative mental type, are easily affected by this aspect, and easily mistake their delight in it for religion. But the feelings which arise from a well-ordered religious service, or from soaring architecture, or from the harmonious blending of dim religious lights, or

Where through the long-drawn aisle and fretted vault
The pealing anthem swells the note of praise —

such feelings may be only æsthetic emotions with no trace of heart love and devotion. Likewise the sad delight, the pensive tenderness, the speechless longings developed in passive contemplation of life and its vicissitudes and mysteries, may have nothing of religion in them. They may even be incompatible with special inhumanity, just as grief over the woes of a character of fiction is no security for tenderness of heart. When these things are cut loose from righteousness, or are viewed as ends in themselves, they become an abomination to the Lord and to every enlightened conscience. It is easy for any one in contemplative moments, or in a religious crowd, or in the presence of religious ideas which make no present demands upon the will, to have pleas-

ing and lofty religious emotions, and to fancy
one's self religious on that account. The practical enmity is asleep, and the evil and forbidden
courses are forgotten. The music, the æsthetic
impressiveness of the service, the contagion of
social excitement, and even the grandeur of the
divine character, combine to impress us and to
hide from us the set rebellion of the will. Nothing but life will reveal this. Balaam had fine
religious feeling and insight, and was something
of a poet withal, but, along with it all and ruin-
ing it all, he loved the wages of unrighteousness.
And he has many descendants in both pew and
pulpit.

And often we find persons who, as a matter
of temperament and constitution, have a devotional, meditative, contemplative religious gift.
They abound in the East. The Catholic Church
furnishes more examples than the Protestant
churches, but specimens are everywhere to be
found. They have a natural talent for religion.
This, too, is to be desired as a preparation for
religion. It secures a religious naturalness and
ease and propriety which can hardly be otherwise obtained. But this is not religion at all
until it is brought into connection with righteousness and the fundamental aim to do the
will of God. So far as it falls short of this it is

purely a matter of temperament, and may be utterly selfish and irreligious. Indeed, some of the Church's subtlest temptations and worst aberrations from the spirit of the Master come from æsthetic feeling and good taste. Unless we are on our guard and are filled with our Lord's love for men, it is easy to be so scandalized with the bad grammar, and stumbling speech, and discordant singing, and generally bad social form and lack of style, as to feel in our hearts that perhaps it would be better if the masses kept by themselves in religion as in other things. And then the spiritual ear can hear the Master saying, " The publicans and the harlots go into the kingdom of God before you."

These facts must be borne in mind by the Christian teacher ; and he must carefully refrain from applying any other test of religion than the filial spirit, or the desire and purpose to serve and please God by keeping his commandments. The grace of God does all the rest. And on this most holy faith of the gospel we are to build ourselves up into all obedience and spiritual growth through the assisting grace of the Holy Spirit. In this way the Christian life will unfold naturally and in accordance with the experience and peculiar type of the individual. Nothing being demanded but the filial spirit, that spirit can manifest itself in various ways and be the same spirit in them all. By fixing our thought on the filial spirit, we shall run little risk of confusing ourselves with theological and metaphysical subtleties on the one hand, or with artificial and impossible experiences on the other. Christian truth is manifold and meets the needs of all; but every phase of this truth does not appeal equally to all, nor even to the same at all times.

Christianity has a religion for all ages and temperaments, and for all sorts and conditions of men. There is a bright and cheerful religion for childhood and youth, and a more sombre and deeper-toned religion for later years. It has matin bells for life's morning and vesper songs for the night. Work and prayer, contemplation and obedience, aspiration and communion, all mix and mingle in the complex experience of the Christian community; but the one thing common to all, the one thing with which all may begin and which none may ever outgrow, is obedient loyalty to the spirit and commands of our Lord. Beyond this there is no common pattern of religious experience; and it is not desirable that there should be. The search for such a thing implies gross ignorance in pedagogy, in psychology, and in religion.

The life of man is very complex, and our

human needs are many. The feeling of dependence and helplessness growing out of the vicissitudes of life and the inexorable necessities which
wall us in on every side, the feeling of awe and fear
springing out of the impenetrable mystery of our
existence, the feeling of loneliness and orphanage
also which sometimes comes over us in the deep
silence of the universe, the heart wailing over
and after its dead, the intellect seeking for knowledge, and the conscience hungering and thirsting
after righteousness, — all of these things enter
into and determine the religious manifestations of
humanity. The Christian teacher will always have
to minister to more than the conscience of men. He
must bind up the broken-hearted, strengthen the
feeble will, and bring a message of life and cheer
and inspiration. I would not then be understood
as saying that conduct or righteousness is the
sum of religion. But I do say it is the sum of
God's demands upon us, the central thing in our
relations to him. Given this, our religious life
may unfold in various ways according to our
special experience or peculiar temper, or the demands made upon us by our position in life; but
without this all else is dust and ashes before
conscience and before God. We are not children
of the kingdom because we are filled with awe
before the midnight heavens, or in some great

cathedral, or at some magnificent religious service. We are not children of the kingdom because we are thrilled or melted by religious music, or delight in devotional exercises, or are emotionally moved by religious contemplation. All of these things are possible without one spark of loyalty to God or love to men. We are children of the kingdom, if at all, because we are bent on doing the will of God.

The teaching and practice of the individualistic churches concerning the religion of childhood have generally oscillated between two extremes of error; either children have been viewed as incapable of religion, or forms of experience have been demanded from them which are possible only to mature life, and often only to abandoned sinners. The words of Scripture were originally addressed to grown men, and often to men who were just emerging from heathen darkness and all manner of filthy practices; but they have been supposed to apply to all, heathen and Christian, young and old alike; and then the attempt has been made to force on the young the experience of the mature, and to find in the young the depravity of abandoned sinners. Enormous pedagogical and psychological error has been common at this point.

All the churches which emphasize personal religion have been more or less guilty of this fault; and they need to bring forth fruits meet for repentance. There is a large body of feelings, much affected by the artificially spiritual, which are not religious at all, but are simply expressions of advancing age. Such are the sense of the brevity of life and of the unsatisfying nature of all earthly things. Feelings of this sort are unnatural to the young; and language of this sort from them can only be an echo, or an expression of artificial sentiment. There are many other feelings of a religious nature which are also impossible to the young. Such are a deep sense of sinfulness, of human weakness, of the depravity of human nature, of the imperfection of our righteousness, and of the constant need of divine grace and forbearance and forgiveness. Such insight is impossible to childhood, for it is born only of the deeper experiences of mature life and of the sterner conflicts of faith. Yet we have not scrupled to gather up these feelings and convictions as preeminently marks of grace, and to look for them in the life of childhood. And sometimes the child repeats the phrases, to our great delight and edification. Or we see that the meaning is really beyond the child, and then we conclude that children are incapable of religion.

Both of these errors are to be avoided. The religion of maturity is impossible to childhood, but the religion of childhood is religion nevertheless. It is largely of the simple ethical type, not without its naïve misconceptions and innocent misunderstandings; but it may be very loyal for all that. A child's conscience may be very tender, and may even see more straight on matters level to the child's mind than the more sophisticated conscience of the mature.

Again, we often misjudge the religion of childhood by misinterpreting the transparency of childhood. The child has not learned self-control, reserve, dissimulation; and whatever is in, comes out. The child finds the Sabbath irksome, and says so. The man finds it irksome, and says nothing about it. The child finds the religious exercise distasteful, and would like to run out into the back yard and play. The man finds it distasteful, and retires into the back yard of worldly thoughts, which are quite as far from spirituality as the child's games, but which do not make such a show in the outward appearance. But to him who looketh at the heart the well-behaved and decorous worshiper is often farther from him than the restless and fretful child. Let any one who is inclined to judge the religion of childhood in this way ask himself how he would seem, if he should act out without disguise the passing feelings, the lawless fancies, the random disinclinations, the transient indifference to the best things, from which none of us are free. We can hardly expect the children to attain to a perfection of constancy and consistency which is beyond the mature; and we should not apply a rule to them which we could not endure ourselves.

The insight that a child must be a child in religion as well as in other things, and the further insight that every normal stage of life is legitimate in the divine plan, should help us to look with a kindlier eye on the child life and prevent any interference with its normal manifestations in the supposed interests of piety. The child life moves within a small circle of activities, desires, and aversions, mostly directed toward physical objects, and thus to many it seems not deep enough and spiritual enough for religion. One speaker at a recent gathering of ministers said he did not wish his children to profess religion until they had outgrown the inconstancy and frivolity of childhood. A minister of my acquaintance was received into the Church when a child, and next day was seen playing ball with some other children. This was a sore offense to a good brother, who saw in the fact a proof that children are incapable of true heart religion. How could a boy play ball with any zest if he had any religion ? Yet the probability is that the boy, in playing ball, was doing the very best thing for himself, religion, and all. Another ministerial acquaintance secured a ticket to the Y. M. C. A. gymnasium for a lad who was spending much time on the streets and was in danger from idleness; but his father forbade him to accept it, as he heard they played checkers and bowls there, and he "would as soon think of sending his son to a saloon to learn Christianity." When the minister said that he played himself sometimes, the poor, ignorant Pharisee replied that he could only think of Christ's words: "Ye compass sea and land to make one proselyte; and when he is made, ye make him twofold more the child of hell than yourselves." This was supposed to show exceeding spirituality.

Christian truth, we have already said, is manifold, and meets the needs of all; but the needs vary with age, experience, temperament, mental type, etc., and the religious life will vary to correspond. This must be borne in mind in dealing with the religion of the young. It is one of God's great mercies that those who have the earthly life before them are generally pleased with it. Hence, to the young, it is a glad thing to live, and we ought not to wish it otherwise. Without

this naïve optimism of youth, life would hardly
be possible; and nothing could well be more false
to Christian truth and the Christian spirit than
interference therewith in the supposed interests
of piety. We must not, then, call upon the young
to have mournful and despondent feelings about
the life that now is, and a desire to depart and
be with Christ, in the fancy that thereby they
become more truly religious. We must rather remind them that this earth also is one of the many
mansions in the Father's house, and seek to help
them to relate this life to God's will. The child's
optimism is really nearer the truth than the old
man's pessimism; for it is God's world after all,
and it is right that we should rejoice in it and be
glad; and instead of rebuking the children for
their simple joy in life, we should rather rebuke
the pessimism of maturity as rooting in a lack of
faith.

Let, then, the children take their vows with a
glad heart; and when life wears on, and experience deepens, and the overturnings come, they
will learn of themselves that this earth is not our
rest, and will appreciate the life and immortality
brought to light in the gospel. They will also
learn the blessedness of the corresponding fact
that we are saved by grace. Any true apprecia-
tion of these things comes only through life.

The formulas may be learned from a catechism, but their meaning comes from experience; and, coming in this way, it is unforced and natural. It is not a sign of grace, which is anxiously to be sought for in all Christians, but an insight which is developed only in the maturer Christian life. And the lacking insight, or the lesser measure of insight, points only to a less advanced religious development, and not to being an alien or stranger in the household of faith.

The churches have no more important duty at present than to make wise provision for the religious training of childhood. Statistics show that the great majority of church members come from the Sunday school. One of our leading individualist churches reports that ninety per cent of its additions come from this source. While, then, we should not relax any wise evangelistic effort of the revival type, it is manifest that Christian nurture and training are to be the great reliance of the Church in the future, and that we must aim to colonize the world through the Christian family and home, rather than to reclaim the world by the conversion of mature sinners. Of course we must do what we can with the old sinner, but this method alone is as hopeless as the plan to save society from drunkenness by reforming drunkards, rather than by pre-

venting the making of drunkards. Prophylactic
measures are the reliance of all modern thought,
both in medicine and in morals. There is a demand here for more psychological insight and
better pedagogical methods than we have had in
the past. Throughout the early years the Church
and the family are responsible for the religious
life of the child, and they should avail themselves of all the means of influence at their
command to prepare the way for and build up
this life. An atmosphere of home piety, the formation and cultivation of religious habits of
thought and action, wise religious instruction,
all reënforced and illustrated by living example,
would go so far to turn the young life toward
God and righteousness that, when reflective consciousness should come, and the soul should
decide its direction for itself, it would have
nothing to do but to ratify what had already
been done, and go on without break or jar into
the fullness of spiritual life.

And even with the mature we need to criticise
and reform our methods. The growth of intelligence, the spread of good taste, a more independent and critical way of thinking, have made
many traditional methods distasteful or ineffective. This is especially the case with revival
methods, many of which, moreover, rest upon an

outgrown theology, and all of which need to be revised in the interest of both good sense and religion. The indications are that hereafter the churches will have to rely mainly on religious training for children, as just said, and "hand-picking" for the mature. In any case, we must remember that there is nothing sacred in methods; that the present value of a method depends on its adaptation to present circumstances; and that the most effective method is the best.

And now we must have a final word with the traditionalist who confuses theology with experience. He will certainly miss, in the previous exposition, a deal to which he has been accustomed. He is not content to find in conversion simply a turning to God in trust and obedience according to the commands and promises of Christ, but discerns in it mysterious forensic relations to the divine justice, and also deep metaphysical changes in the soul itself. The former element is necessary in order to meet the supposed demands of justice; and the latter element is peculiarly necessary for distinguishing the work of grace from mere natural goodness. Such goodness, not being of faith, is of course of sin; and there is needed some sure standard whereby these counterfeits of grace may be detected. Such a standard is at least formally furnished by the view in question. Judged by character and conduct, it is not easy to mark off men into two sharply distinct classes; but if we may suppose some hidden forensic or metaphysical change or event, then the distinction is easy. The converted are those in whom this change has taken place. All others are unconverted, and their righteousness, however fair in seeming, is filthy rags. But as thus conceived, the operation is as mechanical as baptismal regeneration itself. It is taken entirely out of the intelligible ethical realm, and is with difficulty saved from vanishing into abstract hocus-pocus.

We escape this confusion by again reminding ourselves that salvation on the human side must essentially consist in the production of the filial spirit, and that forensic difficulties, if not fictions of abstract theology, are something with which we have no practical concern. Whatever hidden difficulties in the divine nature or government there may be respecting the forgiveness of sins, our faith is that they have all been met, so that our sole duty is to proclaim the forgiveness of sins, to call the prodigals home to the Father's house, and to bring up the children to be the sons and daughters of the Lord Almighty. All beyond this is theology, and is of no practical moment. The great danger to which men are exposed consists in unlikeness to God in sympathy and purpose. If this unlikeness can be removed, everything else will take care of itself. Remembering the form of human development and the universality of the provisions of the gospel, we must say that every one is in the divine family who does not insist on taking himself out. And our effort must be directed to bringing men to recognize their duties, relations, and privileges as members of the family.

But the person who thinks mechanically will continue to ask, Who, then, are the saved? This question is best answered by asking another, Who are the unsaved? To this we can give an answer. The unsaved are all those who are living in unrighteousness and unfilial rejection of the law and grace of God. These are the prodigal sons who must return to their Father or reap the fruit of their doings. All others are saved in this sense, that they are comprehended in an order of divine grace which is working toward their development into the consciousness and acceptance of their place in God's family. But the development is nowhere complete. It stretches all the way from the unconsciousness of childhood to the still imperfect apprehension and devotion of the mature saint. But all alike stand in the divine grace; and the divine love is bearing them on. And our task consists in co-working with this love, that the will of God may be seen and done by us, and on the earth, as it is seen and done in heaven. Beyond this judgment is not ours. Our sole hope is in the mercy and goodness of God.

Not long ago a minister of considerable standing in one of our churches introduced his sermon by emphasizing the importance of knowing the date and place of one's birth; and then went on to argue the greater importance of knowing the date and place of one's second birth, in complete ignorance apparently that the only really important question in either case is, Is the man now alive? In the development of religious thought this question is fast displacing all others; and the answer to it is found solely in the quality and direction of the life. Obedience and the resulting fruits of the Spirit are the only test of spiritual life. All else may be imitated, and is imitated. The study of religious psychology has shown the unreliability of all other tests. We no longer take any man's word as to his spiritual state on the basis of remarkable experiences. We discount them all; we distrust them all, unless accompanied by the appropriate fruit. We are no longer concerned about experiences, but only to live in the spirit of the kingdom and to be about our Father's business. With growing insight into the divineness of the natural, we are no longer anxious about signs and wonders, but find God also in the routine of life faithfully borne, and in intellect and conscience as well. We recognize the order of life as a divinely appointed discipline for our spiritual development; and we never expect anything from God that will excuse us from doing our best, or relieve us from the discipline of life. Not a little of supposedly religious desire is a desire for religious ease and luxury rather than a desire for greater likeness to God and greater spiritual efficiency in the work of the world. But neither prayer, nor faith, nor any other religious exercise whatever may be offered in place of our own effort. There are no short cuts to perfection even in the spiritual field. The foundations of character must be laid, not without our own effort, in the humble virtues of faithfulness, integrity, patience, industry; and until these are learned the higher spiritual attainments would be out of place and impossible. Nothing but religious caricature can result when the higher graces or the " comforts " of religion are sought apart from faithfulness in elementary duties. Any real communion with God must take place through the moral nature and through spiritual likeness to him. And any mysticism that is not to lose itself in barren, if not immoral, subjectivities must be resolutely subjected to this requirement. Yet though we walk by faith and not by sight God is always with us. We must indeed work out our own salvation, or we should be pauperized by our religion; still it is God who worketh in us to will and to work of his good pleasure. And he does not leave himself without a witness in the soul. We have indeed to plod along the dusty road of daily routine, yet not without a growing sense that we are not alone, and that the Spirit of Christ is with us in the way.

IV

THE MODERN CONCEPTION OF THE KINGDOM OF GOD

IV

THE MODERN CONCEPTION OF THE
KINGDOM OF GOD

THE subject as given implies that the religious thought of to-day has advanced beyond that of the past in its conception of the kingdom. This agrees with the teaching of our Lord himself, and also with the facts of history. The kingdom is a growth, both in our understanding of it and in its realization. Our Lord spoke of it as a leaven, which was gradually to leaven the lump. Again, he described it as a seed, which should grow up, first the blade, then the ear, and after that the full corn in the ear. And he even spoke of our knowledge of it as something to be slowly gained under the tuition of the Holy Spirit, whom he would send to guide his disciples into the truth. He brought the leaven, he planted the seed, he spoke the word; but the evolution and the understanding were committed to the ages.

Probably we should all accept this statement for the realization of the kingdom, but still we might think that the knowledge of the kingdom was possessed from the start in the revelation of the Bible. This fancy, however, is quickly dispelled by a moment's reflection. In some sense we have had Christian truth always before us in the Scriptures, but in another sense we are only slowly entering into the meaning, for a revelation is not made until it is understood. If we should send a book on algebra to the king of Dahomey, we could hardly say that a revelation of the higher mathematics had been made to the savage chief; because such a revelation implies not merely the possession of an outward and visible sign, but also an inward intellectual comprehension. In the same way the revelation of God has been conditioned by the mental and moral development of the religious community. Any revelation, even of the purest truth, is sure to be warped by those who receive it into some image of themselves, and thus their narrowness and blindness reappear in their interpretations, and only slowly does the essential truth, through the illumination of the spirit, finally free itself from these distorting media and appear in its true nature.

These considerations prepare us to understand the slow progress of the kingdom. We have slowly come into the spirit of Christ even as a disposition, and still more slowly into the understanding of God's purpose for man. One of the early disciples, when our Lord was still with them, proposed to call down fire from heaven and consume the inhabitants of a Samaritan village who had not, as he conceived, properly received them. Our Lord rebuked him with the words, "Ye know not what manner of spirit ye are of." And ever since, conceit and vanity and malignity have thought themselves to be of the spirit of God and have wreaked no end of mischief upon the world, when all the time they knew not what spirit they were of. St. Bernard favored the Inquisition. Francis de Sales, so very highly spoken of as a saint and much admired to this day by persons who make a specialty of piety, indulged in one of the most inhuman of persecutions. A few hundred years ago all manner of persecution was the rule in the Christian Church. In the time of Shakespeare six hundred unfortunate women were hanged or burned as witches in consequence of one wind-storm in England. Bodin, one of the greatest legal lights of France, was vehement in his denunciation of witchcraft, and Sir Matthew Hale pronounced sentence of death on witches. It is little more than two hundred years since the Salem witchcraft left indelible infamy upon our New England history. These things were the outcome to a large extent of ignorance, — ignorance of natural science and ignorance of the

order of natural law and ignorance of the laws
of disease; but they were by no means always
free from a considerable smack of malignity.

But even in cases where such ignorance was not
in question, men showed themselves equally slow
in apprehending the truth of the gospel. Thus
we have been repeating for nearly two thousand
years that God is a spirit, and they that worship
him must worship him in spirit and in truth;
and yet it would not be hard to find multitudes
of people, and even many denominations, who
regard God as a stickler for etiquette, so that
some external rite or ceremony is a necessary
condition of salvation, or so that only certain
persons can perform the rite or the ceremony.
Again, we have been praying for a long time
" Forgive us our trespasses, as we forgive them
that trespass against us "; but how seldom we
think of the tremendous implications of such a
petition. Or, " Inasmuch as ye did it, or did it
not, unto one of the least of these, my brethren,
ye did it, or did it not, unto me." Yet in the
face of this the Christian world has been full
of indifference and hardness of heart; and the
claims of humanity, its crying needs, its sub-
merged members, the unjust and destructive
conditions under which so many live and die,
have had historically exceedingly little attention;

and it is only recently that anything that could be called enthusiasm for humanity has appeared even in the Church itself. And all this in the face of those tremendous words, " Ye did it not to me."

Similarly, with the Master's doctrine of stewardship, how slow the Christian world has been to receive it, and how much slower to put it into practice. This doctrine does not indeed condemn the simple possession of wealth, — such a view would be fatal to civilization ; but it condemns its misuse, its waste on vanity and folly, on all those things that contribute nothing to human comfort or advancement, instead of using it so that it shall bless both its owner and the community. On this point the Master was exceedingly uncompromising, but his teaching has not found wide recognition among his disciples. And the dream which lies at the heart of Christianity, of a great brotherhood for prayer and labor and mutual help, is all too much ignored, or rather unheard of. The Christian doctrine of stewardship has never come into the thought of the great majority of disciples.

If then we should ask, Is the Christian Church Christian ? the answer must certainly be, The Church is becoming Christian, but in any ideal sense it is not Christian yet. As in the old dispensation God had to wink at many things because of the hardness of men's hearts, so equally under the new dispensation he has to wink at a great many things because of the hardness and dullness of men's hearts. The truth is in the Church as a leaven which is slowly leavening the lump. It is in the Church as principles which are slowly being understood and applied. It is in the Church as a spirit which is slowly leading men out into the light. Only in this sense is the Church Christian even yet. Verily our God is the " God of all patience."

Now these things do not imply that these imperfect saints are hypocrites. They only serve to show how slowly we come to understand the meaning of the truths respecting the kingdom of God. They have been announced for centuries from our pulpits, and have been repeated in prayer and liturgy; but we have lost ourselves in the letter that killeth, and have missed the spirit that alone profiteth anything. Thus we see the truth of the figure that the kingdom is a leaven, a slowly growing seed, and that the truth is only slowly apprehended through the working of the Spirit in the mind and heart of the religious community.

Thus far on the slow growth of the kingdom; but now let us inquire what the kingdom itself means. If the kingdom of God should come on earth, what would the fact be? In our earthiness of thought and lack of spiritual insight we might easily fancy that some concrete manifestation would be made to the senses. The New Jerusalem might descend out of heaven, with its walls of precious stones, its pavements of gold, and its gates of pearl. There would be something that we could see, and the light would shine afar off, and the nations would gather to behold the sight, and thus the kingdom of God would be among men. Probably some such notion as this would be the thought of most men. But a moment's reflection convinces us that this would be only a celestial show, with no more spiritual significance than a splendid circus. There would be nothing moral or moralizing in such a performance. But the Lord looketh at the heart, and the kingdom of God can come with meaning only in the heart. The true kingdom of God is within. It is a mode of living and thinking, not an external show. Hence the coming of the kingdom could only mean the subordination of our hearts and wills to the will of God. It would not appear in the heavens above nor in the earth beneath. It would not come with sense observation at any time. It would appear first of all in the surrendered and obedient will. Men would be loving God with all their hearts and their neighbors as themselves. This would be the essential thing, the doing of God's will on earth as it is done in heaven.

This describes the essential principle of the kingdom. The kingdom comes in the individual when his will is set to do the will of God. It comes in the community in proportion as the members of the community are bent on doing the will of God. And this also defines the subjects of the kingdom. They are those who are on the side of righteousness and who are seeking to know and do the will of God. Whatever others may be, they are not in the present sense children of the kingdom.

Now we might think that this would be all, and indeed it would be very much. If men were loving God with all their hearts and their neighbors as themselves, we should be far on the way toward the coming of his kingdom. A great many evils would disappear at once. All the evils that spring from selfishness and crime and animalism would disappear. Likewise, all those that spring from harshness and bitterness of thought, from envy and superciliousness and evil speaking and evil thinking would disappear. And yet this in itself would not be the full thought of the kingdom of God. It would indeed be its essential principle and vital germ, but still it would only be part of the matter, for we need next to know what God's will is. We must not only have a right attitude of will toward God, but we must have some knowledge respecting him and his purpose concerning man. And without the latter we might well wander in error and superstition, which would prevent the full manifestation and realization of the kingdom. Thus this right principle might conceivably exist in a community of Lazaruses and paupers, or people lost in ignorance and superstition, and in that case no one would say that this represented God's will for men or that his kingdom had fully come. The Coptic or Abyssinian church may possibly be as devoted as any of the western churches, but the lack of knowledge or of moral and intellectual development keeps them on a level with the grossest superstition. In the Middle Ages, when men had no knowledge of natural law, if a pestilence broke out they had no recourse but the performance of some rite, superstitious or religious, commonly both; and meanwhile the pestilence raged and devastated the community. In such cases also it is plain that the kingdom had not fully come, and that it could not come until the religious will had been supplemented by the appropriate knowledge.

The kingdom, then, may be hindered by two

things : first, the evil will, which is the great root of human trouble; and second, by the ignorance of God's will, the failure to understand him, to enter into his spirit, to know what he is and what he means for men. The evil will, then, and the ignorant will, are the great enemies of the kingdom of God, and not until they are both removed can that which is perfect come.

Let us say, then, that the coming of the kingdom would involve not only the exorcism of the evil will and its replacement by the surrendered and obedient will, but also the removal of the multitudinous misunderstandings and ignorances which prevent us from appreciating and positively realizing God's purpose for man. From this point of view the coming of the kingdom would consist in the multitudinous renovations of life and society which the wise good will should accomplish. It would not consist in any other-worldliness or ascetic piety, but in the subordination of the great normal human life with all its interests to the will of God, and the development of that life, individually and socially, into its highest and noblest form, so that the good will within may find perfect expression without, in the human unfolding and social order which are the divine purpose for men.

Thus we see that the kingdom of God in the

concrete has a material, intellectual, and social basis as well as a formally religious one; and both are equally necessary. In God's plan both alike are included, and neither can dispense with the other. The Church must work for the coming of the kingdom, but so must the school, science, invention, and all the rest. It is plain, then, that in the coming of the kingdom of God two factors are involved: first, the exorcism of the evil will and its replacement by the sanctified will; and second, the development of life in all its possibilities and powers as representing God's will concerning us. It involves, then, not only the exorcism of the evil will, but also the exorcism of ignorance, of superstition, of disease, of bondage to physical needs, of the thousand things which hinder full and perfect life. Hence it involves also the development of the individual in all his powers, and the development of social relations into their perfect form, for man comes to himself only in society; and without a developed social order, which makes possible and conserves the gains of the individual, man would never emerge from the savage state. Thus we are introduced to the whole fabric of the social order, and to the entire mechanism of life, as the conditions of man attaining to himself and thus fulfilling his destiny. Not simply to mean well, but to work for the realization of ideal life, is our duty, and whatever that realization evolves is to be looked upon as also God's will.

The view thus set forth is comparatively a recent growth in popular religious thought. Here and there, indeed, prophets and saints have discerned it, but in the main religious thought has not attained to it. This it shares to some extent with ethical doctrine itself. Ethics has largely been one-sided and abstract, and has failed to connect with the great concrete life of the real human world. It has dealt with intentions and principles and categorical imperatives and the absolute value of the good will. Well, these are all important in their place, but at best they are only half the matter. The good will must will something in order to exist at all; the abstract good will that wills nothing is itself nothing. In order to give the good will any contents, or any worthy task, we must bring it out of its abstraction and connect it with life and all our normal human interests.

Let us put the matter in another form. It takes a vast amount of work to keep the world agoing. Think of the work in the millions of homes, the work of the farm, the school, the government, the organization of industrial production, of transportation, of the transmission of news and ideas, etc. These things are the foundation of civilization, and without them man could lead only the narrowest and most miserable existence. Now what is the relation of morals and religion to this world of life? If they ignore it they themselves become unimportant abstractions and should themselves be ignored. The true relation is this: Life represents the field for moral and religious action; and morals and religion are to move out into life and possess it, and develop it into its ideal form. All of this work in its great outlines must go on, if civilization is to endure; but it should go on under the guidance and stimulus of morals and religion. This life is to be moralized and rationalized; it is to be made the expression of right reason and good will. This is the positive moral task of humanity. We are not simply to mean well, but we are to develop our human life into its ideal form, and to live the human life in a wise and worthy way.

The positive aim of action, then, is to be found in the realization of life itself, full and perfect life; and the field is the world with all its activities. Both morals and religion are to be valued only as attempts to realize this aim. As such they presuppose life, with all its possibilities, as something already provided for in our constitution, and needing only to be realized by us in their

highest and noblest form; and for this realization
of humanity physical and mental training is to
be undertaken, schools founded, knowledge increased, the social order improved and perfected,
inventions made, commerce extended, physical
nature subdued, art encouraged, and whatsoever
else there may be that enlarges and enriches life.

The moral spirit, then, has all fields for its own.
Here is where asceticism and monasticism have
made their fearful blunders. They have rightly
enough fixed their attention on the holy will as
the centre of character; but they have mistakenly
sought to cultivate it apart from the natural objects for its exercise set for it in our constitution.
They have cultivated an other-worldliness, which
has sometimes made sad work of this. The result
has been as unsaintly as it is unlovely and un-
happy. And this might have been foreseen, for
such a notion was implicitly an imputation upon
the wisdom and goodness of God, who is the
author of our constitution and of the general
order of life. But the enlightened Christian recognizes that life is the field for our moral and
religious activity. He sees that all things must
work together to the building up of humanity.
Wealth, leisure, learning, culture, taste, art, and
a permanent subjection of physical forces are
needed to build man into his best estate. Hence

instead of denouncing them, with the ascetic, he seeks to bring them under moral control. They are the sources of temptation, to be sure, but to be without them in some measure is to be savages. The conditions, even of an ideal earthly life, exist as yet only to a very limited extent. The race must produce vastly more, and accumulate more, and acquire leisure for development in the upper ranges of existence, and subjugate nature also to human service, so that the drudgery of the race shall be done by cosmic forces. All this must come to pass before the kingdom of man can come upon the earth. And hence the wise Christian welcomes all these things. He looks upon each new discovery, each new invention, each conquest over nature, each subjugation of physical forces, each unloading of human drudgery upon muscles of steel, each extension of commerce, each advance of knowledge, each increased facility for living, as a veritable Baptist messenger before the face of humanity, declaring that the kingdom of man is at hand. To war against these things is to war against civilization and to be an emeny of the human race. In and through these things the Christian spirit manifests and realizes itself, as it labors for the upbuilding and perfecting of men.

And that this is so will appear at once if we

ask ourselves what we conceive to constitute an ideal human life. That would not be an ideal life, however well meaning or devout or consecrated the person might be, which involved disease, ignorance, narrowness, superstition, or the lack or atrophy of any of our powers. A mind which could not interest itself in truth or duty, which found the pursuit of knowledge tiresome, and had no high aspirations, such a mind could never be considered as other than atrophied or a case of arrested development. In God's dealing with such persons we can well believe in his pity, but we cannot believe that they represent his ideal of humanity. And if we should believe that such persons are always to remain in that condition, never emerging into the large and abundant life of knowledge, and the enjoyment of beauty, etc., it would be for us an unrelieved horror.

Thus it is plain that the great natural forms of life are the conditions of a large human life, and are included, therefore, in the divine plan for men. Least of all are they to be viewed as sinful or as the outcome of sin in any way. They are founded in our constitution and our relations to things, and will be necessary so long as this constitution remains, even if the millennium should come. If the millennium came to-morrow, the work of the world would have to go on just the same. All that would be eliminated would be the evil will and the results which flow from it. Education, trade, transportation, farming, mining, the manifold productive industries of the world, the administration of government, all would go on or civilization would perish. These are absolutely necessary conditions of any large human life, as we are at present constituted, and man could not be man without them. Not less trade is needed, but more conscience in the traders; not less production, but a finer spirit in both producers and consumers. We need not less knowledge or wealth or taste, but far more of all—but all of them used for the enlargement and upbuilding of men. God's will concerning us involves activity in all these lines, an activity beyond anything yet attained, but it also involves the subordination of all these activities to the spirit of love and righteousness; and the Christian spirit, instead of withdrawing from this life, is to move out into it and possess it, into the great institutions of humanity, the family, the school, the state, and build them into harmony with the will of God. Then the kingdom of God and the kingdom of man, which are essentially the same, will come.

Religion, we have said, was misled in this matter by the abstractions of theoretical ethics. Both fixed their attention on the holy will as the centre of the moral life. In this they were right; and it cannot be said that they over-emphasized the holy will, but rather that they under-emphasized the natural order of life as the great field of moral activity, and thus left the moral life without any proper object and field. In addition to this source of error, religion was further misled by misconceptions of its own. Salvation itself has largely been conceived in a selfish way as a means of escaping external danger; there was comparatively little desire after God, or after spiritual life, and equally little generous and magnanimous desire to work for and with God. Our native selfishness has won some of its greatest triumphs and made its most odious manifestations in its conception of salvation. A mistaken theology also helped to increase the delusion. The world was supposed to be hopelessly bankrupt, and nothing good could be made out of it. It was mortgaged to the devil, and he had foreclosed. The Church, on the other hand, was a kind of life-raft to save a few here and there from a sinking wreck, but there was little thought that this earth should be made one of the many mansions in the Father's house. Such a view was excusable at a time when the ancient civilization was decaying and the end of the world was supposed to be near, but it became pernicious as history wore on, and the end of the world was indefinitely postponed. It gave rise to the disastrous distinction between the religious and the secular, which has so fatally led men astray. Some things were supposed to belong to religion and some other things to the world, and religious duties could all be performed in a religious field, while secular duties owed little or no allegiance to God. In the Middle Ages this notion led to asceticism and monasticism, and we are by no means clear of it yet. Religion is still largely conceived as a specialty or as a detached movement, which has no gearing with life as a whole. It tends to withdraw itself from the secular, which it calls profane, and to carry on a set of formal rites or services in a vacuum, from which all every-day interests have been excluded. Hence it is no uncommon thing to find in religious circles an indifference to social and civic duties, on the ground of their unspirituality. And the tacit assumption is very general that the higher and finer virtues of character flourish only in holy retirement from life and its clamorous interests. In many circles wealth, intellect, culture, taste are disparaged, especially by those who lack them, as hostile to spiritual growth; and the very distinction of the religious from the secular illustrates or expresses the aberration of religious thought on this subject. Even now the most useful citizens

are not always church members. The men most
concerned for civic and social righteousness, the
men most concerned at social injustice and most
filled with the enthusiam for humanity are by no
means always in the churches — an instructive
illustration of the danger of this distinction. For
one who believes that this is God's world, it is
nothing less than blasphemy to hold such a view.
To hold that the study of God's world or of human society is to turn from God, or to hold that
the normal relations of life are defiling, is of the
same sort.

Now we escape these errors as soon as we
recognize that this is God's world, and that the
great normal forms and interests of life represent
his will and purpose. To think otherwise is to
assume that God did not know what he was doing when he made man and fitted up our earthly
home for the field of our development. The field
is the world; and this life is the means by which
he develops us, or the raw material which we are
to build to its ideal form. The deepest thought
of Christianity and the deepest aim are not salvation, but life, large, full, and abundant, lived,
however, in the filial spirit. This is the deepest
and essential thing. The forgiveness of sins is
essential, but it is only introductory. The forms
of worship and practices of piety are important,

but they are only instrumental. They are not the thing, and their significance consists entirely in what they help us to. The central thing is the recognition of the divine will in all life and the loyal purpose to make that will prevail in life; first of all in the hidden life of the spirit, and then in family life, in social life, in political life, in trade, in art, in literature, in every field of human interest and activity. Religion must be brought out of its abstraction by being brought into relation to every aspect of life. Its concern must be not to make men abstractly good or pious, but to make them concretely good in the complex relations and duties of actual life. The religious spirit must, indeed, have all fields for its own; at the same time we must remember that all that is normal to man has its place and justification in the divine purpose, and would appear in the realized kingdom of God upon earth.

The growing recognition of this fact is one of the good signs of the times. We are not very much concerned to-day about an abstract salvation, but we are concerned for a concrete salvation, which shall bring man into loving relations to God and which shall make human conditions and surroundings and all social forms an expression of righteousness and good-will. It is no longer the desire of man to rescue an occasional sinner here and there from a perishing world, but it is rather to lift that world itself into its ideal conditions. We seek to save the community, to make the social order just, to put away needless inequalities, to remove the obstacles to the development of humanity, to give every one a chance. We aim to set the earth to rights; we pray that God's kingdom may come, and we believe that this prayer commits us to the attitude of trying to make it come, by doing our best. We do not believe that this world is a sinking ship or an insolvent concern. We rather believe that God is in it, and will be in it until it shall be so transformed that we might properly speak of a new heaven and a new earth. We are not very much concerned, either, about abstract sin, but we are concerned about the concrete fact that there are people unwilling to do right and willing to do wrong, and we know that this fact is the great source of our sorrows and woes, and must be removed before the perfect can come. We believe that this earth may be made vastly better than it is, and this fact constitutes our obligation to make it better, and so we seek to work together with God to bring in the better day. The human world is nothing ready-made by God apart from our activity. We must work together with him. He gives us the possibility and leaves us to realize it, and when we set to work in this spirit we shall find that the kingdom will be well on its way. When the kingdom of God has fully come, there will be no grinding poverty, no guilty ignorance, no disease resulting from folly and sin, but there will be peace and blessing and fellowship and helpfulness everywhere.

From our point of view we further see that the Church is not the only institution of humanity or the only instrument through which God is working. It is but one instrument, and by no means the most important. The family, the state, the school, the great ordinance of labor, are also necessary. All of these institutions are of God's appointment, and through them God is working out his will concerning man. Each of these has a function which the Church cannot perform. And in comparison with any of these the Church, as the organization which concerns itself with religious worship, rites, and ordinances, is relatively insignificant. None of these institutions is perfect until it is possessed and pervaded by the Christian spirit, but that spirit in turn misses its own principal aim until it sees that the field is the world. And by world we mean such things as government, national and municipal, the great industries of society, the great professions, the courts of justice, the fine arts, the hospitals, the schools, the work of physical science and its application to life, the domestic economy of our homes, the daily work of all toilers, in short this great complex of secular activity which maintains the world from day to day and keeps society going. This is the field into which morals and religion are to move and control. Here they are to find their field ; and any institution, church or otherwise, that stands apart from this and condemns it as irreligious, or as having no significance for religion, is itself to be condemned as an enemy of God and man.

There is another factor in present thought which also makes for this view, and that is the immanence of God, or the view which regards God as present in all things, as the great administrator of the world, as being its continual source on whom all things forever depend and from whom they all proceed. Our occidental religion generally for many generations has been of a crude deistic type, with the conception of a self-running world and an absentee God. Nature was supposed to be made by God and set going in a kind of general way, so that the great mass of events represented no divine purpose but only a sort of by-product of the cosmic machine. The result was that God was perpetually on the point of vanishing, except as he showed his person by an occasional miracle now and then, just to let us know that he still lived. By consequence the presence of God was thought to be revealed only in strange and marvelous happenings, while the ordinary movement of life, the intuitions of conscience, the revelations of reason, the products of education and training, were thought to have no divine character whatever. Now this is passing away, and we are coming to take in strict literalness the words of Paul that in him we live and move and have our being, for he is not far from any one of us. By consequence we are finding God in the orderly movements of the world, in the administration of the laws he has made, in the purpose he has indicated, in the results of education and of all that can be wrought out through the use and application of the laws of things. Thus he works with us and through us to will and to do of his good pleasure, and thus the cosmic mechanism that for a long time was such a terror to many is becoming transformed with the divine presence and expresses a divine meaning.

I dream of a time when humanity shall come to its own, when physical nature shall be subdued to human service beyond all present conception, when want and disease shall have disappeared,

when the social order shall be an expresssion of
perfect justice, when the race shall be rich enough
to afford all its members the opportunity of a
truly human existence, when the bondage of physical drudgery shall have been taken off from human shoulders, when the treasures of knowledge
shall be a universal possession, and when over
against these external conditions there shall be
a moral spirit wise enough to use them and strong
enough to control them. Then the kingdom of
man and of God will have come. And to turn this
dream into a reality is the Christian programme,
the true meaning of the prayer, so often uttered
and so seldom understood, " Thy kingdom come;
Thy will be done in earth, as it is in heaven."

V

THE CHURCH AND MORAL PROGRESS

THE CHURCH AND MORAL PROGRESS

It is one of the paradoxes of our human life that some of our worst woes spring from our higher nature, and even from the moral and religious nature itself. Sympathy, without which there could be no society, is often a pronounced enemy of righteousness and the common good. Hence Kant declared all action springing from sympathy and similar emotions to be non-moral, as rooted in no moral insight and devotion. Conscience is often reactionary and obstructive, and all the more so as being conscientious. Not without reason has a French writer declared that " virtue is more dangerous than vice, as the excesses of virtue are subject to no restraints of conscience." An ordinary sinner may be restrained by considerations of humanity or public opinion, but Pharisaic fanaticism knows no bounds. And when this fanaticism is joined to religion, then we have all the conditions for the persecutions and religious wars which have covered the pages of history with infamy. Unless properly directed, virtue may indeed be more dangerous than vice.

Our more dreadful aberrations in this matter, we may believe, are past; but in minor forms the tendency of the moral nature to lose itself in mischievous reaction or obstruction still remains and needs to be guarded against. Perhaps we shall better understand the problem by taking a concrete case for illustration and guidance.

There was a prominent controversy in the primitive Church respecting meats offered to idols and the duty of Christians in the case. Many of the disciples brought with them their Jewish traditions about the matter and sought to impose them on the Church as of abiding obligation. The Gentile disciples, on the other hand, believed in greater freedom and held the Jewish tradition as no longer binding; and some of the more radical spirits would seem to have treated it with contempt. This naturally bred friction and misunderstanding and uncharity. St. Paul discusses the subject in two places, — in his letter to the Romans and in the first letter to the Corinthians.

This question in its special form has of course no interest for us except as illustrating our problem. This problem, which is perennial, is essentially the problem between conservative and progressive morality. It is the problem of changing

codes of conduct. It concerns, also, the measure
of individual liberty and individual subordination,
the extent to which the individual may assert his
own freedom, and the extent to which he shall
subordinate it out of consideration for others.
This problem continually emerges in social
changes. Old customs are outgrown. Traditions
become obsolete, new duties arise, and our concrete codes of conduct demand revision. Without
this revision conscience falls behind social and
intellectual development, and may even become
an enemy of truth and righteousness. And unless matters be rightly understood, there will be
indefinite confusion and friction. Virtue will be
made odious or ridiculous; and progress, being
made with violence and defiance, will lose much of
its blessing. Hence the interest and importance
of the old debate.

Likewise, Paul's decision of the specific case
has no longer any interest for us; but his mode
of treatment and the principles by which he
sought to solve it have abiding significance. As
to the meat question, he agrees with the disciples
of liberty. He says: An idol is nothing; and
hence meat offered to idols cannot be affected
thereby. He advises his readers to eat what is
sold in the market, or what is set before them by
their hosts, and be thankful. He adds: I know

and am persuaded in the Lord Jesus that nothing is unclean of itself. Neither will he allow
his liberty to be judged of another man's conscience, as a yoke to be imposed upon him from
without. But, on the other hand, if there be any
who have not attained to this insight and liberty,
they must follow their conscience; for if any one
thinketh anything to be unclean, to him it is
unclean; and he that doubteth is condemned if
he eat; because his action is not the freedom of
Christian insight, but the transgression of his
conscience.

But this is not the end of the matter. St. Paul
tries to lift the whole subject to a higher plane
and to view it in the light of principles. In the
first place he says: Let each man be fully persuaded in his own mind. This recognizes that
every one must be faithful to his own conscience.
At the same time this conscience is for himself
and not for another. Let us not, therefore, judge
one another any more. Judgment is not ours, for
we shall all stand before the judgment seat of
God. Instead of this mutual judging, let love
reign. The brother with weak conscience is apt
to condemn the brother who insists on liberty
and to view him as yielding to sin. But the
brother who insists on liberty is apt to set at
naught the weak brother and hold him in con-

tempt. But this also is a mistake; for none of us liveth to himself. We may not, therefore, walk uncharitably and with our freedom grieve or cause to stumble or destroy the brother for whom Christ died. Moreover, the kingdom of God is not eating and drinking in any case, but right-eousness and peace and joy in the Holy Ghost. The radical brother who insists on his freedom should remember this higher meaning of the kingdom. Likewise the brother of uneasy scruples should rise to this larger view. Finally, St. Paul proposes to both parties to consider the question in the light of a new principle: Whether, there-fore, ye eat or drink, or whatsoever ye do, do all to the glory of God.

Thus I have sketched St. Paul's two discus-sions of the topic. As said before, the special problem has no longer interest for us, except as it illustrates a perennial problem of society. Neither is St. Paul's particular decision of any interest to us, but only the principles which he brings to the discussion. The truth is that, ex-cept in the denial of any essential uncleanness in things offered to idols, St. Paul does not reach any decision. He only lays down the principles by which both parties should be guided. The discussion also is not between good and bad people, Christians and idolaters. If it had been, it could easily have been settled. It was rather between progressive and conservative Christians; and the problem of which this ancient debate was only a special case is, as I have said, the problem of progress and conservatism in morals, of the freedom and subordination of the individual. And these problems admit of no definite and final solution. They can be solved only approximately in any case; and no good result can be reached unless they are studied in the light of the Apostle's principles. These are: —

First. The sacredness of the individual's conscience for himself.

Second. The duty of charity toward others who differ from us.

Third. The duty of subordinating life and liberty to love and the glory of God.

The problem in question arises naturally from the form of our moral development. The only thing that is fixed and absolute in morals is the good will and the will to do right. The law of love and the loyalty to what we conceive to be right are of absolute and inalienable obligation. No outside authority and no conceivable change of circumstances can absolve us from this central and basal duty. But this does not tell us what is to be done in any particular case. It only reveals the spirit in which we should live. What this spirit demands in the actual circumstances of life is not decided, and remains a problem for wisdom and experience to solve. Thus a physician may love the patient as himself, but that does not reveal the mode of treating the disease. The legislator may be impartially devoted to the public good, but that does not insure wise legislation. For this he must have practical wisdom, a knowledge of human nature, of social needs, of economic laws, of the political situation. The philanthropist may have the Golden Rule for his motto, and he could not well have a better; but this alone will not reveal how to deal with the problem of public charity. For this he needs not merely a soft heart, but also a hard and wise head, well furnished with knowledge of human nature and social problems and conditions. The physician, the legislator, the philanthropist, who are furnished only with good intentions, are not likely to be useful people, however well they may mean or however good they may be. The concrete code is a function of knowledge as well as of good intentions. If our action is to be wise, it must be adjusted to reality and the present conditions of things. Hence it must vary with knowledge and also with social development.

In these illustrations we see clearly that in

concrete action there are two factors: the moral intention and motive, and a judgment based on reflection and the indications of experience. And the same is true for all practical codes. They have the same double aspect, the moral intention and the judgment of wisdom. They are no original intuition of conscience, but the slowly built-up result of generations of life and experience. The moral nature itself is slowly developed, and the practical insight whereby it reaches the best form of conduct is developed more slowly still. Throughout this development men may be moral, in the sense that they act from moral principles; but owing to their lack of knowledge, both of the inner and outer world, they attain only to very imperfect codes; just as physicians, while always aiming at the cure of the patient, because of ignorance have fallen into great errors of practice.

Now this general fact has for its result that our codes of conduct are no fixed quantities, but are ever undergoing change. The elementary duties, of course, are abiding; but on the outer edges of expanding life change will always be going on. With the growth of knowledge, the increase of experience, the clearer indication of tendencies, there will be a change of judgment as to what should be done or left undone. Some things thought harmful will be found harmless. Some things thought harmless will be found pernicious. Social customs will be modified to meet new conditions. Business practices will be adjusted to public policy or the common good. With the deepening of spiritual insight, also, many things thought essential to religion will be seen to be indifferent; and other things which may have been overlooked will be lifted into perpetual obligation. Thus our codes of life, our social customs, our personal habits, our political practices, are always undergoing criticism in a living community, and are slowly being adjusted to growing knowledge and experience. In this way a great improvement in our codes has been brought about within the historical period, and even within recent years. We need look back only a hundred years to find great advance in Christian codes. The saints of a century ago would hardly be tolerated to-day. Distinguished saints owned distilleries and defended the slave trade. Lotteries were used for the endowment of colleges and the building of churches, but now they are outlawed. Religion has been purified and rationalized, social customs ameliorated, laws humanized, and the empire of conscience has been extended over larger and larger fields of life. We may have no better intentions than our ancestors, and in that sense may be no more moral; but we are wiser, and our codes and customs are better adjusted to life and reality.

And a second result of this fact of development is that there will always be a border of conduct concerning which good men are not agreed. They will all agree that the right thing should be done, but they will differ concerning the thing to do. Some will cling to habit, to custom, to tradition, and will view any departure therefrom with suspicion and alarm. Others, more adventurous, will wish to try the new and to improve the old. Or some with scanty experience and narrow outlook will have no sense of the need of readjustment, and will look upon the demand for it as an expression of lawlessness and disloyalty to the truth. Others of larger life and outlook will feel the inadequacy of the old and the need that it yield to the new as a better expression of the truth.

There would be no objection to this opposition if it were ruled by the spirit of charity. It would then be simply the opposition of conservatism and progress, each of which is needed to keep the other sane and sweet. Without the criticism by conservatism, progress would be unsteady and flighty. And without the criticism by progress, conservatism would slumber in ignorance and sloth. Unfortunately, the matter is not always understood, and charity is often wanting. From lack of understanding the difference is commonly supposed to be a moral one, whereas it is only a difference of judgment as to what is wise in the case. From failure to understand the derived and developed nature of codes, also, the conservative is apt to regard the traditional code as an absolute deliverance of conscience or a revelation from God. Thus the code itself is sanctified as something inviolably sacred, and its critics are made to appear as the enemies of God and righteousness. In this way the authority of God and conscience has been invoked for numberless crudities, imbecilities, and iniquities, and has been made one of the mainstays of political and ecclesiastical oppression. In the larger questions of political and ecclesiastical progress, the untaught and sophisticated conscience has been one of the great obstacles. The divine right of kings, the passive obedience of subjects, the sin of resisting authority, no matter how iniquitous it might be, especially the sin of criticising ecclesiastical authority, the depravity of thinking critically about religious teaching, — all these things have been stoutly insisted upon in the name of God and conscience. In minor matters the same way of thinking has produced a rich variety of

grotesque and artificial notions, which are supposed to be the very gist of morality. Styles of
clothing, forms of speech, social customs, have
been insisted upon, which at best were justifiable
only as temporary reactions against conditions
then existing, but which for the most part were
merely expressions of their authors' ignorance,
poverty, lack of social outlook and spiritual insight. And on this pitiable basis they have often
fallen into Pharisaism and spiritual pride and uncharity beyond anything possible to an ordinary
sinner.

One readily sees that when this dual origin of
concrete codes is overlooked or unsuspected,
conscience may easily become an enemy of progress and even of humanity. Current thought in
religion, current customs in society, even current
whims in our particular sect, are invested with
inviolable sacredness; and the tithing of mint,
anise, and cummin takes its place along with the
weightiest matters of the law. Then the whole
force of the moral and religious nature is invoked
to defend some caricature of good sense or to
justify some hoary folly and iniquity. Such facts
give color to Mr. Mill's claim that the appeal to
conscience is an appeal from reason to prejudice
and superstition. This is true of the conventional
social conscience which, as just said, has often

been the bulwark of blind conservatism and oppression. In such cases the appeal should be not
only to conscience but to science, political economy, and social philosophy as well.

Mr. Mill's claim is still truer of the ecclesiastical conscience, which is very often arbitrary and
artificial. In Russia it is a question with this conscience whether to make the sign of the cross
with two fingers or three. The same kind of conscience is strong on the sanctity of saints' days,
and finds in the cremation of the dead, which is
purely a question of sanitary science, a denial
of the resurrection. What would become of the
"noble army of martyrs" in that case is left un-
decided. Religious casuistry which is not based
on universal rational morality is sure to fall into
whims of this sort. Artificial commands are given
the sanction of eternal principles; and failure to
observe some ecclesiastical regulation is viewed
as worse than a violation of justice or good-will
or any ordinary crime. A striking peculiarity of
these artificial duties is that they are very apt to
overtop the genuine. When one gets to tithing
mint, anise, and cummin, the weightier matters of
the law are likely to be overlooked. The rank and
file of any religious body which has made an artificial issue are pretty sure to regard the rites and
customs which have grown out of it as of more

sacred obligation than the moral law. I recall the case of a man who had been brought up on the notion of the impiety of singing hymns. Once, at the bedside of a dying friend who wished a hymn sung, he consented to start the tune, as no one else present could do it. But his conscience so smote him that he afterward said he felt worse than if he had stolen a horse — a statement which, from my experience with this type of conscience, I am inclined to think was true.

Pseudo-spirituality abounds in this sort of thing in more or less striking forms, and the result is to produce a narrow and sophisticated type of piety, which is very often followed by revolt when the fiction is seen through. One of the most dangerous pieces of mental furniture for an otherwise well-meaning youth, in the present temper of thought, is a conscience which has been sophisticated by this sort of moral teaching. For it is likely to be seen through sooner or later, and then the suspicion will naturally arise that the rest of the teaching is of the same arbitrary sort. And if it is not seen through, the result is even worse. In that case a Pharisaic censoriousness is commonly generated, which is odious alike to God and man. Another result of this pseudo-spirituality is to make religion contemptible in the eyes of all who have some sense of reality

and of the real issues of life. There is a strong
and growing impatience among thoughtful persons with religious pettiness. There is a demand
that religion shall justify itself by a large and
sympathetic grasp of life and by corresponding
effort among the real issues of society. Selfishness,
animalism, thoughtlessness, ignorance, — these
are the things to be combated. Personal integrity,
civic honor and devotion, love in the family, and
justice and good-will in the community, — these
are the things to be secured. And when one is
concerned with these things, with the real kingdom of God which is to be brought in, one
cannot escape a feeling of anticlimax and of insufferable pettiness when confronted with these
artificial issues.

Every one acquainted with ecclesiastical history knows how much of this artificial morality
and pseudo-spirituality there has been in the
Church. And for this state of affairs there is no
speedy cure. Cure must be a vital process, involving the growth of intelligence and the clarifying
of the moral vision. It will help, however, if we
remember that our codes of conduct must vary
with growing knowledge, and that there will always be an indefinite frontier where good men
may differ as to what should be done, without

any prejudice to the sincerity of their moral purpose. Many moral problems are indeterminate in themselves. Thus, who can sharply define what spirituality implies? or mark off in clear outline the exhaustive code of the religious life? Of course the thing is impossible, for this life is a spirit rather than a code, and can never be exhaustively expressed in rules. Again, as soon as we get away from the routine of daily life, the thing to be done is not easily discerned, and good men may and do differ in their judgments.

It will equally help in solving this problem if we recognize the absolute legitimacy of the life that now is, and of all its normal impulses, instincts, interests, and activities. Any legislation is to be condemned which stigmatizes as common or unclean anything which belongs to normal human life; and any such legislation is dangerous which aims to reach a higher spirituality in any other way than by faithfully abiding in the work of life, and by the constant reference of that life to the will of God. The aim of religion is not only to get men to go to church and pray, but also, and much more fundamentally, to make men conscious of the divine will and presence in life, until the world shall become God's temple, in which men perpetually offer up the daily life, with all its interests and activities pervaded and

sanctified by the filial spirit, as their spiritual
worship of God. It was oversight of this fact
which led to the fearful blunders of asceticism
and its monastic outcome. A secret failure to
appreciate this fact underlies the popular identi-
fication of religion with formal rites of worship.
But whatever ascetic renunciation or disciplin-
ary rigor may be possible for a time, or in small
bodies, it is certain that no religious organization
will become general, or long command the lives
of men, which is not as broad as humanity itself.
Narrower conceptions may serve for a time,
and may even seem justified in their origin, as
revolts or protests against a prevailing looseness
or indifference; but even then it may be doubted
whether they do not cost all they are worth by
the time we are done with them.

The Church as a whole has been prone to unwisdom in this regard. It has taken John the
Baptist, the austere and ascetic dweller in the
desert, for its model, rather than the Master,
who came eating and drinking, who knew what
was in man, and who moved about among the
humanities of life, sharing in them, sympathiz-
ing with them, and looking upon them with so
loving an eye as to give place and point to the
charge that he was a glutton and a wine-bibber,
a friend of publicans and sinners. And the Church

will not become the Church of Humanity until it finds a holy place for all the interests of humanity.

Thus we see that the problem in the primitive Church about Jewish feasts and eating meat offered to idols is only a special case of a general problem inherent in the very form of our human life. And now we are ready to apply Paul's principles to its solution.

First, let every man be fully persuaded in his own mind and obey his own conscience. To be sure, conscience is far from infallible, and the conscience of many men is a very curious organ; but such as it is every man must obey it. He must do the thing which to him seems right. He may be mistaken; a broader knowledge might change his mind; but so long as anything seems to him right, he must be loyal to it, no matter who differs from him. If, then, there be any social customs of which he disapproves, he must avoid them; and if there be anything not recognized as duty by society, but clearly presented as such to him, that one thing he must do. No power in heaven or in earth can absolve him from obedience to his convictions of right.

But this conscience is his own, not another's. He may recommend his view to others; he may give reasons for the faith that is in him; but when he insists on imposing it on others he may be assuming a knowledge which he does not possess; and when he concludes that those who differ from him are morally unfaithful, he then assumes a knowledge of the heart which he cannot possess and falls into Pharisaic uncharity. For most of these questions which lie in the field of moral change and progress cannot be settled by talking or by any short process whatever. They often involve profound changes of opinion, mental illumination, changes of personal habit and social usage; and these things are not brought about in a day. Only a person entirely ignorant of the world and life would dream of effecting such changes by a syllogism or an exhortation. Every other person knows that such processes are agelong in duration; every other person knows the entire futility of impatience and browbeating and denunciation in hastening the result; and every other person also knows that until that which is perfect is come, good men will be found on both sides of such questions. It may be from defective knowledge, from insufficient reflection, from one-sided sympathy; but whatever the cause, the fact will long exist.

Now in such a state of affairs we must apply the Apostle's first rule, let every one be fully persuaded in his own mind; and also his second rule, charity of judgment. Who art thou that judgest another? To his own master he shall stand or fall. This second rule is the one most frequently violated in this matter. Reformers especially are not content with having a conscience for themselves and with seeking by rational means to brings others to the same mind, but they denounce those who differ from them, and thus injure their own cause and bring themselves into contempt. The history of reform and reformers is a sad and shocking exhibition of the weakness of good men in this respect. Bitter and violent denunciation takes the place of a good example, temperate reasoning, and gracious charity. Or minor matters are magnified into supreme importance; and a strange blindness to proportion and the relative importance of things is induced, which, when it becomes chronic, is incurable. Thus the reformers themselves get by the ears and waste a large part of their energy in fighting and denouncing one another, instead of combining against the common foe.

This second rule of the Apostle, charity in judging one another, we greatly need to lay to heart. The lack of it is a crying scandal to all good people and one great obstacle to moral progress. We all have known, we all know, of

reforms which are very important to society and
in which every good man must be profoundly interested, which nevertheless have been carried on
with such uncharity and unscrupulousness, with
such practical unwisdom and ignorance of human
nature, as to defeat themselves, or at least most
seriously to thwart themselves. And the conviction is becoming general that nothing will ever
be done until these unwise leaders are cashiered
and replaced by others of more practical insight.

Of course if we postpone reform until it is
done just right, we shall never get it. Even good
things are rarely done in an ideal way ; and the
weakest of all weak beings is the person of such
exquisite taste that he cannot abide any reform
because of the rude and uncultured and unæs-
thetic character of the reformers. But it is equally
sure that we shall get reform a great deal sooner
if we learn charity and eschew malignant philan-
thropy, and have our conscience for ourselves
and allow others to have a conscience for themselves, and penetrate to the unity of the spirit
which may exist behind all diversity of judgment
and custom.

St. Paul himself was on the side of liberty.
He was not willing to have his liberty judged of
another man's conscience. He was quite willing

that another should have a conscience for himself, but not for him. He finds, however, a limitation in the law of love. Hence while all things are lawful, all things may not be expedient. Christian love and wisdom must be considered in the use of our freedom. All recognize this. Thus the truth may rightly be spoken, but he would be a very thoughtless or ignorant person who did not see that wisdom must control our freedom even here. Not all and every truth is adapted to every person and circumstance, and it would be easy to misuse our freedom in this respect so as by our truth to cause to stumble some weak brother for whom Christ died. As good and wholesome food may be destructive when the stomach is unfitted for it, so truth itself might be destructive for one whose mind was not prepared for its reception. Again, love is higher than liberty; and I must not for the sake of liberty needlessly cause any brother to stumble. Liberty apart from love is apt to become uncharitable and contemptuous and as bigoted as bigotry itself. But these considerations are not rules which give definite guidance; they are rather principles in the light of which we are to act, and which each one is to apply for himself. No one can give law to another in this respect; no one can prescribe to another how far for love's sake he shall yield his own liberty; least of all may the weak brother himself have a voice in the decision.

This matter of the weak brother has been very much misunderstood. In deciding what is right or wrong in itself, the weak brother cannot be considered at all. This is a question purely of truth and right reason. To declare obligatory, out of regard for the weak brother, something which is not obligatory, is false and dangerous. It makes ignorance and prejudice and weakness, rather than the truth of things, the ground of legislation. It produces an artificial and fictitious code which is sure to produce revolt when it is seen through. It obscures the eternal obligations of justice and righteousness by petty fussiness about the tithing of mint, anise, and cummin. Now this is undue deference to the weak brother, and must never be allowed. St. Paul would not admit that an idol was anything, or that meats offered to idols were damaged thereby, or that there was anything unclean in itself. He would not needlessly offend, but he would not conceal the truth. And this is as far as Christian wisdom allows us to go. In the confusion of this human world it must needs be that offenses come, but in the long run the truth is the line of least resistance and of fewest offenses. Weak brethren abound on all sides of every question. If one is offended by the enlargement of liberty, another is offended by its limitation. Defect is as dangerous as excess. Only the truth is safe, and only the truth makes free. The weak brother, then, is not to be considered at all in deciding the questions of essential right and wrong; but he is to be taken into account in the use of our freedom. We must not walk uncharitably, but in Christian wisdom and love. But the weak brother himself may never prescribe the measure of consideration to be given to his notions. That would simply encourage him in his whims and make him a still greater nuisance. He needs to be told the truth about himself now and then, lest he remain in error; and the truth is that he has mistaken his own ignorant notions for universal principles; and the probability is that he has confounded his native conceit and pugnacity with zeal for the kingdom of God.

The problems are indeterminate. The principles given show the spirit in which we should deal with them, but they give no final solution. The application must be made by each for himself and at his own risk. Each stands or falls to his own Master. St. Paul himself manifestly felt the impossibility of any hard-and-fast decision; and he leaves the matter with a final suggestion designed to change the entire point of view. He says the kingdom of God is not eating or drinking, but righteousness and peace and joy in the Holy Ghost, and he urges his readers to give up haggling and wrangling about eating and drinking and fast days, and make the glory of God the principle of all their living. All things, therefore, whatsoever ye do, whether ye eat or drink, do all to the glory of God. Thus the apostle sought to bring them to an insight into the spiritual nature of obedience, which should vacate their discussions by revealing a higher principle. God looketh at the heart. He takes account only of that; and if that be right, he accepts or overlooks all the rest. A life of scruples is always weak; and there is no end to them, if we allow them to begin. Scruples beget scruples and grow upon scruples until the moral life itself is lost in a Pharisaic casuistry to which there is no end. The only remedy is to reject this method of mechanical rule and scruple altogether, and simply seek to live in the love of God and man. This is the true and only law of Christian living.

To covet earnestly the best things for men is the Church's great obligation. Whatsoever things are just and true and lovely and gracious and pure and helpful are to be secured in the largest possible measure. Nothing is to be held or cherished because it is old, but because it is true and helpful. Nothing is to be held because it is new, but because it is true and helpful. As soon as a better is assuredly in sight, the old, no matter how good, must go. With this principle firmly grasped and with the faith that this is God's world, the Church would take its place, where it really belongs, at the head of all the forces in life that make at once for social permanence and social progress.

VI

THE CHURCH AND THE TRUTH

THE CHURCH AND THE TRUTH

To the question, What is the relation of the
Church to the truth? one might reply by quoting
the text, " The Church of the Living God, the pillar and ground of the truth." And then another,
with some knowledge of ecclesiastical history,
might be led to inquire, Is this so? Possibly the
statement might be maintained for old and accepted truth, but what of new truth? St. Stephen,
addressing some orthodox people of his time, said:
" Ye stiff-necked, and uncircumcised in heart and
ears, ye do always resist the Holy Ghost: as your
fathers did, so do ye. Which of the prophets
have not your fathers persecuted? and they have
slain them which showed before of the coming of
the Just One; of whom ye have been now the
betrayers and murderers." And one acquainted
with history might with equal truth address the
Church, considered as an ecclesiastical organization, and say: Which of the prophets has not the
Church persecuted? What new truth is there
that the Church has not opposed? What mental
or moral or social or political progress is there

that the Church has not protested against; and what tyranny or oppression is there that the Church has not espoused and supported? Consider the present relation of Greek or Roman orthodoxy to human progress, political, intellectual, or religious. Who expects to find either of these churches, as an organization, in sympathy with progressive movements. And consider also the attitude of many Protestant bodies to those larger ideas which advancing thought and study are forcing upon us, and which have long been the property of educated and impartial minds. Whether in government, or in humanity, or in morals, or in social forms and religious thinking, the most bitter and determined enemy of progress has been the ecclesiastical organization. About this there can be no question. The facts look out of myriad pages of history and make up many of its blackest infamies. Are they not written in the books of the Chronicles by Buckle, by Draper, by Lecky, by White, and many another? Clearly in the light of such facts we cannot call the Church the pillar and ground of the truth without very great limitations.

This question, however, cannot be discussed to edification by partisan defenses or by hysterical belaborings. As a matter of fact the Church has commonly lagged behind the intellect of the

time and very often behind the progressive conscience of the time; so much so that orthodoxy
has frequently been a synonym for ignorance,
dullness, narrow-mindedness, and narrow-hearted-
ness generally. The intelligent Christian should
know this fact, and he should also know how it
comes to be a fact, so that he may finally know
how to deal with it and remove the scandal.

The fact itself is the outcome of various causes
which are deep-seated in the order of our human life,
and which produce analogous effects in other fields
as well as in religion. This we now proceed to show.

The human world is an evolving one; and in
such a world both permanence and progress are
alike necessary. If there were no permanence we
should have simply chaos, and if there were no
progress we should be confined to a social monotony which would be destructive. These two
elements may be called the conservative and the
progressive, and their necessity in normal society
under human conditions is manifest.

If society developed normally these two factors would go side by side, and there would be
no friction. Permanence would hold fast all that
is good, and conserve whatever of value has been
gained in human experience. The progressive
element, on the other hand, would remember that

the permanent element merely conserves whatever has been gained, and would point out that in changing human conditions it is necessary to adapt society to those conditions. Thus it would seek to produce the adaptation, and keep society adjusted to its circumstances. Unfortunately, this is seldom the case in actual life. We have an excess of permanence or we have an excess of the critical and progressive element, and the result is that human development is very often accompanied by a great deal of friction. Permanence becomes monotony, as in China; or progress becomes lawlessness and anarchy, as not infrequently happens.

Both elements, then, tend to be caricatured in life. We find in society, for example, vested interests becoming indifferent to justice and humanity, unwilling to make any progress and resisting it with all their might. But, on the other hand, we find wild reformers without any sense of social continuity, and unaware of the complex interests of society, who suppose that anything can be brought about to order by law. Tennyson thus describes them, —

> Men loud against all forms of power,
> Unfurnished brows, tempestuous tongues,
> Expecting all things in an hour,
> Brass mouths and iron lungs.

We find the same caricature in the world of thought. It is evident to every one who thinks, that habit takes the place of thought with the great majority of people. Of course this must be the case with children. They live necessarily by the community intellect. They assent to the ideas about them. Instead of understanding them, they rather catch them by a sort of social contagion. The same thing is true to a large extent of persons of mature growth. They also live by the community intellect. They are averse to the labor and the pain of thinking. Indeed, they are unable to think. Instinct and imitation, fixed in custom and habit, are the only safe guide in this stage of development. Another source of mental inertia is self-interest. A new thought very often demands readjustment of life and conduct, and cannot be admitted without bringing far-reaching consequences with it. All such thoughts are sure to be resisted. Two sorts of people are always conservative. The crass obstinacy and inertia of stupidity will be found in the conservative camp as a matter of course. The conservatism of self-interest is equally intelligible. The former is impervious to new ideas, perhaps congenitally; the latter adjusts beliefs, not to truth, but to desired ends. If necessary, new ideas can always be kept out in one way or another. A Hindoo, according to Macaulay, was once setting forth the sin of destroying animal life and insisting on the duty of a vegetable diet. Some one showed him his vegetable diet under a microscope, but the Hindoo managed the matter, not by changing his diet, but by smashing the microscope.

On the other hand, the progressive element tends to draw to itself various undesirable people, not merely those who are seeking for new truth, but flighty persons, persons who insist on thinking for themselves before they have learned to think at all. And thus the progressive camp tends to become a sort of cave of Adullam. It would be very desirable if these two elements, the conservative and the progressive, could be united in the same persons, who seek at once to prove all things and to hold fast all that is good. In society they would recognize the things of permanent value in our inheritance from the past, and would conserve them with all energy, but they would also recognize that the world is moving, that we are entering upon new social conditions, and that the social order must be adjusted to correspond. In the thought world the same persons would recognize that the thoughts of men are widened with the process of the suns, and they would seek to retain the truth of the old and also keep their minds open for new truths from every quarter.

If this were done we should then have a peaceful progress. Instead of having society divided into two rather hostile camps, we should have the two factors of permanence and progress united, and progress would be by evolution, and not by revolution. Or it would proceed by organic unfolding from within, instead of being mechanically imposed from without.

Thus in the nature of human development we find provision for conservatism in the instincts, habits, imitation, and inertia which underlie society. Without these society could never begin, to say nothing of maintaining itself. Religion, too, by its nature tends to conservatism, at least in its earlier stages. Indeed, that fixity of custom which was the first condition of emerging from savagery seems to have been primarily of a religious nature. The safety of the tribe and its success in any of its enterprises were bound up with a species of religious orthodoxy ; and the tribe had to defend this orthodoxy at all hazards. In more developed times religion becomes more wisely conservative, but remains conservative still. The consciousness of having truths of supreme importance makes religion jealous of any departure from them in the realm of thought, and equally opposed to attacks on the social order. Hence the enemies of society have commonly found in the Church one of their most determined opponents. It is not until a high degree of intellectual and moral development has been reached that the Church becomes a factor of progress as well as one of permanence. In the religious history of the race, religion has commonly been opposed to progress.

Conservatism, we have seen, is rooted in human nature; it becomes still more deeply rooted in institutions. Our native conservatism does not reach its full strength until it has embodied itself in institutions. These abide, and by their continued presence give law to life and thought. The institution by its very nature is conservative, and equally so are the managers. All rulers and administrators have a natural interest in maintaining the existing order. They are used to it; they know how to work it. Besides, they often have an inside knowledge which the outsider lacks, and they see there are more things to be considered than the newspaper critic suspects. This broader knowledge and the sense of responsibility tend to conservatism. It is often remarked that Lord Morley, who, as John Morley, wrote a book denouncing " Compromise," has become notably considerate since he became Secretary for India and a member of the Upper House. But in any case " fear of change perplexes monarchs," large and small. They lie snug and safe in the harbor, and dread the risks of the open and unknown sea. They resent change and dread it. They are full of old saws about " bearing the ills we have " rather than " flying to others that we know not of." And these considerations apply to religious institutions and organizations as well as to political and social ones. And thus arises a new danger to the truth. The single eye, without which there is no light, is often replaced by the evil eye, and then the whole body is full of darkness.

This fact is abundantly illustrated in religious institutions. Custom, rite, tradition, all organize in the religious community as a matter of course, and any departure from them easily appears as irreligious and destructive. Then, again, there is a tendency in all organizations to fall into the hands of men of a certain type, and to be warped from their essential aim and nature by various subordinate factors. Thus political parties tend to fall into the hands of bosses, and government tends to fall into the hands of inferior men, and in all organizations a certain poor type of man often comes to the front. The same is seen in ecclesiastical organizations when they become at all extended. Men of mediocre intellect and sub-mediocre character, but having a certain man-

aging quality and a considerable regard for the
loaves and fishes, become unpleasantly prominent. It is not easy in any such body to put
the best men in power, men of the highest intellect and highest character. Such men commonly have opinions and principles, and therefore
are not the most pliable people, and are often
distasteful to persons of quality, especially of opposite quality. And when the inferior men are
brought to the front, then lower interests become
prominent. The financial aspects of religion are
brought forward and emphasized. The value of
place likewise becomes significant, and we tend
to have men in prominence who have very little
interest in the truth as such, but rather in maintaining the present order, in securing position
and the perquisites of religious place. In the old
temple an authority on the subject declared that
this had resulted in changing the house of prayer
into a den of thieves. The money-changers and
the sellers of doves and the makers of shrines for
the temple were unpleasantly prominent in the
old days, and their descendants are still with us.
Even these people have their place and function,
but they are not fit to be rulers in the temple.
St. Demetrius, who knew that " by this craft we
have our wealth," is their patron saint. Such persons are always thoroughly orthodox. They have

no interest in the truth, but they have an interest in the organization, and in what can be made out of it. And hence they are averse to change and they will resist change, even if it be progress, by all the means in their power. So it has been, so it is, and so it will be until human nature has very much improved. And this is a fact which we need always to bear in mind when we seek to combine religious progress with religious permanence. We must observe that the organization itself, unless we carefully guard it, tends to become an enemy of the truth. Obsolete traditions, worn-out notions, antiquated customs, are elevated into things of eternal obligation, and change is resisted either from what we have called the crass obstinacy of ignorance, or else from the interested obstinacy of self-seekers. This is especially the case with state churches and with all great ecclesiastical organizations. One cannot follow the present ecclesiastical war against modernism without perceiving that much more than the simple love for the truth is in play and in evidence.

This study of the natural history of conservatism shows that the problem of conservatism and progress is not a simple one. Both elements are important and both are justified; but in the confusion and complexity of human life both are often allied with unworthy agencies that discredit them. It is, then, the problem for the wise man to hold fast all that is good, and at the same time keep an open mind for all new truth or needed change. He must be able to read history, and he must also be able to discern the signs of the times. He must look both before and after. A man with eyes only in the back of his head will certainly make a poor guide; and a man who ignores the past will be no better. The problem, then, is complex, and there will always be a point where discussion is going on and where there will be a division of opinion until events have clearly declared themselves.

The great instrument of progress in all fields is discussion and criticism. Society roots back in human instincts and impulses, which of themselves set us going and give life a certain form on their own account. We could not dispense with these, but they never make anything perfect. Man's instinctive life and its habits and products all need revision by intelligence before they can be finally approved. This is true alike of the physical, the mental, the social, and the political life of man. There must be testing criticism and discussion of the past, in order to see what is to be kept and what is to be improved or set aside. The present is preëminently a period of this kind. At last we are beginning to take an inventory of our inheritance, with the aim of rationally appraising it. We are beginning to apply intellect to the problems of life and society more systematically and comprehensively than ever before. The laws of health are being studied and applied; the problems of disease are being attacked with unprecedented vigor; social and economic laws are being investigated with unexampled precision; and the social order itself is subjected to thorough scrutiny. Of course this critical activity extends to religion also, in all its forms and doctrines. This movement, of course, will meet with ignorant and interested opposition, but nothing but good can come of it, if it is conducted in the right spirit. Knowledge will be enlarged, old diseases will be driven away, social injustice will be diminished, beclouding superstitions will disappear, and life will become broad and sane and joyous.

But here we are met by the fancy that the Christian religion at least is not subject to this critical movement or law of progress. In the Bible we have the truth once for all delivered unto the saints; and thus the truth becomes a constant quantity, with no variableness or shadow of turning. Macaulay once said, mischievously or otherwise, "Theology is not a progressive science"; and certainly a great many could be found to agree with him for the reason just given.

This, however, is purely a product of closet thinking, as a look into Christian history shows. There is a certain constancy or continuity in Christian thought, and there is also a great deal of change. Provision is made for this fact in the distinction between a doctrine and the mode of conceiving it. In some sense Christian doctrines remain what they always have been, and we can find the fundamentals of the faith in the earliest creeds. But in some other sense we find our modes of conceiving these doctrines exceedingly various. Thus no one would conceive the divine sovereignty to-day as was done two centuries ago. Similarly, the doctrines of inspiration, atonement, moral retribution, are very differently conceived now from what they were then. It is in this way that provision is made for combining fixed doctrines with a changing world. The doctrines remain the same, sometimes the words remain the same, but the conceptions vary from one generation to another, from one person to another, and even from one stage to another in the life of the same person. The contents we put into a doctrine, or our way of thinking of it, necessarily vary with our own mental and moral development. In the very nature of the case this cannot be escaped. An old scholastic maxim has it, " Whatever is received, is received according to the nature of the receiver." Which means simply that our understanding of things depends upon our mental make and mental stage. We have had the Bible with us now for many hundreds of years, but there has been a most distressing slowness in understanding it. Its spiritual doctrines have been warped and distorted into some likeness of the student, and manifestly the fact could not be otherwise. A glance at the history of interpretation shows how men have read their own notions into the Bible. It is plain, then, that the possession of the Bible in no way removes the fact that this is a changing world in religious thought as well as in other things.

We have before pointed out, what every educated person knows, that the Church very frequently falls behind the intellect of the educated community and appears as an enemy of truth, or as something reactionary and hostile to knowledge. If the Church could have had its way, modern civilization would never have developed, and humanity would have been ruined. We should have been living in filth and squalor and superstition and intellectual abjectness of every kind. The Church saves the world ; and the world saves the Church. Only the instinctive and irresistible impulse of human nature, whereby it has vindicated its own rights, has saved humanity from destruction by religion. This intellectual backwardness of the Church is nothing less than a calamity to religion, because it begets and continues the notion that religion is essentially a thing of inferior intellect, and that it is afraid to come out into the open field of the world where plain secular daylight shines, and be tested. This notion is something seriously to be deplored. It tends to produce a separation between the educated intellect and the religious world, which is of damage to both.

So far as conservatism rests on ignorance and selfish interests, this intellectual scandal cannot be speedily removed; but so far as it has a genuine rational root and interest, much could be done toward the removal of the scandal by simplifying Christian teaching. We should reduce the fundamental Christian doctrines to a statement of what we conceive the essential Christian facts to be, and should distinguish these, as facts to be proclaimed, from the various conceptions or theories of these facts, which make up the bulk of so-called doctrine. Such statement might run somewhat as follows: I believe in God the Father Almighty, and in Jesus Christ his Son

our Lord. I believe in the Holy Spirit, in the forgiveness of sins, in the kingdom of God on earth,
and in the life everlasting. Let this be the Christian platform; and for our programme let that
run, Thy kingdom come. Thy will be done on
earth as it is in heaven. It is perfectly plain that
this platform contains in principle all that is essential to Christianity; and that all who stand on
this platform and work for this programme are
in the truest sense of the word Christians. It is
equally plain that this platform would command,
with scantiest exception, the assent of all the
churches.[1] This is the true continuity of Christian
thought, the same yesterday, to-day, and forever.
This is the true faith received everywhere and
by all. This is the true orthodoxy, and the only
thing that should be called orthodoxy. All else
is theology, perhaps good, but in any case relatively unimportant, and in most cases absolutely
unimportant. For the victories of Christianity
have been and always will be won on this platform. It is by these mighty conceptions that we
triumph; and it is by bringing them into the

---

[1] This is not meant to imply that no other churches are Christian, but only that all churches that stand on this platform are
in the most orthodox sense Christian. When it comes to practical Christianity, the essential thing is not naming the name, but
doing the will; and when it is a question of membership in the
kingdom, nothing is decisive but the affinities of the spirit.

minds and lives of men that we spread the gospel, the good news of God. And against the Christian programme there can be equally no objection. The aim is not to build up an ecclesiastical hierarchy, or a churchly domination, but to do God's will on earth as it is done in heaven. Against this there is no law and no opposition, except from the selfish side of our nature. This programme commands the assent of every lover of men in the Church or out of it. It has been the dream of every good man from the beginning and is the dream of every good man to-day. Finally, it is clear that no one standing on this platform and working on this programme will ever get far or dangerously astray. Here the pragmatic test comes in with decisive effect. The vital interest in the kingdom of God will perpetually generate right practical thinking. A church with no other theology and programme, if it were vitally interested in this, would not fail to give a good account of itself as a church of Christ.

This is the true Christian orthodoxy, the thing on which the Church must insist as the condition of its existence. Historically, however, orthodoxy has been of another sort. It arises in this way: There is a natural desire to formulate Christian doctrine so as to show its philosophy. We seek

to pass from the revealed facts of God's grace to
a theory about them; and this theory becomes
the orthodox one. Of course this formulation
must take place in accordance with the reigning
philosophy of the time; and when the progress
of thought displaces the philosophy there is a
conflict of reason and faith. Again, the Christian
facts cannot lie in the mind unrelated to all its
other beliefs, but is spontaneously adjusted to
them. Thus it becomes complicated with the
science of the time; and when the science progresses we have a conflict of science and religion.
Further, Christianity tends to adjust itself to
existing social customs, and views any departure
from them as dangerous and irreligious. Then
when society progresses the Church is left behind, vainly protesting against the "spirit of the
times" as the "spirit of Antichrist," itself ap-
pearing meanwhile as the foe of humanity. In
this way the various orthodoxies arise; and we
have an orthodox philosophy, an orthodox astronomy, an orthodox geology, an orthodox medicine,
an orthodox political economy, and an orthodox
politics. These are mainly obsolete phases of
thought once current, to which Christian thought
attached itself, but which now are outgrown and
impossible. And Christian thought finds itself
greatly enlarged and liberated when it avails itself

of the larger intellectual conceptions. Who would now think of going back to ancient geology, or astronomy, or physics, or medicine, or chronology, or economics as aids to faith? The only possible reason any one could find for such a notion would lie in the belief in the verbal infallibility of the Bible; and this belief has largely disappeared as unnecessary and groundless.

Thus we see how the false orthodoxies arise and what they are. There are some of hierarchical origin, but these we have no call to consider. Generally the false orthodoxies do not touch the essential Christian faith, but are interpretations of that faith in the imperfect thought of their time. In the nature of the case they lie in the realm of opinion rather than of faith; and, equally in the nature of the case they are subject to change with the growth of thought and experience. From the mode of their origin it follows that the most ignorant will always be the most orthodox in this sense. Having themselves little knowledge and no intellectual interest, they will desire to "stand in the old paths," that is, the old formulas, or, still more accurately, the old phrases. All that is needed for this is a competent and active ignorance and a belligerent conceit. With this furnishing, they read out to their own satisfaction all modern science, modern history, modern sociology, modern political economy, and modern thought in general; and know not meanwhile that they are poor and miserable and blind and naked, and know nothing as they ought to know it. This has been so largely the character of self-styled orthodoxy, that one might almost have ground for a suit for slander or libel at being called orthodox.

Now the way out of this scandal lies in distinguishing the true orthodoxy of the essential Christian facts from this orthodoxy of opinion and interpretation. At its best it is only an attempt to theorize on Christian doctrine, and might be exchanged for a Christian agnosticism with no loss whatever in many cases. Essential Christian teaching is independent of any or all of these orthodoxies, and they commonly only serve to obscure the good news of God. We can believe in the Father and the Son and the Holy Spirit without going into the metaphysics of the Trinity, and even while renouncing such metaphysics as beyond us. We can thus believe without saying, "Theology teaches that there are in God one Essence, two Processions, three Persons, four Relations, five Notions, and the Circumincession which the Greeks call Perichoresis." We can believe in the forgiveness of sins without going into the "theories of salvation," or the "order of salvation" under theological guidance. There has been a deal of theology of this kind which was worthless even in its own field, and which constituted one of the worst aberrations of Christian thought; but we are getting clear of it. It is only a few years since a theological professor was complained of for getting the " order of salvation " wrong, but we are coming to see that if we secure salvation the " order" will take care of itself. Many of these orthodoxies are so petty that they could by no possibility begin to-day but, being here, they are maintained only by force of custom.

There will always be need of theology, but its field will be very much restricted in the future. The elaborate deductive constructions of the past will be abandoned as outrunning our data and our knowledge, if not our faculties. But the theologian will always have the function of formulating our Christian ideas and adjusting them to the current stage of thought and knowledge. In this way our ideas will fit harmoniously into the existing intellectual and social order, and will have their proper influence. But the results thus reached are never to be stiffened into an orthodoxy " which if any man hold not he shall without doubt perish everlastingly," or made into an "article of the standing or falling of the faith." These results are relative

to conditions. They have varied greatly in the
past; they will vary greatly in the future. In few,
if any, departments of theology has finality of
conception been reached. For instance, the problem of eschatology has hardly been rationalized
or moralized at all, and awaits its adequate discussion. This, however, does not mean that everything is at sea, or even that anything of much
importance is at sea; for still and all the while the
Church believes in God the Father Almighty, in
the Son, our Lord, in the Holy Ghost, the forgiveness of sins, and the life everlasting; and this
is all that is essential for faith or practice.

Still there is an important field for the theologian. The realization of Christian ideas in life
belongs to the individual disciple and the Christian community; their formulation and systematic presentation belong to the Christian scholar
and thinker. And these ideas cannot have their
full effect until this work is done; and because
of the progressive order of life and thought this
work will wait long for its completion. Knowledge is growing, human nature itself is developing, society is unfolding, experience is enlarging;
and our religious conceptions must change to
correspond. Hence there should be in every
church a large place for freedom of thought
within the limits of what I have called true or

essential orthodoxy, for it is only by free discussion that we can advance to new truth. It is now plain to every one that truth is not given all at once, and in the nature of the case cannot be, but is slowly developed through long processes of thinking as experience accumulates and knowledge advances. Every church, therefore, needs to be very hospitable to new truth from whatever quarter it may come, whether from science and from advancing history or from the criticism of history, secular and religious, or from the developing moral nature and insight of the religious community. Of course if any church is founded on some petty whim or prejudice, or if any church has staked its authority on obsolete science or disproved history, such church must object to freedom of thought, with the sure result that sooner or later it will be abandoned of God and man, unless it bring forth fruits meet for repentance. But all other churches, if they have faith in God, must also have faith that truth will do no harm and cannot itself be finally harmed. As Lowell has it, "God's universe is fire-proof and it is safe to strike a match."

Probably all of the larger Protestant bodies would in a way assent to this, but none of them is fully awake to its duty to the truth. The great body of church members have little real intellectual interest, just as the mass of men have little intellectual interest. Even the leaders are mainly taken up with the multitudinous routine of the religious community, and this bulks so large as to exclude all thought of anything else. The minister has his two sermons a week and the mid-week service. Then there are the funerals, the finances, the church organizations, the public demands, — what time has any one to think in such a whirl as this? Or the minister may be busy with more spiritual interests. He has an institutional church, or is managing a rescue league, or organizing a social reform movement; and then the questions of the troubled intellect seem almost impertinent, if not unintelligible. Any one, then, who finds fault with received and traditional formulas is likely to be a troubler of Israel, and we have no time to attend to him in any case. All this is true for a time but not forever. The still small voice of intelligence will at last be heard; and the gates of popes and bishops and general assemblies and general conferences shall not prevail against it. At last the outraged intellect and conscience revolt against religion itself; and then it is seen that there are questions perhaps even more important than who shall be made bishop, or when the Sunday-school picnic shall be held. Fiddling while Rome is burning is rational and praiseworthy in comparison with this dull indifference, while the intellect of a nation is being alienated from the Church and from religion.

Questions of scholarship can be settled only by scholarship. Questions of fact can be settled only by evidence. The very notion of deciding them by authority is absurd. How many papal bulls, or how big an ecclesiastical club, or how large a majority of ignorant votes would be needed to overturn the Copernican astronomy? Ignorance, in high or low places, is entitled to no opinion on these matters. Authority only makes itself ridiculous when it assumes to dictate. Majorities are equally absurd, unless they rest on the facts and the evidence.

The Church, then, has need of a body of scholarly investigators to do its intellectual work. They will have the function of formulating the spiritual life so as best to express it and keep it from losing its way in swamps of ignorance and superstition. They will also have to adjust religious thought to the ever-advancing thought of cultivated intelligence so as to remove needless misunderstanding. The rank and file of the Church, or even of the ministry, cannot be expected to do this or even to be deeply interested in this work. Most of them lack the ability, more of them

lack the time. They may make good day-laborers
in the Church, but they never can be master builders. As in science and general scholarship they
must depend on others to guide them, so in theological and biblical scholarship they must depend on others for leadership and guidance. This
most obvious fact makes it the duty of the
scholar to bear witness to the truth in all proper
ways. He must resist the conservatism of bigotry
and enlighten its blindness, and never permit the
religious life of the Church to be crippled and
thwarted by outgrown formulas, no matter who
utters them.

The same fact makes it important that the
nominal leaders of the Church shall also be leaders in the intellectual world, or at least be aware
of what is going on in that world, so as not to
put themselves continually in the wrong. When
the Copernican astronomy is everywhere received
in the educated world, it is not wise or safe for
the Church to be teaching the Ptolemaic doctrine.
In the midst of twentieth-century physics it is
not well for the Church to be teaching physics
of the sixteenth century. Simply as a piece of
policy, one could hardly imagine anything more
futile and fatuous than that. In the presence of
modern medicine the Church must not repeat its
old theory about demoniacal possession. And now

that the facts of hypnotism and suggestion are common property, the Church must not bring out its ancient doctrine of witchcraft. It is nothing less than pathetic to find persons harping away on obsolete knowledge in the idea that thereby the ark can be saved. They only do mischief and imperil the ark, which, if it be the real ark, must be able to stand alone.

And here, too, we are by no means out of the woods yet in this matter. It is not uncommon to find nominal leaders in our church organizations who have failed to keep up with the times, and who seek to cover up their ignorance by authority, or by assumption, or by the various forms of ecclesiastical imposition which are so familiar to the student of ecclesiastical history. What shall we say of a bishop in these days who addresses a conference of young men thus: "I beg you, I beseech you, not to read any works on evolution or higher criticism; but live and die in the faith of your mothers. And if it be said that then you will die in ignorance, be it so, and praise God for an ignorance that will give you peace." This is simply a recurrence of the dear old doctrine that ignorance is the mother of devotion. And what shall we say of a body of bishops that can issue pastoral letters in one of which the doctrines of the virgin birth and the infallibility

of Scripture are declared to be fundamental doctrines of Christianity, and in another of which
all those who do not accept the traditional teachings of the Church are commanded to keep silent
or depart? Clearly we have here an outbreak of
mediæval ignorance and not a worthy utterance
of people who know what is going on in the intellectual world to-day. Such persons are the
worst enemies of the faith. While claiming to be
its defenders, they really betray it in the house
of its friends, and show absolute blindness to the
intellectual conditions and needs of our time.

Now with respect to the first doctrine which is
mentioned, I have, myself, no difficulty. So far as
I know I believe it. I certainly do not deny it,
and I am in no way embarrassed by it. At the
same time I should strongly protest against making it an article of the standing or falling of the
faith of the Church. Manifestly it is a doctrine
which can be received only by faith, and can
never be put to any decisive test. I think in all
probability that those who accept Christianity
as a revelation of God will generally accept this
doctrine; and it will be held because of its
beauty and æsthetic fitness as inaugurating a
new era in the great order of divine revelation.
But at the same time it is clear that there are
considerable difficulties on the face of the nar-

rative in accepting it. Jesus himself never refers to it, neither does John nor Paul refer to it, and even the two genealogies which are given in the gospels that report the miraculous birth are curiously puzzling. For instance, it is somewhat difficult to tell why Matthew should give the genealogy of Joseph when Joseph himself is supposed by the doctrine in question to have had no part in the matter. But in any case the doctrine itself is nothing which affects our fundamental Christian ideas at all. Nothing whatever of importance depends on it. The divinity of Christ and his incarnation are absolutely independent of it. And those persons who try to connect these doctrines with the miraculous birth, in order to secure his sinlessness, always use a very limping logic. For if human paternity is incompatible with the sinlessness of Jesus, a human maternity must be equally so. The Roman church has shown its sense of this fact and has sought to provide for it by its doctrine of the sinlessness of Mary. But if that be needed, then the sinlessness of Mary's parents must also be assumed, and so on indefinitely.

Historically, this discussion of the virgin birth has generally been based on the assumption of the undivineness of the natural. This view is ruled out by the doctrine of the divine imma-

nence in all natural processes, so that God is not
excluded from any fact or process by calling it
natural. The person of Christ and his incarnation are the important thing, not the mode of
his birth. As already said, Paul and John laid
all emphasis on the former, and never mentioned
the latter.

As respects the technical infallibility of the
Scriptures, probably no doctrine is the source of
more difficulty and unbelief than this. That it
cannot be maintained every one knows, that
knows anything about the subject, and it is
nothing less than astounding to find the leaders
of a great church, supposed to be scholarly and
intellectual, setting forth as late as 1894 in a
pastoral letter this doctrine as a fundamental of
the Christian faith. This is worse than blind
leaders of the blind.

Such leaders should confine themselves to
deciding and condemning; it is always a mistake for them to give reasons, that is, of the
scholarly sort. They have, however, an argument
of an ethical type of which they are very fond
and which deserves some notice. In the second
pastoral letter referred to, it is said that persons
who do not accept the traditional views of the
Church should keep silent or depart; and it is
very common to hear such persons accused of

being untrue to ordination vows, or common honesty, or something or other which is supposed to be rhetorically effective. This makes it necessary to devote a word to the ethics of creed subscription.

It is commonly supposed that this matter of truthfulness can be settled offhand by easy appeals to what is called the "plain man" or the "man on the street." And it is easy to say, If you do not accept this, get out; if you do not accept this, it is dishonest for you to remain in a church that does accept it. To the plain man or the man on the street of course this sounds very conclusive, and the dishonesty of any doubter on this point is very manifest. However, all who have occasion to examine this general question of veracity know that when we get away from some very simple every-day affairs it is one of the most slippery and difficult notions possible. I have recently had a letter from an anxious inquirer asking if the divine veracity is not hopelessly impugned by the general illusiveness of life, the sense world, etc. And in our human world there are very few questions which can be answered by yes or no, and particularly is this the case when we come to these larger and more complex questions of interpretation of creeds and documents. It is well known that all creeds are historical compromises, which at best are to be accepted only for substance of doctrine, and which, moreover, always allow of a broad and a strict interpretation. It is only as this is understood that any creed whatever can serve as a working platform for a body of men.

In the interpretation of the Constitution, the same fact appears. We have the State Rights interpretation and the Federal interpretation, and we have one great political party inclining toward the stricter interpretation and another great political party inclining toward the Federal interpretation. It would be in the highest degree absurd for members of these parties to twit those of the opposite party with being traitors or perjurers. The fact and its necessity are perfectly recognized by intelligent people. Similarly with creeds: a fixed creed in a changing world must admit of being interpreted in accordance with the new conditions under which it is applied, or the new facts which emerge; otherwise it could not endure from one generation to another. This, again, is understood by intelligent persons, and they know that the creed is to admit of the various interpretations as a condition of being a creed at all. Change of creed from one day to another would be impossible. To change it every few years would be scarcely better. Under those circumstances we have to do with creeds just what we do with laws and constitutions. We must interpret them not merely in accordance with past beliefs, but also in accordance with present conditions and present knowledge.

Here, again, the stickler for what he thinks is veracity may interpose that creeds must be interpreted in accordance with the original intention, and here, again, he only shows his ignorance. For the fact is that no creed of any age and complexity is or can be interpreted in strict accordance with the original intention. The simple progress of astronomical knowledge makes it impossible for us to interpret, say, the Apostles' Creed in strict accordance with the original intention. Thus, " He descended into Hell," " He ascended into Heaven," and so on. We know very well what the notions of the original formers of this creed were in these clauses, for they were based upon the fancy of a flat earth with the hell down below and the heaven up above. But since the Copernican astronomy those notions of course have disappeared. Similarly we could find psychology, philosophy, and moral and political science setting aside many a notion of older writers, so much so that we agree with them, if at all, in the essential spirit of their thought and only to a slight extent in the real contents which they had in mind.

And that this must be so is further clear from the fact that the opposite view is to make truth itself a heresy. If we could suppose that a completed and final system of orthodoxy had been once for all delivered unto the saints, then we might say that the church in possession of this precious treasure might rightly require all who differ from it to depart. But then we know that nothing of the kind has existed. Orthodoxy itself historically has been a very changeable quantity. There are very few of the stoutest defenders of the faith who would not be ashamed of things once held orthodox and counted important. It is plain, then, that we must provide for the entrance of new truth into our system of religious thinking, and any church which does not do so and which insists that those who have progressed in thought shall keep silent or depart, condemns itself ; and its leaders show thereby that they have no insight into the truth themselves, and make it very probable that their pretended interest is of the vested kind, an interest in the financial aspects of the case, or an interest in their own dominance or something of that sort.

And yet persons talk so ignorantly on this subject that we have had heresy trials conducted on the principle that the truth or falsehood of the statements tried was not to be considered at all, but only whether they agreed with the profession of faith. At the trial of Professor Henry Preserved Smith some years ago this principle was announced and was received with very great satisfaction by the General Assembly, as it made it exceedingly easy to dispose of the professor. For plainly his views on higher criticism could hardly be expected to agree with the profession of faith made hundreds of years before higher criticism had been dreamed of. And at a still later trial for heresy the same principle was announced with equal satisfaction, as being something like a revelation from above. But what a pitiable comment on the pretense of high veracity and zeal for the truth! If this principle of interpretation which makes truth itself a heresy unless it agrees with traditional formulas were strictly applied, it would result in turning over all our churches and their property to a few ignoramuses, so dull and so ignorant as to be scarcely above the brute. Meanwhile the churches would exist not to seek and proclaim the truth, but to maintain a profession of faith, although it had been proved to be false! If that is what the churches are for, they ought to spare us their reflections on truth and honesty. We commend as an interesting problem for ecclesiastical casuists the question, How long may a church continue to teach what is known not to be so?

Plainly when the professional ark-saver begins to make rhetorical flourishes about truth and truthfulness, he soon gets out of his depth. It is indeed engaging to find such show of zeal, but veracity has never been a prominent orthodox virtue. And we need not go back to the times of Huss when it was declared, to the scandal of the secular authorities, that faith need never be kept with heretics, for we can find illustrations much nearer our own day. A legal friend lately remarked that he had had somewhat to do with ecclesiastical trials and had never found one conducted with much regard for right or truth, certainly none conducted in a way required in secular courts. An illustration: A ministerial acquaintance of mine some time ago was on a committee to report on the orthodoxy of a certain book. When the committee met this person asked how many of the committee had read the book in question. The question proved embarrassing, and he insisted upon an answer. Then it turned out that four men of the seven composing the committee had never seen the book. But they were perfectly ready to pass judgment upon it. Such a thing could not have happened in any secular court under the sun, and in a secular court such a committee would have been dismissed with severest rebuke and most likely heavily fined for contempt of court. But these godly people did not need to take into account such commonplace matters as fairness and truth and justice. They had the witness in themselves. They had not to discuss, they needed only to decide. They had not to refute; it was theirs to condemn. Now people of this sort must not talk too much about veracity or twit with inveracity those who are trying to mediate between the old and the new; for in my opinion there is no person less careful of the truth and more willing to give ear to evidence that jumps with his disposition, and more unready to deal impartially with evidence, than precisely this ecclesiastic who talks about veracity and calls upon those who differ from him to be silent or depart. On the contrary, they owe it to the truth and the Church alike neither to be silent nor to depart, but to stay where they are and bear witness to the truth in all wise and proper ways. Only thus can religious thought progress. To depart would be to deprive the Church of intelligence and leave it to flounder and smother in superstition, like the brainless monsters of ancient times that floundered and perished in palæontological swamps.

But surely, it will be said, there is, or ought to be, such a thing as loyalty to ordination vows. Of course there is, and it lies in loyalty to what I have called the fundamental platform and programme of Christianity. Whoever departs from this must be judged to have renounced our distinctively Christian teaching and should seek some other fold. But generally these so-called heresy cases are not properly such, but rather cases of practical wisdom and efficiency, and they should be dealt with on that line. When any minister differs so widely from his brethren that he cannot work with them, his place is elsewhere, not because he is a heretic, but because of his inability to stand on the same working platform. Be he heretic or orthodox, he is impracticable, and in so far undesirable as a Christian teacher. A man must have some measure of sympathy with the aims of a political party in order to be a member of it. If he is purely and only and always a mugwump, he must go elsewhere. The same is true of church affiliation.

Again, a minister may have sundry advanced views on biblical or doctrinal matters, and may be quite correct in holding them. At the same time he may become so obsessed by them as to make them practically false and make himself a nuisance. He may be persuaded of the post-Mosaic

origin of the Pentateuch, or the plurality of Isaiahs,
and similar matter, and thereafter be unable to see
or say anything else. He denies that Moses wrote
the Pentateuch, or that there was a single Isaiah,
or the historicity of the book of Daniel, or the
virgin birth of our Lord ; and these denials bulk
so large in his mind that he forgets the gospel
itself. Such a minister might rightly be cashiered,
not on the ground of heterodoxy, but for practical unwisdom. His views are not properly hetero-
dox, but he is not a useful, and may be a mischievous, person. Undoubtedly this is sometimes
the fact in what are called heresy cases; and it is a
great mistake to raise the question of heresy instead of the practical question of efficiency. The
indictment is wrongly drawn.

In another point the advanced thinker often
fails as a religious teacher. He overlooks the instrumental character of language and supposes
that language itself says something. Of course
language is only a means for expressing thought,
and that language is best which best expresses
the thought. It follows that the value of language
is relative to the person addressed. It further
follows that the language for scholars may not
be the best language for the " plain man " or
the " man of the street." Even shibboleths may
have their use at times, and may more accurately

convey our thought than the more careful language of the schools. The religious teacher should understand this. He should aim to be understood, and in order to this he must use "language understanded of the people." If any one can find religious help in some crude form of speech or some crude symbol, I should be willing for him to have it. If any one cannot believe in God the Father and in his Son without believing in the whale of Jonah or the ass that spoke, or the talking serpent and other saving truths of that kind, I should say, By all means believe in them. If these are the only things that hold you to the deeper truths of religion, hold on to them with all your might; only you must not insist that others also must believe in them.

So far the Church may go in condescension to ignorance, but no farther. The Church should always be a church for the ignorant, but it should never be an ignorant church. Ignorance can do little for the ignorant in any field, and least of all in religion. Ignorance left to itself must tend to grovel in superstition. Nothing but the clear, dry light of intellect can save religion from this fate which has overtaken, not only the outlying non-Christian religions, but Christianity itself in a great many places, say the churches of Abyssinia and northern Africa and western Asia. The

Christianity of these churches is scarcely higher than sorcery and incantation, and the reason is the lack of intellect and its free play. Among ourselves as soon as the control of intellect is withdrawn we have the fantastic excesses of the multitudinous sects, such as the Holy Jumpers, etc., who fancy that God is pleased with their ignorance and mistake their religious indecency for a special mark of divine illumination. "God don't need your book-larnin'," one such saint said to Dr. South. "No," was the reply, "and he does n't need your ignorance, either." We are not saved by taste, good or bad; but good taste is preferable, even in religion.

The Church certainly has other interests than those of the intellect, and our nominal leaders are by no means sinners above all men that dwell at Jerusalem. But they are seldom intellectual leaders, and they are required by their position to decide on questions beyond them. And this is an evil thing under the sun. Ignorance in high places is increasingly dangerous. Had our churches in the last generation had real leaders, who were equal to their position, and who commanded the respect of the churches by their scholarship and their character, to speak about the disturbing religious questions of our time and to say to the churches: These questions at best are of only subordinate importance and do not affect the fundamentals of the faith, we should have been saved much confusion, friction, and disgrace. But instead of that we had men who were not equal to their position, men whose scholarship and character did not command the respect of the community, and the result is familiar to all of us.

These things ought not so to be, but so they are, and so they will continue to be until the Church gets a deeper sense of its relation to the truth and of its obligations to it. Only thus can this age-long scandal of a church hostile to the truth and perpetually compelled to surrender with dishonor be done away.

The Riverside Press

CAMBRIDGE · MASSACHUSETTS

U · S · A